Robert G. Thonen
Church in Cleveland
12/24/91

THE CHURCH

The Vision and Building Up of the Church

A LESSON BOOK - LEVEL FIVE

*Based on and Compiled from
the Writings of*
WATCHMAN NEE
AND
WITNESS LEE

Living Stream Ministry
Anaheim, California

First Edition, 1,000 copies. June 1990.
Second Edition, 1,000 copies. July 1991.

ISBN 0-87083-525-4

Published by

Living Stream Ministry
1853 W. Ball Road, Anaheim, CA 92804 U.S.A.
P. O. Box 2121, Anaheim, CA 92814 U.S.A.

Printed in the United States of America

TABLE OF CONTENTS

INTRODUCTION
TO THE LESSON BOOK

Concerning the Lesson Books

This lesson book is one in a series originally designed to teach the truth to junior high and high school students during their summer school of the truth. Because the lesson books were written over a period of several years, the books may vary in style and format.

Concerning This Lesson Book

This is the fifth lesson book in this series. This book is based upon and compiled from the writings of Brother Watchman Nee and Brother Witness Lee and these brothers have not reviewed it.

This book is divided into two main sections of twelve lessons each. The first section covers the vision of the church. The second section describes the practical way for building up the church.

The church is one of the most crucial yet misunderstood matters in the Bible. Many people may see Christ as the Savior. Some may see Christ is for our daily experience. Very few see that the church is the Body, the enlargement, and the extension of Christ. We have been saved for the church. The processed Triune God's dispensing is to produce the church. Our experiences of life and growth in life are not for our own spirituality, but for the building up of the church. God, man, and the universe are all for the building up of the church.

We need to see this vision of the church and the way the church is built up. If we see this vision we will always be in the practical expression of the church to build up the church. Having seen this vision, we will never leave the church due to distractions in the world or "problems in the church. We will continually pray to be in spirit and to let the word of Christ dwell in us richly so that the Lord may use us in the building up of the church. May the Lord grant us this vision.

The Structure of the Lessons

The title conveys the subject of the lesson. The verses are for reading or pray-reading. The outline gives you an overview of the lesson. It is good to read the outline first to get an overview of the lesson before you proceed to the text of the lesson. The text is organized according to the outline. The writing contained inside the brackets [ ] are quotes from Brother Nee or Brother Lee's publications. The questions are intended to help you better understand and apprehend the lesson. A list of books with the author, publisher, and page number is included for all quoted materials. Finally, a list of books is included for further reference on the subject of each lesson. Nee represents Brother Watchman Nee. Lee represents Brother Witness Lee. LSM represents Living Stream Ministry. CFP represents Christian Fellowship Publishers.

The Versions Used in Quotes

When quoting verses, we used the American Standard Version of the Bible for the Old Testament and the Recovery Version of the Bible for the New Testament. We sometimes replaced New Testament quotations found inside the brackets [ ] with the corresponding Recovery Version verse.

The Proper Attitude Needed to Study the Word with the Help of the Lesson Book

This lesson book is not the Bible. It is a lesson book based on the Bible. It can be used as a study aid for the Bible. Do not quote the lesson book as the authoritative source for biblical truths or teachings. You must learn to reference the appropriate source - which book, which chapter, and which verse, etc. You must also learn how all the key verses relate to one another in presenting the vision of the church and the way to build up the church. Take the time to know the Word of God with certainty.

The Way to Study the Word with This Lesson Book

The Word of God embodies the essence of the Spirit. Therefore, when you come to the Word, you must use your spirit. The best way to use your spirit is to pray. You must pray before, during, and after the studying of this lesson book. It is also important that you fellowship as you are studying. It is not adequate to read by yourself without fellowshipping with others. The fellowship of the Body is necessary to help you comprehend the heavenly vision.

Suggestions on the Summer School of the Truth

It is suggested that the summer school of the truth be six weeks in length. Each week should be divided into four days, each day lasting three hours. Twenty-four days, each with three hours, will provide adequate time to pray, to cover all the lessons, and to fellowship. We recommend that all the students practice to write prophecies for each lesson, and also practice prophesying to speak for Christ and speak forth Christ. Each student should endeavor to experience individually and corporately what he has learned.

We have prayed and will continue to pray for you, that you may have an enjoyable time together during your summer school of the truth, that you will progress towards the full knowledge of the truth, and be built up in your locality. Amen!

June, 1990   Paul Hon

Pleasant Hill, California

Lesson One
THE VISION CONCERNING THE CHURCH

Scripture Reading

Eph. 3:10-11; 1:22-23; 1 John 1:2; 5:1; Eph. 2:6; Rev. 21:9-10; Col. 3:1-3; Eph. 2:20; 5:25-27.

Outline

I. God's eternal purpose being the Church

II. The church being the building up of all God's chosen, redeemed, regenerated, and transformed people, not a physical structure.

III. The church being the organism of the Triune God, not an organization

IV. The essence of the church is of life, not of knowledge

V. The nature of the church being of heaven, not of earth

VI. The foundation of the church being Christ

VII. The church being glorious

Text

In the past four lesson books, our emphasis had been on the side of the individual. This year we are going to emphasize something corporate—the church. God's full salvation is to redeem, regenerate, and transform His chosen people for the church. The Triune God desires to dispense Himself into His chosen people for the church. Christ's person and work is to build the church. The Spirit's regeneration and transformation work is to produce the church. Our knowing and experiencing the divine and eternal life of God is for us to be built up in the church. What God is, what God has, what He has passed through, what He has accomplished, and what He has obtained and attained are all for the church. We who are chosen, predestinated, redeemed, forgiven, washed, justified, reconciled, and regenerated to be sanctified, transformed, conformed, and glorified are material for the building up of the church. We are not only individual Christians, we are also a corporate entity—the church.

I. GOD'S ETERNAL PURPOSE BEING THE CHURCH

[God's eternal purpose is to have the church. His purpose is not just to create man, to rescue him from his fallen condition, and to bring him to heaven. Furthermore, God's purpose is not simply to have us be holy, spiritual, and victorious. Creation, salvation, sanctification, spirituality, and victory are all part of God's procedure to reach His goal, but they are not the goal itself.]

[Ephesians 3:10-11 unveils the fact that the existence of the church is according to the eternal purpose of God which He purposed in Christ. The church is something of God's eternal purpose. It did not come into existence by accident, but was planned in eternity. Before time began, in eternity, God purposed to have the church.

The word "purpose" here in the Scriptures is equivalent to the word "plan." God's eternal purpose is God's eternal plan. God has a plan which He planned in eternity—He is not purposeless; He is a God of purpose.

What did God plan? He planned to have a church composed of a group of human beings coordinated together as a corporate Body with which He may mingle Himself in His divine nature. In other words, this corporate Body would be a corporate vessel, into which He would put Himself. This is the very thing God planned and this is the very center of His purpose. God planned to have a corporate Body, a corporate vessel, with which he could mingle Himself and all that He is. This vessel is called the church.

The church, therefore, is the center of God's eternal plan. Why is the church so dear, so lovable, and so precious to God? It is because the church is the desire of God's heart, which He purposed before time began. God in eternity planned to have the church.]

II. THE CHURCH BEING THE BUILDING UP OF ALL GOD'S CHOSEN, REDEEMED, REGENERATED, AND TRANSFORMED PEOPLE, NOT A PHYSICAL STRUCTURE

[Many in Christianity have made the church something outward. When some speak of the church, they mean a physical building. If they speak of going to church, they mean going to a chapel or cathedral or some kind of sanctuary. These are material things constructed of bricks, stones, steel, or wood. What a mistake this is.] Have you made this mistake in the past? If you have, you will not make the same mistake after studying this lesson book.

The church is a building, but the church is not a physical building. The church is a building of all God's chosen people. He first created His people. His people, as a result of the fall, fell into sin. He then had to redeem them back to Himself. After being cleansed from sin, they needed to be regenerated with the life of God in their spirit. After being regenerated in their spirit they are suitable for the building, but their soul still needs sanctification and transformation. The sanctifying and transforming work is done by the Triune God to produce material for the building of His church. These building materials are living. They are the chosen, redeemed, regenerated, and transformed people of God.

III. THE CHURCH BEING THE ORGANISM OF THE TRIUNE GOD, NOT AN ORGANIZATION

The church is the organism of the Triune God. [We need to see that the church as the Body of Christ is altogether organic, absolutely of life, with nothing organizational. The body of Christ is the organism of the Triune God. The Triune God has an organism. An organism and an organization are entirely different. To illustrate this difference, we may compare a living person to a wooden stand. The wooden stand is without life, while a living person is full of life. The wooden stand is an organization of pieces of wood put together, but a living person has many members which are joined together organically. A person is a living, moving, functioning organism, unlike a robot, which is an organization of inorganic parts. The church is not an organization without life, but an organism with life.]

We are born of God into the church. We do not join the church as we would join an organization. Because the church is a living organism ruled by life, there is no need of a hierarchy to organize or rule over the church. There are leading ones in the church. They are not organizational leaders, but ones who are more mature in life to shepherd the younger, the newer, and the weaker ones in life. Praise the Lord for His organic church.

IV. THE ESSENCE OF THE CHURCH IS OF LIFE, NOT OF KNOWLEDGE

[The divine life, God's life, the eternal life, the uncreated life, the indestructible life, is the very essence of the church, and this divine life generates the church (1 John 1:2; 5:1).] Anything that is not of life is not of the church.

Man left God in the garden of Eden because he took in knowledge. From there man sinned, developed the world, lived in the flesh, loved only himself, and became separated from one another. Before we were saved, we were alienated from the life of God and were not in the church. When we were saved, we received the life of God into us. This life immediately made us a part of the church. From that point on, we must feed the life in us and grow in this life so that we may be in the church life. Anything other than life does not belong in and is not part of the church. Saints who care for knowledge bring death into the church. They not only deaden themselves they also deaden others. We should never bring anything other than life into the church. We also should stay away from anything that is not life. The best way to be in life is to pray, read the Word, fellowship things of life, and preach the gospel.

V. THE NATURE OF THE CHURCH BEING
OF HEAVEN, NOT OF EARTH

Since the source of the church is the Triune God, the nature of the church is of heaven and not of earth. We began by being seated in the heavenlies with Christ (Eph. 2:6). The New Jerusalem, the ultimate consummation of the church, will descend out of heaven from God (Rev. 21:9-10). This tells us that the church is not of earth but of heaven. Therefore, the Apostle Paul told us in Colossians 3:1-3, "If therefore you were raised together with Christ, seek the things which are above, where Christ is, sitting at the right hand of God. Set your mind on the things which are above, not on the things which are on the earth; for you died, and your life has been hidden with Christ in God." We should live our life on this earth as a heavenly people, not bound or distracted by earthly things like the unsaved, but to be occupied with the Triune God, His life, and the things above—Christ Himself. As we live this way, we will be good material for the building up of the church.

VI. THE FOUNDATION OF THE CHURCH
BEING CHRIST

[The church's foundation is Christ, revealed and ministered through the apostles and prophets. Ephesians 2:20 speaks of the foundation of the apostles and prophets. This foundation is the very Christ whom they ministered to others. Paul said that Christ was the unique foundation which he had laid. No one can lay another foundation (1 Cor. 3:10-11). The Christ who is the foundation of the church is the unique Christ revealed and ministered by the early apostles, as recorded in the New Testament.] We should lay hold of this Christ. We should not live in ourselves or become distracted by the world.

VII. THE CHURCH BEING GLORIOUS

God [wants a church of glory. Glory is the expression of God and it is altogether different from human morality and behavior. When God filled the tabernacle and the temple, both of them were filled with glory, with the very manifestation of God.][The only way God can have a glorious church is through Christ's sanctifying, cleansing, nourishing, and cherishing. As we experience these things in a personal and practical way, the church becomes glorious.]

The church is God's eternal purpose. The church is the building of all God's people. The church is the organism of the Triune God. The essence of the church is life, the very life of God. The nature of the church is of heaven. The foundation of the church is Christ. This means the church is a corporate entity that is completely involved with the Triune God; therefore, the church is glorious. It can only express God. Sometimes we may see some problem in the church. Those problems are not part of the church, they are the blemishes and wrinkles the Lord is cleansing in this age. Eventually the church will be "glorious, not having spot or wrinkle or any such things" (Eph. 5:27).

CONCLUSION

We praise the Lord, that by His mercy, He brought us into the church. Let us treasure the church as God treasures her. Do not take the church for granted. The church is according to God's plan. Christ died for her. The Spirit is transforming her. We should consecrate ourselves—all our time, all that we are, all that we have, and all that we can do—to Christ and the church so that God can accomplish His plan. This is the highest matter in the universe. Let us press on for this.

Questions

1. Use several verses to describe how God's eternal purpose is the church.

2. Use different portions from the Bible to prove that the church is a building of people and is not physical.

3. What is the difference between an organism and an organization?

4. What does the term "glorious church" mean?

Quoted Portions

1. Life Study of Ephesians (Lee/LSM), p. 565.

2. The Practical Expression of the Church (Lee/LSM), p. 7.

3. The Organic Building Up of the Church as the Body of Christ (Lee/LSM), p. 10.

4. Organism of the Triune God in the Organic Union of the Divine Trinity (Lee/LSM), p. 7.

5. The Organic Building Up of the Church as the Body of Christ (Lee/LSM), p. 11.

6. Basic Revelation in the Holy Scriptures (Lee/LSM), p. 70.

7. Life Study of Ephesians (Lee/LSM), p. 495.

Further References

1. Basic Revelation in the Holy Scriptures (Lee/LSM), p. 59.

2. The Body of Christ a Reality (Nee/CFP), p. 4

3. A Brief Definition of the Kingdom of the Heavens (Lee/LSM), p. 7.

4. Building Up of the Body of Christ (Lee/LSM), p. 7.

5. Completing Ministry of Paul (Lee/LSM), p. 105

6. Conclusion of the New Testament (Lee/LSM), p. 2045.

7. The Economy of God and the Building Up of the Body of Christ (Lee/LSM), pp. 13, 35.

8. The Exercise of the Kingdom for the Building of the Church (Lee/LSM), p. 11.

9. Further Light Concerning the Building Up of the Body of Christ (Lee/LSM), pp. 47, 55, 58.

10. The Glorious Church (Nee/LSM), pp. 7, 131.

11. The God-ordained Way to Practice the New Testament Economy (Lee/LSM), p. 32.

12. Life Study of Ephesians (Lee/LSM), pp. 29, 59, 68, 73, 208, 347, 664, 730.

Lesson Two

GOD'S PURPOSE FOR THE CHURCH

Scripture Reading

Eph. 1:4-5, 9-11; 3:9-11; 1 Peter 1:2-4; 2:2; 1 Cor. 3:6;
2 Cor. 3:16-18; 4:16-18; 1 Thes. 5:16-18, John 2:19.

Outline

I. To express God through the sonship

II. To make God's wisdom known to the enemy

III. To head up all things in Christ

Text

[Nearly all of the things revealed about God's eternal plan for the church are found in the two books of Ephesians and Colossians. The book to the Ephesians is the revelation of the Body, and the book to the Colossians is the revelation of the Head. When put together, these two books reveal a universal man, composed of Christ the Head, and the church the Body!

In Ephesians 1:10 and 3:9, the words "dispensation" and "fellowship" should be translated "economy." They are both the same word in the Greek. The church is something of God's economy, and this word "economy" is very important. It means dispensation, arrangement, stewardship, and administration. God has something to dispense, so He needs an arrangement and an administration in order to carry out this dispensing. The very substance that God is going to dispense is Himself. God is going to dispense Himself into man, so He arranged and administered the church. The church is the central matter in God's economy. Putting it into human terms, the church is God's business.

We all know that business is the key to any economy. Such a large corporation as General Electric has an economy in order to do business. In other words, business reveals the economy of this large corporation. In a similar way, God

Himself is a corporation with an economy, and in this economy God's divine business is the church.

Many Christians do not have such an awareness of the church. Their thought is that the church is a group of fallen people who are saved and who come together to worship God. This is right, but it is a concept far below God's economy. The heavenly and eternal view of the church is much higher than this. It is the very central matter of God's economy. In God's dispensation, in God's administration, in God's arrangement, in God's governmental stewardship, He has eternally planned the church.]

I. TO EXPRESS GOD THROUGH THE SONSHIP

[There are three main items concerning the church in the economy of God. The first is that the church might have the sonship, and that God might be expressed through this sonship. Ephesians 1:5 says that God predestinated us unto sonship. What does this word "sonship" mean, and what does it include? Briefly, it means the birth, plus the growth, plus the birthright. First of all, we must be born of God. By this divine birth we become the sons of God, because we have the life of God. This is the very beginning of God's mingling with us.]

[God's eternal purpose is to work Himself into us that He may be thoroughly mingled with us and expressed through us. When God is born into us, He begins this mingling process. But this is only the start! There must be the growth. If we have the birth, but not the growth, we could never enjoy the birthright. God is born into our spirit, which is the very center of our being. Then His desire is to spread from our spirit to transform all the parts of the soul, and eventually to transfigure our physical body. By this process our whole being will be saturated and permeated with the essence of God Himself.] This is the growth in life.

[After receiving the birth of God's life and the growth of this life, the Lord will grant us the enjoyment of the birthright.] The birthright is the special portion of the firstborn. According to the Bible, the birthright includes the double portion of the land, the kingship, and the priesthood. [Hebrews 12:15-17 warns us to be careful because there is the possibility of losing the birthright. We may have it, but we may also lose it. Having been born of God, there is the possibility of enjoying the birthright if we are matured, but there is also the possibility of losing the birthright. There will be many Christians who will lose the birthright because they do not have the proper growth. They have the birth of life, so they are the children of God, but they still need the growth of life, the maturity in life, for them to be the heirs of God] in order to enjoy the birthright. By having the birth, growing in life, and enjoying the birthright, we will be able to express God, not only individually, but also corporately as the built up church.

You have been born of God. Would you like to participate in the full sonship? I am sure that you would, since the full sonship is the most enjoyable thing any human being can attain to and experience. All of your friends are seeking enjoyment of some kind; some good and some evil. You too are seeking enjoyment. Imagine, that one day God will fill your spirit and soul and body, and that you will be a priest to God and a king to the inhabitants of the earth eternally. If you seek enjoyment, nothing is more enjoyable than this. This is our birthright. This is our rightful portion, given to us when we were born anew of God in our human spirit. The way to experience the full sonship is by the growth of the divine life in us. Even this process of growth is an enjoyment to us. All of humanity, including you and your friends, experience some sort of suffering every day. All of these sufferings are temporal, and are working for us daily to cause us to grow in life (2 Cor. 4:16-18). Therefore, in 1 Thes. 5:16-18, Paul charges to "Always rejoice; Unceasingly pray; In everything give thanks." We thank Him for all our situations, because through prayer we can rejoice always in our spirit to grow in life. We not only do this individually, but also with one another corporately. By His mercy with our diligence, we will receive the full sonship on the day of the Lord.

II. TO MAKE GOD'S WISDOM KNOWN TO THE ENEMY

[The second item of the purpose of God for the church is to deal with His enemy. In chapter one of Ephesians there is the positive side of God's purpose for the sonship; and in chapter three there is the negative side against the enemy, that the enemy may be subdued and come to know God's manifold wisdom. God is not sorry that there is such an evil one as Satan, because without such a one, God's manifold wisdom could not be manifested. It is through all the troubles originating from Satan that God has a chance to show forth His wisdom. Suppose you have a car, and this car never gives you any trouble. If this is the case, no one could know how wise you are. A car without problems would not demonstrate your wisdom. But if you have a car which needs wisdom to handle, your wisdom will be brought to light, and all of your passengers will marvel. It is a problem car, but what a wonderful driver! The whole universe has been damaged by Satan, but God needs such a one in order that His wisdom might be shown.]

In Ephesians 3 verse 10 [Paul declared that God's multifarious wisdom is made known to the rulers and authorities in the heavenlies through the church. The church is the Body of Christ, the joint-heirs, and the joint-partakers. The church is composed of those who once were ruined, corrupted, and damaged. Before we were saved, we were vipers, poisonous serpents. Furthermore, we were dead in trespasses and sins. Moreover, we were scattered and divided, utterly unable to be one. Thus, all the members of the church were in a hopeless situation. Nevertheless, God in His wisdom is able to make us the church. Now we are not only redeemed, saved, cleansed, freed, liberated, and regenerated—we are also united. We are one with God and with one another. Therefore, we are the church.

The church is God's greatest boast. Although you may not care that much for the church, God cares very much for the church. Sometimes God may say, "Look, Satan, I have taken the very people whom you have ruined and I have made them into the church. Do you have the wisdom to do such a thing? You do not have this wisdom, but I have it."]

[God created man in His own image and gave him authority to have dominion over all the earth. The image is related to the sonship, to the expression of God; and the dominion is related to dealing with God's enemy. The sonship is the fulfillment of God's image, for it is by the sonship that we will eventually be in the full image of God to express Him.]

[But God not only created man in His image to express Himself, He also committed His full authority to man for the purpose of subduing His enemy. So the second item of the purpose of God for the church is related to the second aspect of God's creation of man.

The church was predestinated to the sonship of God, and it was also purposed to subdue the enemy. The church is built up by the sonship, and through the building up of the church, the enemy is subdued and God's wisdom is displayed. There is a real order here. The more life we have, the more built up we will become as a display to Satan. This is a real challenge to the enemy, a shame to him and a glory to God.

Satan is so subtle. He causes many children of God to think that it is impossible to have the church built up on this earth. He persuades them to believe that it is not to be built up on this earth, but far away in the future. But is Ephesians 3:9 only for the future? I believe it must include this present age. In this present age and everywhere on this earth, the Lord must work out something as a challenge to Satan. Then God will say: "Satan, look! Even in the territory which you are utilizing, I have built up many lampstands which shine with the light of my life and bring things into order." This display is a challenge and a shame to Satan, but a glory to God. If our eyes are really opened, we will be ready for this at any cost. We will pray, "Lord, I am willing at any cost for the building up of your church in my locality." This is not a small matter, but something very strategic. All of the struggling of the enemy is over this strategic point. Satan will allow people to be saved, as long as they are not built up. Satan will even allow them to seek spirituality, as long as they are not built up. Satan will allow them to be anything, as long as they are not built up. This is because God's ultimate consummation is a building.]

[In the eyes of the Lord, Satan has already been defeated. If we have this insight, day by day we will sing, "Hallelujah for the victory!" We can tell Satan that even his small victory is just a preparation for our greater victory. Eventually, he will be the one that is completely defeated. We do not care how much he attacks and damages. The Lord Jesus said if people destroyed His body, He would build it up in three days (John 2:19). The more Satan destroys, the more Christ will build up. His destroying is just a preparation for the Lord's building up. We need the vision of how the Lord will use the church to defeat His enemy and to recover the whole earth.] In this way, God is using His church to display His multifarious wisdom to His enemy.

III. TO HEAD UP ALL THINGS IN CHRIST

[The third main aspect of the church in God's economy is the heading up of all things in Christ. We have seen that the first item of the sonship is for the church positively. The second item is that the church might make known to the principalities and powers the manifold wisdom of God, in defeating the enemy negatively. Now the third item is the heading up of all things in Christ universally. The church has to have the sonship, Satan has to be subdued and cast out, and the whole creation has to be brought into the proper order and oneness.

In Ephesians 1:10, the phrase "gather together in one" is best translated, "head up." It is God's eternal purpose that in the economy of the fullness of times He might head up all things in Christ.]

[God created the heavens and the earth as a realm within which He placed countless creatures, and at the center God created man as the vessel to contain Himself. But before God could come into man, Satan, the enemy of God, injected himself into man by tempting him to take the fruit of the tree of the knowledge of good and evil. When man took of that tree, the fruit went into his body. This is why we read in Romans 7 of sin being in the members. The Apostle Paul says in verse 20, "But if what I do not will, this I do, it is no longer I that do it but sin that dwells in me." Here sin is a personified thing; it is something living, because it can dwell in us and have dominion over us. This is the law of sin which is in the members of the body. Sin brings in death, death brings in darkness, and darkness brings in confusion. This influences the whole universe because man was made the head of all things. The head has been damaged, so all of creation is damaged. Sin brings in death and death brings in darkness. We all know that where there is darkness, there is confusion. If we did not have the sunlight or the electric lights, everything would be confused. We are controlled unconsciously by light. If there were no light, there would be no order and everything would be in confusion.]

You have probably witnessed this confusion in your own life, family, neighborhood, and school. There is much confusion. Many of your friends come from broken homes. That is confusion. Some in your school may be ruined by drugs, alcohol, or boy/girl relationships. That is confusion. In God's ordination, there is no divorce. According to God's creation, the human body does not need alcohol or drugs. These things ruin people. Boy/girl relationships are a form of fornication which is sin before God. There is confusion and division everywhere you look. This was brought in by the fall.

[God's way to recover the oneness among His creation is to impart Himself into us as life. Satan injected himself into us as death, but God imparts Himself into us as life. When life comes, there is light. John 1:4 says, "In Him was life, and the life was the light of men." Then in John 8 the Lord Jesus says, "I am the light of the world; he who follows Me shall by no means walk in darkness, but shall have the light of life" (v. 12). When God comes in as life, there is the light that shines within us as the light of life. This life swallows death, and this light expels the darkness. When we are in the life and under the light, then we are delivered out of confusion and brought into order, harmony, and unity. God's way of recovery is Christ versus Satan, life versus death, light versus darkness, and order versus confusion. When we are filled with Christ, we will be full of life, and completely under the light. Then we will have the harmony and the unity. If we are not filled with Christ as life, then, at least to some extent, we are in darkness. As long as there is some part under darkness, there is confusion, and no order or harmony. When everyone is full of Christ as life, we all are under light, and there is no need of outward control. Spontaneously, everyone is controlled by this light of life, and there is unity and harmony.]

[God's purpose with the church is to work Himself into us as life that we may be full of light. When we are controlled by this light, then we have oneness and harmony, which will be the real building. By this building God will shine upon all creation to bring it out of confusion. This will be the fullness of time when creation will be liberated. The old serpent will be cast into the lake of fire; and even death, the last enemy to be dealt with by God, will be cast away. Then the universe will be full of light, and under this light all creation will be liberated from the bondage of corruption in vanity and brought into the liberty of the glory of the sons of God. The shining of the New Jerusalem is the glory of the manifestation of the sons of God, and all the nations will be brought into that light. By this light they will be controlled, and there will be no more confusion, vanity, bondage, or corruption.

But all of this depends on the work of God within us. God is working out such a city as a corporate vessel, that He might be the life and the light to shine through this city to liberate the whole creation. How important it is that the church be built up! Without the building up of the church, God could never head up all things in Christ. It is by being life to the church, and the church being built up by this life, that the light of God shines out as the controlling factor. This will release all creation from confusion and bring it into a liberty under the shining of the sons of God. Then Christ will be the Head of all things through the church. All of God's problems will be solved, and all creation will be brought into the liberty of the glory of the sons of God.

This will be the consummation of God's eternal purpose for the church: when the sonship of God is fully fulfilled that God may be fully expressed, when the enemy of God is cast out that all of God's problems may be solved, and when all things are headed up in Christ through His Body that all of the creation may be in full harmony, freed from the bondage of corruption and brought into the liberty of the sons of God. Even today we can realize this in a miniature way here on this earth. When we know how to enjoy the sonship, how to defeat the enemy, and how to be filled with Christ under His headship, there will be the light shining out from us enlightening others and giving a foretaste of the coming consummation of the New Jerusalem.]

You and I must take the lead to live under the light of life to be a testimony against this evil world around us. We should not participate in things of darkness with our friends. Rather, not only should we separate ourselves by this life, we should also testify to our friends how we have been saved from the confusion of Satan into the oneness of God, that is the church. Hallelujah! We have been saved to take the lead to head up all things in Christ. We get headed up first, then we help others around us to be headed up, and finally, we head up the whole universe as the church, the Body of Christ. The three main items concerning God's purpose for the church are: expressing God through the sonship; making God's wisdom known to the enemy; and heading up all things in Christ. These items are universally great. We must consecrate ourselves to the Lord and His church as members of His Body so that He will have His builded church to fulfill His purpose. Amen!

Questions

1. What is "sonship"? What does it include?

2. How does the church make known God's wisdom to His enemy?

3. What does it mean "to head up all things in Christ"?

4. Write a prophecy of about 200 words concerning God's purpose for the church. Make sure that you include the three key points with verses to back up your prophecy.

Quoted Portions

1. God's Purpose for the Church (Lee/LSM), pp. 3-9.

2. Life Study of Ephesians (Lee/LSM), p. 270.

3. God's Purpose for the Church (Lee/LSM), pp. 9-20.

Further References

1. Basic Revelation in the Holy Scriptures (Lee/LSM), pp. 83, 142, 144-146.

2. Body of Christ (Lee/LSM), p. 28.

3. The Body of Christ a Reality (Nee/CFP), p. 23.

4. The Divine Economy (Lee/LSM), p. 120.

5. The Economy of God and the Building Up of the Body of Christ (Lee/LSM), p. 70.

6. The Glorious Church (Nee/LSM), p. 10.

7. On Home Meetings (Lee/LSM), p. 26.

8. Life Study of Ephesians (Lee/LSM), pp. 74, 265, 268, 809.

9. The Living Needed for Building Up the Small Group Meetings (Lee/LSM), p. 73.

10. The One New Man (Lee/LSM), p. 44.

11. The Practical Expression of the Church (Lee/LSM), p. 10.

12. Scriptural Way to Meet and Serve for the Building Up of the Body of Christ (Lee/LSM), p. 10.

13. The Spirit and the Body (Lee/LSM), pp. 63, 65.

Lesson Three

THE STATUS OF THE CHURCH (1)

THE ASSEMBLY, THE HOUSE OF GOD, AND THE KINGDOM OF GOD

Scripture Reading

1 Cor. 1:2; Matt. 18:20; Gen. 28:12, 16-17; John 1:51;
1 Tim. 3:15; Heb. 3:6; 1 Pet. 4:17; 1 Tim. 3:15;
Eph. 2:22, 19; Rom. 14:17.

Outline

I. The assembly of the called out ones—ekklesia

II. The house of God

III. The dwelling place of God

IV. The kingdom of God
   A. Being the living of the Church
   B. The entrance into the kingdom of God

Text

In this lesson we come to the status of the church. [As we consider the status of the church, we shall see the reality concerning the church and the real definition of the church. Therefore, we need to get into the depth of each aspect of the status of the church.] We will use four lessons to see the main aspects of the status of the church.

I. THE ASSEMBLY OF THE CALLED OUT ONES—EKKLESIA

[We all have to admit that since the time of the apostles until at least the sixteenth century the church was going downward. By the sixteenth century the church had fallen to the bottom, into the dark ages. It could not go any lower. At this time the Lord came in to start His recovery. He started the recovery from the very base of the biblical truth, justification by faith. Luther did see something concerning the church as well, but he did not have much time to care for this matter. He saw something of the church, yet he did not see enough.

A little more than two centuries later Count Zinzendorf, with so many other brothers, the so-called Moravian brothers, saw something more concerning the church. In Bohemia, on the land owned by Zinzendorf, they started to have the practice of the church. That was the first step of the Lord's recovery of the church practice. By reading church history, you could realize that before Zinzendorf, no one was so clear concerning the church practice. Their practice was good, yet it was not complete.

One century later, in the early 1800's, the Lord went on from Bohemia to England, raising up a group of seekers, including John Nelson Darby and other brothers. They began to practice the church life. Their practice was a great improvement over that which was practiced under the leadership of Zinzendorf at Bohemia. These brothers began to see that the church is the assembly of God's called out ones (Eph. 1:22; 1 Cor. 1:2). The church is the gathering of all the dear saints who have been called in Christ out of this world. Thus, they began to drop the English term "church," because they realized that it had been damaged through wrong usage. At that time fallen Christianity considered the church to be a physical building, perhaps with a "high tower" and a bell. Even today, many parents say to their children on Sunday morning, "Let us go to church," referring to the wood, the stone, the brick, and the glass. How pitiful that was, and how pitiful it still is today. The Brethren dropped this wrong concept, and they even dropped the term church. They began to use the word "assembly." After this the Assembly of God followed them to use the word assembly.]

[Because the church has the status of the assembly, the ekklesia, we need to gather together. We must assemble and meet in order to have a congregation for God to work and move among us. When God's called out ones meet together, this is the church. Without such a gathering together of the believers in a locality, there is no practical church life. The practical church life consists in the gathering of the saints in a certain locality. If believers live in a particular city but do not assemble, then in a practical way there is no church in that city. The basic concept of the church as the assembly is that the church is a gathering of the called out ones.]

[We need to be impressed with the fact that, as used in the New Testament with respect to the church, the Greek word ekklesia indicates that the church is a congregation called out of the world so that God may carry out His purpose. According to Genesis 1:26, man was created by God to bear His image and to carry His authority. However, man fell again and again. Eventually, in the last stage of his fall, man fell into the world, the system of Satan. In the eyes of God, as a result of the fall the entire human race has actually become the world. In John 3:16, human beings as a totality are called "the world." Since fallen man is in the world and has even become the world, how can God fulfill His purpose with man and through man? The only way is for God to call out a part of the human race. God has done this very thing. In applying His salvation to us, the first thing God does is to call us. Therefore, the first status of the church is that of the assembly of those who have been called out of the world by God to Himself for the fulfillment of His purpose.

Because the church as the assembly is separated from the world, we may say that the church is composed of the real Hebrews. The root of the word "Hebrew" (Gen. 14:13) means "to pass over"; it especially means to pass over a river from one region to another and from one side to another. Hence, the word "Hebrew" denotes a river crosser, one who crosses a river. The church is composed of the believers who, as real Hebrews, have been called by God out of the world and have "crossed the river" from one realm to another. Now as believers in Christ we are the called out ones, the assembly, the congregation called out by God, the ekklesia in opposition to the world, which is on the other side of the river we have crossed. Just as our forefather Abraham was called out of the land of Chaldea, so we have been called out of the world by God to be His assembly.

Whenever we speak of the church as the assembly, the ekklesia, we need to realize that this means that the church has been separated from the world. The first status of the church indicates a thorough separation of God's called out ones from the world. There must be a great and thorough separation between the church as the ekklesia and the world as the system, the cosmos, of Satan. As the assembly, the church is separated entirely for God so that He may have a means to carry out His eternal purpose.]

II. THE HOUSE OF GOD

[The first mention of the house of God in the Bible is in Genesis 28. One night, when Jacob was escaping from his brother, he had a dream. In his dream he saw "a ladder set up on the earth, and the top of it reached to heaven: and behold the angels of God ascending and descending on it" (v. 12). When he awoke from sleep, he said, "Surely the Lord is in this place; and I knew it not. And he was afraid, and said, How dreadful is this place! This is none other but the house of God, and this is the gate of heaven" (vv. 16-17), which means the house of God.

This first mention of the house of God in the Bible is a seed that grows and develops elsewhere in the Scriptures. The Lord Jesus refers to Jacob's dream in His word to Nathanael in John 1:51. "He said to him, Truly, truly, I say to you, you shall see heaven opened and the angels of God ascending and descending on the Son of Man." This is the fulfillment of Jacob's dream, for Christ as the Son of Man with His humanity is the ladder set up on the earth and leading to heaven, keeping heaven open to earth and joining earth to heaven for the house of God—Bethel.]

[Three verses which reveal that the church is the house of God are 1 Timothy 3:15; Hebrews 3:6; and 1 Peter 4:17. In 1 Timothy 3:15 Paul says, "If I delay, that you may know how one ought to conduct himself in the house of God, which is the church of the living God, the pillar and base of the truth." As God's dwelling place, the church is both God's house and His household, His family. In the Old Testament the temple and

God's people were two separate things, but in the fulfillment in the New Testament the dwelling place and the family are one. According to God's New Testament economy, God's house is His family.

Another verse that speaks of the church as the house of God is Hebrews 3:6. This verse refers to "Christ, as a Son over His house, whose house we are." In Old Testament times, the house of God was the house of Israel (Lev. 22:18; Num. 12:7), symbolized by the tabernacle or the temple among them (Exo. 25:8; Ezek. 37:26-27). Today the house of God is the church. The children of Israel, as people of God, are a type of us, the New Testament believers (1 Cor. 9:24—10:11). Their history is a prefigure of the church.

The church has a twofold function. To Christ, the church is the Body; to God, the church is the house. Christ is the Head, and the church is the Body of the head. This is one function of the church. God is the Father, and the church is His house. This is another function of the church. Just as Christ is the Head and the church is His Body, so God is the Father and the church is His house. The church as the Body of Christ is an organism. In like manner, the church as the house of God is a living entity, a living house.

First Peter 4:17, another verse that refers to the church as the house of God, says, "Because it is time for the judgment to begin from the house of God." Here we see that disciplinary judgment begins from God's own house. God's house, or household, is the church composed of the believers. From this house, as His own house, God begins His governmental administration by His disciplinary judgment over His own children, that He may have strong ground to judge, in His universal kingdom, those who are disobedient to His gospel and rebellious to His government.

In speaking of the church as the house of God, Paul specifically refers to God as the living God. The living God who lives in the church must be subjective to the church and not merely objective. The God who not only lives but also acts, moves, and works in His house, the church, is living. Because God is living, the church is also living in Him, by Him, and with Him. A living God and a living church live, move, and work together. The living church is the house of the living God. Therefore, in our meetings, service, and ministry we should give people the impression that the living God is living, moving, speaking, and acting among us.]

[The first characteristic of the status of the church is that it is an assembly called out of the world. The second characteristic is that the church is God's house composed of those who have been born of God. This second characteristic is a matter not merely of separation but of a spiritual, divine birth. In order to be the assembly, we need to be sanctified, that is, separated from the world. But to be a component of the house of God, we need to be born of God. Anyone who has not been born of God cannot be part of His house, part of His family.]

III. THE DWELLING PLACE OF GOD

[As the house of God, the church is the dwelling place of God. Ephesians 2:22 says, "In whom you also are being built together into a dwelling place of God in spirit." The word "you" here refers to the local saints. Paul is saying that the local saints, the saints in Ephesus, were being built together in Christ into a dwelling place of God.

The church, the dwelling place of God on earth, is the place in which God can have His rest and put His trust. In this dwelling place God lives and moves to accomplish His will and satisfy the desire of His heart.

Because the church is God's dwelling place, the church is where God expresses Himself. A house is always the best place for a person to express himself. The kind of person you are is expressed by your house. Hence, if you look at a person's house, you will be able to tell what kind of person he is, because a person's house is his expression. The principle is the same with the church as the dwelling place of God. In His house, His dwelling place, God expresses Himself on earth. This is the reason 1 Timothy 3:16 reveals that the church is God's manifestation in the flesh. God not only desires to make home in the church and to have a resting place there; He also wants to express Himself in the church. He wants to practice His New Testament economy, speak forth His desire, and manifest His glory in the church. All that He is, all that He is doing, and all that He wants to obtain are to be manifested, expressed, in the church as His dwelling place.]

IV. THE KINGDOM OF GOD

[Ephesians 2:19 says, "You are no longer strangers and sojourners, but you are fellow citizens of the saints and members of the household of God." The term "fellow citizens" indicates the kingdom of God. All the believers, both Jewish and Gentile, are citizens of God's kingdom, which is a sphere wherein God exercises His authority. As long as anyone is a believer, he is a citizen of the kingdom of God. This citizenship involves rights and responsibilities, two things that always go together. We enjoy the rights of the kingdom, and we bear the responsibilities of the kingdom.]

[Although the church today is God's kingdom, we are in the kingdom in reality only when we live and walk in spirit. Whenever we behave according to the old man or live in the flesh or the self, we, in a practical way, are out of God's kingdom. This means that when we are in the flesh, we are in the old realm of the fallen human nature, which has been fully usurped by Satan to form his kingdom. Therefore, a genuine Christian, if he lives in the flesh instead of in the spirit, may live in a practical way not in the kingdom of God but in the kingdom of Satan. Only when we live, walk, behave, and have our being altogether in our spirit, not in our natural man, are we in the kingdom of God and, in reality, are the kingdom of God.

The kingdom of God, like the house of God, is a corporate person. The church as the house of God is a corporate person because this house is the family of God, the household of God. The kingdom is likewise a corporate person because it is also a corporate entity. Whether we are living in the church as the house of God or as the kingdom of God depends on whether we are living as members or as citizens. To live as members of the house of God is a matter of enjoyment, but to live in the kingdom of God is a matter of bearing responsibility and of being regulated. We are members of our Father's household, and we are citizens of our God's kingdom.]

A. Being the Living of the Church

[The kingdom of God is the living of the church. A verse that strongly proves this is Romans 14:17. "The kingdom of God is not eating and drinking, but righteousness and peace and joy in the Holy Spirit." According to some Bible teachers, the kingdom has not yet come. They claim that now is the dispensation of the church, and the next dispensation will be that of the kingdom. But in 14:17 Paul does not say that the kingdom of God shall be; he uses the present tense and says that the kingdom of God is. According to the context of Romans 14, which speaks of receiving the believers, the kingdom is today's church life. The reality of the church life is the kingdom. Romans 12 speaks of the Body life and Romans 14, of the kingdom life. This indicates that, in Romans, the kingdom life is the reality of the Body life.

In a sense, it is correct to say that the present age is the church age and that the coming age will be the kingdom age. However, in another sense, the kingdom of God is here today, for the kingdom is the reality of the church and the living of the church. Hence, the church is the kingdom. Since the church is the kingdom today, it is not correct to say that the kingdom has been suspended altogether until the coming age. Romans 14:17 proves definitely that the kingdom is the living of the church today.]

[In Romans 14:17 we see that the kingdom of God as the living of the church is righteousness, peace, and joy in the Holy Spirit. When the authority of God's kingdom operates in us, righteousness, peace, and joy will characterize our daily life.

Righteousness, peace, and joy are actually the expression of Christ. When Christ is expressed, He is our righteousness toward ourselves, our peace toward others, and our joy with God.

As the believers live the kingdom life in the church, they will live righteously toward themselves. This means that we must be strict with ourselves and make no excuses for ourselves.

To live the kingdom life in the church also means that we live peacefully toward others. Our relationships with others must be characterized by peace. Toward others we must endeavor to pursue peace, continually seeking to be at peace with them. This peace is Christ Himself lived out from our being.

Living the kingdom life in the church also requires that we live joyfully to God in the Holy Spirit. The Holy Spirit is a Spirit of joy. If we are not joyful, this indicates that we are not in the Holy Spirit. If we are truly living the kingdom life, we shall be joyful with God, praising Him. Whenever we live righteously toward ourselves and peacefully toward others, we shall live joyfully to God in the Holy Spirit. Such a living is the kingdom of God as the living of the church.]

B. The Entrance into the Kingdom of God

[In 2 Peter 1:3-11 we see that those believers who develop and grow in the life of God in the church life shall be richly and bountifully supplied with the entrance into the kingdom of God. After we have entered into the kingdom of God through regeneration, we need to go on to have a rich entrance into the eternal kingdom of our Lord and Savior Jesus Christ. On the one hand, we have entered the kingdom; on the other hand, we still need a rich entrance. The initial entry into the kingdom is regeneration, but the rich entrance is through the full growth and development of the divine life revealed in 2 Peter 1:5-11.

Verse 11 says, "For so shall be richly and bountifully supplied to you the entrance into the eternal kingdom of our Lord and Savior Jesus Christ." The bountiful supply we enjoy in the development of the divine life and nature (vv. 3-7) will bountifully supply us a rich entrance into the eternal kingdom of our Lord, which will be a reward to His faithful believers, who pursue the growth in His life unto maturity and the development of the virtues of His nature, so that they participate, in the millennium, in His kingship in God's glory (2 Tim. 2:12; Rev. 20:4, 6).]

[According to Peter's word in 1:5-11, to grow to maturity is to develop what we have already received. We have been allotted the like precious faith, which is an all-inclusive seed. All the divine riches are in this seed, but we must be diligent to develop them into virtue. Then we need to develop in our virtue, knowledge; in knowledge, self-control; in self-control, endurance; in endurance, godliness; in godliness, brotherly love; and in brotherly love, love. Through such a growth and development we eventually shall reach maturity and shall have a rich entrance into the eternal kingdom of our Lord and Savior Jesus Christ.

The fact that those who develop and grow in the life of God in the church life will have a rich entrance into the coming kingdom implies that certain believers will not have a share in the coming kingdom, because they have not been living in the proper church life and have not had the adequate growth in the divine life. For this reason, at the time of the manifestation of the kingdom, they will have no participation in the kingdom. But those who grow and develop in the divine life to the full extent will be supplied with a rich and bountiful entry into the coming kingdom.

We have seen three aspects of the status of the church: first, the church as an assembly separated from the world; second, the church as the house of God composed of those who have been born of God; and third, the church as the kingdom of God, which is the reality and living of the church today. We all need to grow in the divine life in the church life so that in the coming age we may have a rich entrance into the kingdom of God.]

Questions

1. How does the first status of the church show that the church is not a physical building, but the built-up believers?

2. In this age the church is the reality of the kingdom. What is God's requirement for us to be in this kingdom today?

3. What is required of us in this age to enter into the manifestation of the kingdom in the next age?

4. Write a prophesy (100 words) listing each status of the church. Write a brief explanation of each status.

Quoted Portions

1. Conclusion of the New Testament (Lee/LSM), p. 2215.

2. The One New Man (Lee/LSM), pp. 7-8.

3. Conclusion of the New Testament (Lee/LSM), pp. 2216-2218, 2225-2229, 2235-2241, 2243-2244.

Further References

1. Basic Revelation in the Holy Scriptures (Lee/LSM), pp. 57-58, 75, 83, 87, 93, 94, 127.

2. Body of Christ (Lee/LSM), pp. 23, 24.

3. A Brief Definition of the Kingdom of the Heavens (Lee/LSM), pp. 9-16.

4. Completing Ministry of Paul (Lee/LSM), pp. 42-45, 47, 49.

5. The Exercise of the Kingdom for the Building of the Church (Lee/LSM), p. 65.

6. Experiencing Christ as the Offerings for the Church Meetings (Lee/LSM), pp. 7, 22, 30, 134-135.

7. Further Talks on the Church Life (Nee/LSM), p. 66.

8. Life Study of Ephesians (Lee/LSM), pp. 231, 624-625.

9. The One New Man (Lee/LSM), p. 9.

10. The Practical Expression of the Church (Lee/LSM), p. 20.

11. Scriptural Way to Meet and Serve for the Building Up of the Body of Christ (Lee/LSM), p. 259.

12. Vision of God's Building (Lee/LSM), pp. 182-183, 223-224.

Lesson Four

THE STATUS OF THE CHURCH (2)

THE BODY OF CHRIST

Scripture Reading

Eph. 4:4; Eph. 1:22-23; 5:23; 1 Cor. 12:12-13, 15, 21; Eph. 3:8; 3:19; Col. 3:11; John 6:48, 57, 63.

Outline

I. Christ being the Head

II. We being the members of the Body of Christ

III. The Body receiving from the Head

IV. The fullness (expression) of Him Who fills all in all

V. The fullness (expression) of God

Text

[The organism of the Triune God is a Body (Eph. 4:4). The very abstract and mysterious God has an organism. God is invisible, yet He has a visible organism, the Body of Christ. The church as the Body of Christ is for His fullness, His expression. The definition of the church as the fullness of Christ may be illustrated by a cup that is filled with water to the extent that it overflows with water. The water within the cup is seen and expressed when it overflows from the cup. The overflow of the water is the fullness of the water, and the fullness of the water is the expression of the water that is inside the cup. John 1:16 says, "For of His fullness we all received, and grace upon grace." We received of the fullness of the incarnated Christ who came as grace and truth (v. 17). The Word became flesh, and He was full of grace and truth (v. 14). The fullness of grace and truth is the fullness of the incarnated Christ. To fill a cup with water until it overflows is to have "water upon water." The Lord Jesus was full of grace, grace upon grace. Of His fullness we all have received, grace upon grace. The fullness is the expression of the riches. A person's body is his fullness, his expression. A husky American man who has enjoyed so much of the rich foodstuffs of America, the riches of America, may be considered as the fullness of America, the expression of America. The church as the Body of Christ is the expression, the fullness, of Christ.]

The church is the Body of Christ. Jesus Christ, being the embodiment of the Triune God, is rich in all that God is. He is also rich in what He has gone through and accomplished. He is wonderful and marvellous. Such a universally great Person needs an equally wonderful and marvellous Body to contain and express Him. After He went through His process and ascended to heaven, He became the Head of the church, His Body. The church therefore is universally great having the Head on the throne in the heaven and the Body on the earth expressing the Head as His fullness.

I. CHRIST BEING THE HEAD

[Christ is the Head of the Body. In Ephesians 5:23 Paul says, "Christ is Head of the church, being Himself the Savior of the Body." The Savior is a matter of love, whereas the Head is a matter of authority. We love Christ as our Savior, but we must also be subject to Him as our Head.

As the Head of the church, the Body, Christ is joined to the Body. Just as in one's physical body the head and the body are one, so Christ, the Head, and the church, His Body, are joined and therefore are one. The Body is one with the Head in the divine life and in the divine Spirit.

All that Christ has accomplished, obtained, and attained as the Head is not only for the Body but also to the Body (Eph. 1:22-23). This means that what the Head has gained now belongs to the Body, for it is transmitted to the Body. The Body, therefore, comes into existence from the transmission of the Head. Whatever Christ has passed through, obtained, and attained is now being transmitted into the Body.]

II. WE BEING THE MEMBERS
OF THE BODY OF CHRIST

A body must have members. Who are the members of the Body of Christ? We are! We, the God-chosen, Christ-redeemed, and Spirit-regenerated people are the members of the Body. We do not join the Body by signing up. We become members by being saved and baptized into the Body. First Corinthians 12:13 says, "For also in one Spirit we were all baptized into one body." Therefore, the Body is organic, of life; it is not formed organizationally.

Like the human body, not one member is hired and not one member can be fired. Every member is of life. The Body of Christ is the same. We were not hired nor can we be fired. None of us were admitted into the Body, so we can not remove anyone from the Body. This is wonderful. We can be assured that we will remain in the Body of Christ forever.

We may have different functions in the Body, yet we are still one Body. The foot cannot say, "Because I am not a hand, I am not of the Body" (1 Cor. 12:15). Neither can the head say to the foot, "I have no need of you" (1 Cor. 12:21). Because we are organically in the Body we cannot be discharged. We are in the Body forever to enjoy all the riches of the Head.

III. THE BODY RECEIVING FROM THE HEAD

Ephesians 1:22b says, "and (God) gave Him (Christ) to be Head over all things to the church." Christ is the Head of the church to direct the church's every move; and in order for the church to express Christ as His Body, the church must be connected to Christ all the time to receive all that Christ is. The phrase "to the church" implies a continuous transmission from Christ the Head to the church His Body. All His divine riches are ours to enjoy continually. All that He is, all that He has, all that He has accomplished, and all that He has obtained and attained is being transmitted into all the members all the time. We need to open to Him to receive all these divine riches all day long.

When you get up in the morning, you may pray, "O Lord Jesus, You are my Head. I want to enjoy all that you are. Flow into me." As you are praying, the Spirit will flow from the Head into you to revive your spirit. Then you should pray-read the verses for the day. The Head on the throne will be your rich supply for you to live Him out that day. God will be expressed in your manner of living. You will be energized to preach the gospel to save sinners that they may become new members of the Body. You and your newly saved ones, may prophesy and testify to exhibit Christ in the church meetings to build up the Body of Christ. The most enjoyable and fulfilling way to live our human life and our Christian life is to live as a member of the Body of Christ.

IV. THE FULLNESS (EXPRESSION) OF HIM WHO FILLS ALL IN ALL

[The church as the Body of Christ is the fullness of Him who fills all in all. Ephesians 1:23 says that the church "is His Body, the fullness of the One who fills all in all." Grammatically, "the fullness" is in apposition to "His Body." This indicates that the Body is the fullness and the fullness is the Body. The Body of Christ is His fullness. The fullness issues from the enjoyment of the riches of Christ (Eph. 3:8). Through the enjoyment of Christ's riches, we become His fullness to express Him.

This fullness is the fullness of the One who fills all in all. Christ, who is the infinite God without limitation, is so great that He fills all things in all things. Such a great Christ needs the Body to be His fullness for His complete expression.]

[Many Christians do not understand what the word fullness means in Eph. 1:23 and 3:19. They think the word fullness means riches. Fullness does not mean the riches. In Ephesians the unsearchable riches of Christ are mentioned in 3:8. We must differentiate between the riches and the fullness. The United States has supermarkets full of the riches of America. The riches of America are its products, but the fullness of America is a husky American. This fullness is the expression.

The fullness comes out of the riches. However, if we do not eat and digest the riches, we may have them without having the fullness. The riches issue in the fullness through eating and digesting. If we do not eat and digest the riches, we shall remain skinny and short. In like manner, the church is not only the Body of Christ, but also the fullness, the expression, which issues from the enjoyment of the riches of Christ.

This fullness is the expression of the very One, the universal Christ, who fills all in all. Colossians 3:11 says that Christ is all and in all. All, both times in this verse, refers to people. In Ephesians 1:23, however, the "all in all" which Christ fills is something universal. Christ is unlimited (Eph. 1:23; 3:18). The dimensions of the universe are actually the dimensions of Christ. How long is the length? How high is the height? How deep is the depth? How broad is the breadth? No one can tell. The dimensions of Christ in Ephesians 3:18 are unsearchable and unlimited. These dimensions are the description of Christ.

Christ fills all in all, and we the church, by enjoying His riches, eventually become His fullness. If I had only a head, without a body, I would have no fullness. This fullness is my expression. We must realize that the church as the Body of Christ is Christ's fullness as His expression.]

V. THE FULLNESS (EXPRESSION) OF GOD

[In Ephesians 3:19 the King James Version says we are "filled with all the fullness of God." The preposition "with" literally means "unto, resulting in." We are filled unto all the fullness of God. We are filled, resulting in an expression of God. Fullness here means expression. Paul said he prayed that the Father would strengthen us with power through His Spirit into the inner man that Christ might make His home in our hearts, and that we might know Christ's dimensions—the breadth, length, height, and depth—that we might be filled unto, resulting in, the fullness of God, the expression of God (Eph. 3:14-19).

The entire book of Ephesians deals with the church. It is the house or household of God (2:19), it is the Body of Christ (1:23), and it is the fullness as the expression of Christ and of God (1:23; 3:19). According to chapter three, the church can be such an expression, not only of Christ but also of God, when Christ makes His home in our hearts that we may experience His unsearchable riches. While we are enjoying Him in such a way, we are being filled with all the riches of Christ, resulting in an expression of God.

The church today should be such an expression, issuing out of the rich enjoyment of the unsearchable riches of Christ. We are burdened for the situation among Christians. Where is there an expression of God? I hope that among us there will be such an expression. We all need to pray for ourselves as Paul did for us in Ephesians 3. We should bow our knees to the Father that He may strengthen us into our inner man that Christ may make His home in our hearts, fully settling down in every avenue, every part, of our inner being. Then we may enjoy His love, and we may touch and possess His dimensions. We will be filled with Him unto the fullness of God, the expression of God. This is not just an assembly or a called-out congregation of Christians. This is a group of people fully possessed by Christ and enjoying Christ to the uttermost, being saturated by Him and filled with Him to such an extent that they become an expression of God.

Whatever we eat we express. When I was young, I would sometimes visit my grandparents who lived at the seashore. They often ate fish, whereas our family hardly ever ate fish. Whenever I went to my grandparents' home, I smelled nothing but fish. One day I asked my mother why everyone there smelled like fish. My mother replied, "Do you not know that they eat fish every day? That is why they smell like fish!" What we eat we become and we express.

When we eat Jesus, we "smell of" Him (2 Cor. 2:15), we express Him, and we become Him. What is the church? The church is the expression of the very Christ whom we eat. All the fullness of the Godhead is embodied in this Christ, and this very Christ is our bread of life (John 6:48). He said, "He who eats Me shall also live because of Me" (John 6:57). When we eat Christ, we live by Him. This Christ is the embodiment of the Triune God; when we eat Christ, we eat the Triune God. Our Savior, Jesus Christ, the embodiment of the Triune God, is our daily manna, our daily food. We eat Him, so we express Him. This expression is the fullness of the One who fills all in all. Eventually this is the fullness of the Triune God. We can be such an expression by eating Jesus. Let Him saturate your entire being. Let Him settle in every room, every avenue, and every corner of your inner being—in your mind, your emotion, your will, your conscience, your soul, and your spirit; in your loving, your decisions, your intention, and your motive. Whatever you do must be filled with Christ.

To eat Jesus is simply to take Him in and let Him be assimilated into our being. To eat means to receive food into our being; to eat Jesus means to receive Him into our being. The issue of our eating Him is the fullness of the One who fills all in all and also of the very Triune God. This fullness is the church. The church is not only an assembly, nor is it only the house of God, the family of God; it is also the Body, an organism of this living One, which eventually becomes His fullness and the fullness of the Triune God.]

Do you know how to eat Jesus? He went through the process of incarnation, human living, crucifixion, resurrection, and ascension to be the life-giving Spirit (1 Cor. 15:45b). According to John 6, He went through the process to be embodied in the Word. That is why He said in John 6:63, "It is the Spirit who gives life; the flesh profits nothing; the words which I have spoken unto you are spirit and are life." The word is spirit and life. The Spirit is His person. The word has His essence. Whenever we come to the word with our spirit, we may touch the Spirit. When we mix our reading of the Word with calling and praying, we touch the Spirit. This is the way to eat Jesus. Eph. 6:17-18a confirms this. It says, "And receive the helmet of salvation, and the sword of the Spirit which is the word of God, By means of all prayer and petition, praying at every time in spirit." By praying in spirit, we take in the Spirit which is the word of God. This is the way to eat Jesus. You can eat Jesus by yourself and with your companions. This is the way for us to take in His riches to become His fullness. Right now, practice pray-reading the two verses quoted in this paragraph.

Questions

1. What is the significance of Christ being the Head of the Body?

2. We have seen that the Body of Christ is composed of organic members. Could you hire or fire anyone for a particular function in the Body? Why?

3. How do we as members of the Body of Christ become His fullness?

Quoted Portions

1. Organism of the Triune God in the Organic Union of the Divine Trinity (Lee/LSM), p. 8.

2. Conclusion of the New Testament (Lee/LSM), pp. 2265, 2270.

3. Basic Revelation in the Holy Scriptures (Lee/LSM), p. 61.

Further References

1. Basic Revelation in the Holy Scriptures (Lee/LSM), pp. 59, 62.

2. Body of Christ (Lee/LSM), p. 30.

3. Building Up of the Body of Christ (Lee/LSM), pp. 8-9.

4. Completing Ministry of Paul (Lee/LSM), pp. 35, 77.

5. Conclusion of the New Testament (Lee/LSM), pp. 2245, 2099-2100.

6. Life Study of Ephesians (Lee/LSM), pp. 156, 624.

7. The One New Man (Lee/LSM), p. 9.

8. The Organic Building Up of the Church as the Body of Christ (Lee/LSM), pp. 17, 31-32.

9. Practical and Organic Building Up of the Church (Lee/LSM), pp. 8-9.

10. The Practical Expression of the Church (Lee/LSM), pp. 14-15.

11. The Problem of the Unity of the Church (Nee/LSM), pp. 39-41.

THE STATUS OF THE CHURCH (3)

GOD'S MASTERPIECE, THE NEW MAN, AND THE COUNTERPART OF CHRIST

Scripture Reading

Eph. 2:10; 2:15; 4:22-24; Col. 3:10-11; Gen. 1:26-27; Eph. 6:12; 5:22-33; Gen. 2:21-24; John 3:29-30; 2 Cor. 11:2; Rev. 19:7-8; Rev. 21:2, 7-9, 17.

Outline

I. God's masterpiece

II. The new man
   A. Created by Christ on the cross
   B. Bearing God's image to express Him
   C. Fighting as a warrior

III. The counterpart of Christ
   A. The church as the bride, the wife, of Christ as the Bridegroom, the Husband
   B. To be married at Christ's coming back
   C. To be consummated in the New Jerusalem for eternity
   D. To be a couple in eternity

Text

I. GOD'S MASTERPIECE

[Ephesians 2:10 says, "For we are His workmanship." The Greek word for workmanship, poiema, can also be translated masterpiece or poem. It conveys the thought of a piece of work that expresses its maker or author. The church is a poem! In the whole universe the church stands out as an expression of God's wisdom; its design cannot be improved upon. It is like pleasant music or a lovely poem. What a matchless display of divine wisdom! Who can improve on this supreme handiwork of God!

When it comes to the way a building is designed, there can always be changes and improvements. An architect often modifies his designs, as he becomes aware of their shortcomings. But what God designs has no room for improvement. Man cannot imitate it. Any adjustment would be for the worse. Consider the way the human body was designed. What a work of art the facial pattern alone is! The placement of our two eyes, our two ears, our nose, and our lips makes a beautiful appearance. Our body with two shoulders, two lovely hands, and so forth, is worthy of admiration. The church is a far greater, more magnificent design than the human body! The church is a poem declaring and demonstrating God's wisdom and design.]

[God has made many things, but none of them is as dear, precious, valuable, and desirable as the church. The church is God's masterpiece. Writers, composers, and artists often attempt to achieve a masterpiece, an outstanding work. God created the heavens and the earth, but neither the heavens nor the earth is God's masterpiece. Likewise, God created man, but not even man is God's masterpiece. Only one item of God's work in this universe is His masterpiece, and this masterpiece is the church. As God's masterpiece, the church is the Body of Christ, the fullness of the One who fills all in all. What could be a greater work than this? Furthermore, the church as God's masterpiece is the corporate and universal new man (2:15). Because we see things from the side of the messed-up "kitchen" of the church life, we may not realize that the church is such a masterpiece.]

II. THE NEW MAN

[The church is also the new man (Eph. 2:15; 4:24; Col. 3:10). There is a sense in which the whole human race is just one corporate man. All the different peoples on earth comprise this one man, who in the Scripture is called the old man or Adam. God at the beginning did not create two men, but only Adam. This one man was mankind. In Genesis

1:26-27 the whole human race was created. But on the cross, through Christ and in Him, God created another man, a new man! This man is also corporate; we are included in him. Adam was the old man; Christ with the church is the new man. This new man is not only Christ, but also the church. Christ is the Head of this universal man; the church is His Body.

As the body exists for the expression of the head, so the church as the Body of Christ is Christ's expression. As man exists for the expression of God, so the church as the new man is God's expression. The whole church is a corporate yet single man. There are many local churches all over] the earth, [yet altogether they are only one man. Throughout the earth today, this one universal man expresses God. As the Body, the church expresses Christ. As the new man, the church expresses God.]

[Ephesians 2:15 says that Christ through the cross "abolished in His flesh the law of the commandments in ordinances, that He might create the two in Himself into one new man." Then in Ephesians 4:22-24 we are told to put off the old man and to put on the new man. This new man is the Body of Christ. To put on the new man means to live a life by the Body. Before our salvation we were living in the old man, in the old society, but now we are members of Christ, living in His Body. We should put off the old man with the old social life, and we should put on the new man, the church.]

As the church people, we have left the old man through baptism into the new man; however, we may still think, act, talk, and look like people from the old society. We have left the old man through baptism; therefore, we should walk in newness of life (Rom. 6:3-4). We must spend more time in prayer, in reading of the word, in the gospel, and in the meetings to be transformed by the renewing of the mind and to live in the practical church life. If we remain in the old way of life, we cannot be renewed and we have little participation in the new man church life.

[In this new man there is nothing natural, nothing Jewish, nothing Greek, nothing of social rank; everyone is full of Christ, so Christ is everyone and Christ is in everyone (Col. 3:10-11). There is nothing but Christ in the new man. Our life is Christ, our living is Christ, our intention is Christ, our ambition is Christ, our will is Christ, our love is Christ, and everything else about us is Christ. He saturates our entire being.]

A. Created by Christ on the Cross

[Ephesians 2:15 reveals that the church as the new man was created by Christ. Christ created the one new man with God's nature wrought into humanity. This action was something new. In the old creation God did not work His nature into any of His creatures, not even into man. In the creation of the one new man, however, God's nature has been wrought into man to make His nature one entity with humanity.

The new creation, like the old creation, is not something individual but something corporate. In the old creation God did not create millions of men; on the contrary, He created one man Adam, who includes all men. The principle is the same with God's new creation. In the new creation we are all parts of the new man, the church, composed of the many sons of God.

There is a basic difference between the new creation and the old creation. God's life and nature are not wrought into the old creation, but the new creation does possess the divine life and the divine nature. Although the old creation came into being through the work of the mighty God, He Himself does not reside in it. Hence, the first creation has no divine content. The divine nature does not dwell in the old creation, and that is why it has become old. Adam did not have the life of God or the nature of God. We can receive the divine life and the divine nature only by believing in the Lord Jesus Christ and being regenerated by the Spirit. When we believed in Christ, God's life and nature were imparted to us and made us a new creation.

Second Corinthians 5:17 says, "If anyone is in Christ, there is a new creation; the old things have passed away;

behold, they have become new." Anyone who is in Christ is a new creation. The old things of the flesh have passed away through the death of Christ, and all has become new in Christ's resurrection. To be in Christ is to be one with Him in life and in nature. This is of God through our faith in Christ (1 Cor. 1:30; Gal. 3:26-28).

The words, "Behold, they have become new," are a call to watch the marvelous change of the new creation. The word "they" refers to the old things. The old creation does not have the divine life and nature; however, the new creation, composed of the believers born again of God, does have the divine life and nature (John 1:13; 3:15; 2 Pet. 1:4). Hence, the believers are a new creation, not according to the old nature of the flesh but according to the new nature of the divine life.

The new creation is actually the old creation transformed by the divine life, by the processed Triune God. The old creation was old because God was not part of it; the new creation is new because God is in it. We who have been regenerated by the Spirit of God are still God's creation, but we are now His new creation. However, this is real only when we live and walk by the Spirit. Whenever we live and walk by the flesh, we are in the old creation, not in the new creation. Anything in our daily life that does not have God in it is the old creation, but what has God in it is part of the new creation.

If we would be in the new creation, we must enter into an organic union with the Triune God. Apart from such a union we shall remain in the old creation. But now, by the organic union with the Triune God, we are in the new creation. As believers in Christ, we are the new creation through an organic union with the Triune God.

In Adam we were born into the old creation, but in Christ we were regenerated into the new creation. Here in the new creation we are not only God's assembly, God's house, and God's kingdom and not only Christ's Body and counterpart—we are also the new man. God's intention is to have a corporate, universal man. God wants such a man for the fulfillment of His eternal purpose. On the one hand, we were created in God's old creation and became the old man; on the other hand, we have been re-created in God's new creation and have become the new man.]

[The new man was created by Christ in Himself in a particular way. This particular way was Christ's death, for Christ created the new man when He was on the cross. While Christ was being put to death, He was working to create the one new man. In His death He created the different peoples into the new man. His death, therefore, was a tool used to work out the new creation.]

B. Bearing God's Image to Express Him

[God's creation of man in Genesis 1 is a picture of the new man in God's new creation. This means that the old creation is a figure, a type, of the new creation. In God's old creation the central character is man. It is the same in God's new creation. Therefore, in both the old creation and the new creation man is the center.

God created man in His own image (Gen. 1:26) and then gave man His dominion. Image is for expression. God wants man to be His expression. Dominion, however, is a matter not of expression but of representation. God wants man to represent Him in His authority for His dominion. In the old creation man was created to have God's image to express Him and also to have His dominion to represent Him.

The image refers to God's positive intention, and dominion to God's negative intention. God's positive intention is that man would express Him, whereas God's negative intention is that man would deal with God's enemy, Satan, the Devil. In the universe God has a problem, the problem of dealing with His enemy. Since God's enemy, the Devil, is a creature, God will not deal with him directly Himself; instead, He will deal with him by man, a creature of His creation. God deals with His enemy through man. Hence, in God's creation of man there were two intentions. The positive intention is that man would bear God's image for His expression; the negative intention is that man would have God's dominion to represent Him to deal with His enemy.]

C. Fighting as a Warrior

[The new man has the obligation of fighting against God's enemy. Therefore, the church as the new man is a warrior fighting against God's enemy, for the new man is now fulfilling God's purpose to express God and to fight against God's enemy for God's dominion, God's kingdom.

In Ephesians 6:12 Paul says, "Our wrestling is not against blood and flesh, but against the rulers, against the authorities, against the world-rulers of this darkness, against the spiritual forces of evil in the heavenlies." "Blood and flesh" refers to human beings. Behind men of blood and flesh are the evil forces of the Devil, fighting against God's purpose. Hence, our wrestling, our fighting, must not be against men but against the evil spiritual forces in the heavenlies. The principalities, the authorities, and the world-rulers of this darkness are the rebellious angels who followed Satan in his rebellion against God and who now rule in the heavenlies over the nations of the world. "This darkness" refers to today's world, which is fully under the dark ruling of the Devil through his evil angels. "The world-rulers of this darkness" are the princes Satan has set up to rule the various nations. Because of the working of Satan, who is the authority of darkness, the earth and its atmosphere have become "this darkness." "The spiritual forces of evil in the heavenlies" are Satan and his spiritual forces of evil in the air. The warfare between the church and Satan is a battle between us who love the Lord and who are in His church and the evil powers in the heavenlies. We must fight against these spiritual forces.]

III. THE COUNTERPART OF CHRIST

[In his exhortation in Ephesians 5:22-33, Paul presents the church as the counterpart of Christ. This reveals that the church is actually a part of Christ, for the church comes out of Christ and is unto Christ, just as Eve came out of Adam and was unto Adam (Gen. 2:21-23).

The first couple in the Bible, Adam and Eve, is a picture of Christ and the church. In His creation, God did not create a man and woman at the same time. He first created a man, and then from the man He created a counterpart to help him (Gen. 2:18). When the fowl, the beasts, and the cattle were brought before Adam, Adam named them one by one. But for Adam "there was not found a help meet for him" (Gen. 2:20). Adam desired to have a counterpart, to have someone to match him. However, among the fowl, the beasts, and the cattle, he could not find his counterpart. In order to produce such a counterpart, God caused a deep sleep to fall upon Adam (Gen. 2:21), and He took a rib out of Adam and built a woman with the rib (Gen. 2:22). The name of the woman was Eve. Eve was the same as Adam in life, nature, and form. Therefore, she could be his counterpart. When God brought Eve to Adam, Adam exclaimed, "This time it is bone of my bones, and flesh of my flesh" (Gen. 2:23, Heb.). At last, Adam had found one who could be his counterpart.

Genesis 2:24 indicates that a man and his wife are one flesh. The husband and the wife are two halves of a whole person. This is a marvelous picture of Christ and the church. Eve had the same life and nature that Adam had. This signifies that the church has the same life and nature that Christ has. Furthermore, Eve had virtually the same image and nearly the same stature as Adam. This indicates that the church bears the same image and has the same stature as Christ.

The church as the counterpart of Christ implies satisfaction and rest in love. Every husband needs satisfaction and rest, which are found in love. The brothers who are husbands can testify that our satisfaction and rest can only be in our wives. If we say that we are the church, then we must ask if Christ has His rest among us. This is a serious matter. A group of Christians should not be so quick to claim that they are the church. To be the church is to render to Christ the adequate satisfaction and rest in love. Christ needs such a counterpart. The church is not merely a gathering of God's called ones. The church, as Christ's counterpart, is a satisfaction and rest to Christ in love.]

A. The Church as the Bride, the Wife, of Christ as the Bridegroom, the Husband

[The church is the bride, the wife, of Christ, who is the Bridegroom, the Husband. The word of John the Baptist in John 3:29 indicates that Christ is the Bridegroom. "He who has the bride is the bridegroom." The bridegroom is a most pleasant person, who comes for the bride. The church should be a corporate bride prepared for Christ. To us He should be the attraction, the pleasure, and the satisfaction. As those who constitute the counterpart of Christ, we should enjoy Him as such a pleasant Bridegroom.

In 2 Corinthians 11:2 Paul speaks concerning Christ as the Husband. "I am jealous over you with a jealousy of God; for I betrothed you to one Husband, to present a pure virgin to Christ." Here we see that Christ is the believers' Husband, the unique Husband for us to love. We should belong only to Him, and we should appreciate Him and love Him. As our Husband, Christ has attracted us, and we have been presented as a pure virgin to Him. Now we should care only for Him, allowing nothing to replace Him in our hearts. Our love for Him should be pure, and our whole being should be focused on Him.

As Eve was Adam's increase, so the church as the bride, the wife, of Christ as the Bridegroom, the Husband, is Christ's increase. After John the Baptist referred to Christ as the Bridegroom, he went on to say, "He must increase, but I must decrease" (John 3:30). The increase in verse 30 is the bride in verse 29. For the Lord to increase means that He must have the bride. All the following must go to Him. All those who believe in Him should follow Him to be His bride as His increase.]

B. To Be Married at Christ's Coming Back

[In Revelation 19:7 and 8 we see that Christ and His counterpart, His bride, will be married at His coming back. Verse 7 says, "Let us rejoice and exult, and let us give the glory to Him, for the marriage of the Lamb is come, and His wife has made herself ready." The marriage of the Lamb is the issue of the completion of God's New Testament economy. God's economy in the New Testament is to obtain for Christ a bride, the church, through His redemption and divine life. By the continual working of the Holy Spirit through all the centuries, this goal will be attained at the end of this age. Then the bride will be ready.

The words "His wife" in Revelation 19:7 refer to the church (Eph. 5:24-25, 31-32), the bride of Christ. However, according to Revelation 19:8 and 9, the wife, the bride of Christ, here consists only of the overcoming believers during the millennium, whereas the bride, the wife, in Revelation 21:2 is composed of all the saved saints after the millennium for eternity.

As the Lamb, Christ needs a wedding. The Gospel of John reveals that Christ is the Lamb who came to take away sin (1:29) and also the Bridegroom who came that He might have the bride. Christ's goal is not to remove sin; His goal is to have the bride. In the book of Revelation we see that Christ is the Lamb and the coming Bridegroom. As the Bridegroom, He must have a wedding.

We need to emphasize the marriage of Christ and His bride so that we may know that our position is that of the bride and the position of the coming Christ is that of the Bridegroom. We are on earth preparing to become the bride to meet Him, and He is on the throne in the third heaven prepared to come as the Bridegroom to meet us. Therefore, He is coming as the Bridegroom, and we are going as the bride. When we meet Him at His coming back, we shall have a wedding.

Revelation 19:7b says, "His wife has made herself ready." The readiness of the bride depends on the maturity in life of the overcomers. Furthermore, the overcomers are not separate individuals but a corporate bride. For this, building is needed. The overcomers are not only mature in life but are also built together as one bride.]

C. To Be Consummated in the New Jerusalem

[The consummation of the church as the counterpart of Christ will be the New Jerusalem in the new heaven and the new earth for eternity. Revelation 21:2 says, "And I saw the holy city, New Jerusalem, coming down out of heaven from God, prepared as a bride adorned for her husband." The New Jerusalem is a living composition of all the saints redeemed by God throughout all generations. It is the bride of Christ as His counterpart. As the bride of Christ, the New Jerusalem comes out of Christ and becomes His counterpart. She is prepared by participating in the riches of the life and nature of Christ.

Revelation 21:9b and 10 say, "Come here, I will show you the bride, the wife of the Lamb. And he carried me away in spirit onto a great and high mountain and showed me the holy city, Jerusalem, coming down out of heaven from God." Whereas the bride is mainly for the wedding day, the wife is for the entire life. The New Jerusalem will be the bride in the millennium for one thousand years as one day (2 Pet. 3:8) and then the wife in the new heaven and new earth for eternity. The bride in the millennium will include only the overcoming saints, but the wife in the new heaven and new earth will include all the redeemed and regenerated sons of God (Rev. 21:7).]

D. To Be a Couple in Eternity

[Revelation 22:17a says, "The Spirit and the bride say, Come." This verse reveals that Christ and the church as His counterpart will be a couple in eternity. The Spirit, who is the totality of the processed Triune God, becomes one with the believers, who are now fully matured to be the bride. Therefore, the Spirit is the ultimate expression of the processed Triune God, and the bride is the ultimate expression of the transformed tripartite man. By the time of Revelation 22:17, the processed Triune God—the Spirit—and the transformed tripartite man—the bride—will be one and speak as one.]

[The Bible begins and ends with a marriage. The Bible begins with the marriage of Adam and Eve in Genesis and ends with the marriage of the Spirit and the bride in Revelation. This final marriage is the marriage of the processed, consummated, and dispensed Triune God as the Husband with His regenerated and transformed people as the bride. For eternity this universal couple will be the full manifestation of the Triune God expressed in all His glory. Therefore, the transformed tripartite man will match the processed Triune God forever for His full expression and satisfaction. This is the conclusion of the New Testament and also of the entire Bible.

At the conclusion of the Bible there is a couple—the Spirit as the consummation of the processed Triune God with the bride as the aggregate and consummation of the redeemed, regenerated, transformed, and glorified tripartite man. Here is an eternal, universal couple expressing the Triune God for eternity.]

Questions

1. What does the term "masterpiece" imply when referring to the church?

2. What is the difference between the old man and new man?

3. How did Christ's death on the cross create the new man?

4. List as many parallels as you can between Eve as the bride of Adam, and the church as the bride of Christ.

Quoted Portions

1. Completing Ministry of Paul (Lee/LSM), p. 39.

2. Life Study of Ephesians (Lee/LSM), p. 186.

3. Completing Ministry of Paul (Lee/LSM), p. 37.

4. Basic Revelation in the Holy Scriptures (Lee/LSM), p. 64.

5. Conclusion of the New Testament (Lee/LSM), pp. 2303, 2301, 2302, 2321, 2275.

Further References

1. Basic Revelation in the Holy Scriptures (Lee/LSM), pp. 65-66, 110, 117-118.

2. Body of Christ (Lee/LSM), pp. 21, 24, 55.

3. Completing Ministry of Paul (Lee/LSM), pp. 38-40, 46-47.

4. Conclusion of the New Testament (Lee/LSM), pp. 2305-2306, 2308-2321, 2293, 2395-2396, 2399-2300.

5. The Glorious Church (Nee/LSM), pp. 46-71.

6. Life Study of Ephesians (Lee/LSM), pp. 210-212, 223, 612, 624-625, 722, 798, 814, 816-817.

7. The New Way to Carry Out the Increase and Spread of the Church (Lee/LSM), pp. 41-43.

8. The One New Man (Lee/LSM), pp. 10, 19-20, 32-36, 39-42, 44-46, 48-49, 59, 61, 65-66.

9. The Organic Building Up of the Church as the Body of Christ (Lee/LSM), pp. 32-33.

10. Vision of God's Building (Lee/LSM), pp. 163, 183, 195.

THE STATUS OF THE CHURCH (4)
THE GOLDEN LAMPSTANDS

Scripture Reading

Exo. 25:31-40; Zech. 3:9; 4:2-10; Rev. 1:11-12, 20b; 4:5;
5:6; Col. 2:9; 1:15; Gen. 1:26; 1 John 5:11-12;
Rev. 21:18b, 23; 22:1, 5.

Outline

I. The golden lampstands typifying Christ as the embodiment of the Triune God
   A. Gold signifying the Father's divine nature, the divine substance, essence
   B. The form signifying the Son as the embodiment of the Godhead in His humanity
   C. The seven lamps signifying the Spirit as the expression

II. The golden lampstands signifying Israel as God's testimony in the Old Testament and in the millennium
   A. Shining through the Seven Eyes (Spirits) of Jehovah
   B. As the Seven Eyes of Christ (the Stone-Savior for God's Building)

III. The golden lampstands signifying the seven local churches as God's testimony in the New Testament
   A. Shining in the dark age as in the night, bearing the testimony of Jesus
      1. With the Father's divine essence
      2. In the Son's human form
      3. Through the Spirit's expression
   B. To be consummated in the New Jerusalem

C. Expressing the processed Triune God
in eternity

Text

In this lesson we shall consider the final aspect of the status of the church—the church as the golden lampstands.

[One of the crucial symbols in the Bible is that of the lampstands. Revelation 1:12 says, "I turned to see the voice that spoke with me; and having turned I saw seven golden lampstands." Revelation 1:20b explains that "the seven lampstands are seven churches." The church, therefore, is signified by a golden lampstand.]

[The revelation concerning the golden lampstand is found in Exodus, Zechariah, and Revelation. In Exodus the lampstand signifies Christ as the embodiment of the Triune God. In Zechariah the lampstand signifies the nation of Israel as God's testimony. In Revelation the lampstands signify the church as God's living embodiment for the testimony of Jesus. Hence, the lampstand is a symbol of Christ, the nation of Israel, and the church. Furthermore, as we shall see, the lampstand signifies the embodiment of the Triune God. With Christ, with Israel, and with the church the golden lampstand is a portrayal of the embodiment of the Triune God.]

I. THE GOLDEN LAMPSTANDS TYPIFYING CHRIST AS THE EMBODIMENT OF THE TRIUNE GOD

[The lampstand in Exodus 25 typifies Christ as the embodiment of the Triune God. As a type of Christ, the lampstand portrays Christ as the resurrection life growing, branching, budding, and blossoming to shine the light. Jesus Christ is the embodiment of the Triune God. God is in Him, and apart from Him no one can find God.]

A. Gold Signifying the Father's Divine Nature, the Divine Substance, Essence

[With the lampstand as a type of Christ as the embodiment of the Triune God, there are three important things: the gold, the stand, and the lamps. These three matters imply the significance of the Triune God. Gold is the substance with which the lampstand is made, the stand is the embodiment of the gold, and the lamps are the expression of the stand.

According to Exodus 25:31, the lampstand was made of pure gold. Gold was the substance, the element of the lampstand in its entirety. In typology, gold signifies the divine nature, the nature of God the Father. If we consider this substance, this element of the lampstand, we shall see that it signifies the divine nature. Therefore, by this we can see God the Father, the One whose nature is the substance of the lampstand. The golden lampstand exists in the nature of God the Father.]

[God the Father is signified by the gold with which the lampstand was made. Hence, with the gold we see the first of the divine Trinity, the Father.]

B. The Form Signifying the Son
as the Embodiment of the Godhead in His Humanity

[In Exodus 25 the lampstand made of pure gold had a definite form or shape. The form of the golden lampstand signifies the Son as the embodiment of the Godhead in His humanity (Col. 2:9). Hence, the form, the shape, of the lampstand signifies the second of the Trinity, the Son.

God the Father is invisible and abstract. God the Son is the embodiment of this invisible One. The stand is a form signifying God the Son as the embodiment of God the Father. This solid form of the lampstand is the embodiment of the gold. According to the New Testament, God the Father is embodied in God the Son. Therefore, in the lampstand we have the substance signifying the Father, and the solid form signifying the Son.

The gold of the lampstand was made into a prescribed form, which indicated its function. This form is Christ, who is the image of God (2 Cor. 4:4; Col. 1:15). When God created man, He created him in His image (Gen. 1:26). Since Christ is God's image, man was created according to Christ. God does not have a physical form, but He does have an expression of His image. Christ, the beloved Son, is the image of the invisible God. The function of this image, this form, is to express God. "No one has ever seen God; the only begotten Son, who is in the bosom of the Father, He has declared Him" (John 1:18).]

C. The Seven Lamps Signifying the Spirit as the Expression

[Exodus 25:37 says, "Thou shalt make its lamps, seven." These seven lamps signify God the Spirit being the seven Spirits of God for His expression (Rev. 4:5; 5:6). The shining of the lamps denotes expression.]

[Substantially the lampstand is one, but expressively it is seven, because it is one lampstand with seven lamps. In substance the lampstand is one piece of gold, but it holds seven lamps. This indicates that, mysteriously, in substance the Triune God is one but in expression He is the seven Spirits. The Father as the substance is embodied in the Son as the form, and the Son is expressed as the seven Spirits.

We can prove from the Scriptures that the seven lamps of the golden lampstand signify the Spirit expressing Christ. If we had only the record in Exodus, it would be difficult to realize that these seven lamps are the Spirit. But as we proceed from Exodus to Zechariah, we see that the seven lamps are the seven eyes of Christ, the seven eyes of Jehovah (Zech. 3:9; 4:10). As we continue to Revelation, we see that the seven eyes of the Lamb are the seven eyes which are the intensified Spirit of God (Rev. 5:6). Hence, we have a strong basis for saying that the seven lamps are the seven Spirits, that is, the sevenfold intensified Spirit, as the expression of Christ.]

Thus, the seven lamps are the expression of God the Son as the embodiment of God the Father. The gold signifies the Father as the substance, the stand signifies the Son as the embodiment of the Father, and the lamps signify the Spirit as the expression of the Father in the Son. Thus, the significance of the Triune God is implied in the lampstand.

II. THE GOLDEN LAMPSTAND SIGNIFYING ISRAEL
AS GOD'S TESTIMONY
IN THE OLD TESTAMENT AND IN THE MILLENNIUM

[The lampstand is first mentioned in Exodus 25. Near the end of the Old Testament, the lampstand is mentioned again in Zechariah 4:2. "What seest thou? And I said, I have looked, and behold a lampstand all of gold, with a bowl upon the top of it, and his seven lamps thereon, and seven pipes to the seven lamps, which are upon the top thereof" (Heb.). Here the lampstand signifies Israel as God's testimony in the Old Testament and in the millennium. In Old Testament times, whenever the nation of Israel was in a normal condition, it was God's testimony. In the coming millennium, the restored nation of Israel will once again be God's testimony symbolized by a golden lampstand.

In Exodus 25 we only have the lampstand with the seven lamps; there is no mention of what the seven lamps refer to. In Zechariah, however, we are given a definite interpretation of the seven lamps, for in this book we are told that the seven lamps are the seven eyes of Jehovah (4:10) and the seven eyes of the stone (3:9).]

A. Shining through the Seven Eyes (Spirits) of Jehovah

[In Zechariah we have the seven eyes and the seven lamps but not the seven Spirits. But in Revelation the seven lamps are developed into the seven Spirits. "Out of the throne come forth lightnings and voices and thunders; and seven lamps of fire are burning before the throne, which are the seven Spirits of God" (Rev. 4:5). Here we have a new and further development of the seven lamps as the seven Spirits, for we are told clearly that the seven lamps are the seven Spirits of God. Since the seven lamps are the seven eyes and also the seven Spirits, then the seven eyes in Zechariah 4:10 are the seven Spirits. This gives us the ground to say that the lampstand in Zechariah 4 shines through the seven eyes, the seven Spirits, of Jehovah.]

B. As the Seven Eyes of Christ
(the Stone-Savior for God's Building)

[The seven eyes, the seven Spirits, of Jehovah are the seven eyes of Christ, who is the Stone-Savior for God's building. Zechariah 3:9 says, "For behold the stone that I have laid before Joshua; upon one stone shall be seven eyes: behold, I will engrave the graving thereof, saith the Lord of hosts, and I will remove the iniquity of that land in one day." The reference to engraving the stone indicates that this stone is Christ. The Lord Jesus as the building stone, was engraved, dealt with, by God on the cross for the iniquity of God's people. In one day, by that engraving on the cross, the Lord Jesus took away all the sins of God's people (John 1:29). Hence, the stone with the seven eyes is Christ, the Stone-Savior.

We know that Christ is the Stone-Savior by the fact that the seven eyes of the stone in Zechariah 3:9 become the seven eyes of the Lamb in Revelation 5:6. "I saw in the midst of the throne and of the four living creatures, and in the midst of the elders, a Lamb standing as having been slain, having seven horns and seven eyes, which are the seven Spirits of God, sent forth into all the earth." The Lamb here has seven eyes, which are the seven Spirits of God. In Revelation 4:5 the seven lamps are the seven Spirits of God, and in 5:6 the seven eyes of the Lamb are the seven Spirits of God. Here we have a further development over Zechariah, for the seven eyes are not only the seven eyes of the stone but also the seven eyes of the Lamb. These seven eyes of the Lamb are the seven Spirits of God sent forth into all the earth. This is a reference to Zechariah 4:10, where we are told that the seven eyes of Jehovah run to and fro through the whole earth. In Zechariah 3 and 4 we have the seven eyes of the stone, the seven lamps of the lampstand, and the seven eyes of Jehovah, all of which are the seven Spirits of God.]

III. THE SEVEN GOLDEN LAMPSTANDS
SIGNIFYING THE SEVEN LOCAL CHURCHES
AS GOD'S TESTIMONY IN THE NEW TESTAMENT

[Both in Exodus and Zechariah the lampstand is uniquely one. But in Revelation, the book of consummation, there are seven lampstands signifying seven local churches (Rev. 1:12, 20b). This indicates that Christ as signified by the lampstand in Exodus and the Spirit of God as signified by the seven lamps of the lampstand in Zechariah are for the reproduction of the local churches. One lampstand is reproduced in the seven lampstands. Actually, there were more than seven local churches on earth at the time of Revelation. Hence, the number seven in Revelation 1 is a representative number. All the local churches as the many lampstands are the reproduction of Christ and the Spirit as the one lampstand. This reproduction is actually a multiplication of the wonderful expression of Christ as the life-giving Spirit in a practical way.

In Exodus 25 the emphasis is on the stand—on Christ. In Zechariah the emphasis is on the lamps—on the Spirit. Eventually, in Revelation both the stand and the lamps, that is, both Christ and the Spirit, are reproduced as the local churches. The lampstands with their lamps in Revelation are the reproduction of Christ and the Spirit.]

A. Shining in the Dark Age as in the Night,
Bearing the Testimony of Jesus

[As golden lampstands, the churches shine in the darkness. The word "lampstand" enables us to understand much about the church and its function. The church is not the lamp; it is the lampstand, the stand which holds the lamp. Without the lamp, the lampstand is vain and means nothing. But the lampstand holds the shining lamp. Christ is the lamp (Rev. 21:23), and the church is the lampstand holding the lamp. God is in Christ, and Christ as the lamp is held by the stand to shine out God's glory. This is the testimony of the church.

The churches as golden lampstands bear the testimony of Jesus. "The testimony of Jesus" (Rev. 1:2, 9; 20:4) is an all-inclusive expression. The testimony of Jesus is the testimony of the Son coming with the Father by the Spirit to live on earth, to die on the cross to clear up the universe, to release the divine life, and to resurrect from the dead to become the life-giving Spirit, who then comes as the Son with the Father compounded with divinity, humanity, human living, crucifixion, and resurrection, including all the divine attributes and the human virtues. Such a compound testimony is the testimony of Jesus. This testimony has a symbol—the golden lampstand. The golden lampstand is the testimony of Jesus.

The lampstands shine in the darkness. If there were no darkness, there would be no need for the shining of the light of the lamp. The shining of the lamp is quite particular. In order for the lamp to shine, it must have oil burning within it. If the oil burns within the lamp, the light will shine out through all the darkness. This is the function of the church. The function of the church is not simply to preach or to teach doctrine. In the dark night of this age, the church must shine out the glory of God.]

1. With the Father's Divine Essence

[As the testimony of Jesus, the golden lampstands are the embodiment of the Triune God. In the golden lampstand there are three main factors: the substance, the shape or form, and the expression. The substance, the material, of the lampstand is gold, which signifies the Father's divine essence.

There was no dross in the lampstand, for it was made of pure gold. In typology, dross signifies something other than God brought in to cause a mixture. The fact that the church is a golden lampstand indicates that we should not bring anything other than God into the church life. Even good things such as ethics, culture, education, and proper religion are dross, because they are not God Himself. Only God, the divine Being, is the gold which is the substance of the lampstand. No doubt Paul had this realization when he told us in 1 Corinthians 3 that upon Christ, the unique foundation of the church, we should build not with wood, hay, or stubble but with gold, silver, and precious stones.

As the local churches, the lampstands are golden in nature. In typology, gold signifies divinity, the divine nature of God. All the local churches are divine in nature; they are constituted of the divine essence. These stands are not built of clay, wood, or any inferior substance; they are constructed out of pure gold. This means that all the local churches must be divine. Without divinity, there can be no church. Although the church is composed of humanity with divinity, humanity should not be the basic nature of the local churches. The basic nature of the local churches must be divinity.]

2. In the Son's Human Form

[The golden lampstand is not a lump of gold but gold in a definite form and purposeful shape. The form, the shape, of the lampstand signifies the Son's human form. Christ, the Son, is the embodiment of the Godhead, the embodiment of the Father's nature (Col. 2:9). Therefore, the church should have not only the Father's divine essence but also the Son's human form.

The fact that the form of the lampstand signifies the Son as the embodiment of the Godhead indicates that the church should not be vague but should have a definite shape. In chapters two and three of Revelation the Lord Jesus, as the embodiment of the invisible God, was clearly standing as He spoke to the churches. All the churches should also stand, having the Son's shape.]

3. Through the Spirit's Expression

[Furthermore, the golden lampstands as the testimony of Jesus have the Spirit's expression. The seven lamps of the lampstand shine for God's expression. These seven lamps are the seven Spirits of God. Thus, with the lampstand are the Father's essence, the Son's human form, and the Spirit's expression. Since the golden lampstand has these three aspects, we can say that the golden lampstand signifies the embodiment of the Triune God, with the Father as the substance, the Son as the form, and the Spirit as the expression.

To say that the church is the embodiment of the Triune God is not to make the church a part of deity or an object of worship. We mean that the church is an entity born of God (John 1:12-13), possessing God's life (1 John 5:11-12) and enjoying God's nature (2 Pet. 1:4). The church has the divine substance, bears the likeness of Christ, and expresses God. Because we have been born of God, we have God's life and possess His nature. Now we may enjoy this life and nature day by day and learn to live not by our natural life but by the divine life and nature. As we live this way and are transformed, there will be the fullness, the expression, the form, the appearance of Christ. Furthermore, we shall shine by the sevenfold, intensified Spirit.

As symbolized by the golden lampstand, the church is the embodiment of the Triune God to express Him. As members of Christ, we are sons of God born of Him, having His life and possessing His nature. Now we are learning to live by this life and nature that we may be filled and saturated with the processed Triune God to become His corporate expression through the sevenfold, intensified Spirit.]

B. To Be Consummated in the New Jerusalem

[The churches as golden lampstands will be consummated in the New Jerusalem. The New Jerusalem, the holy city, is the aggregate of all the lampstands. If we consider the facts that the New Jerusalem is a golden city (Rev. 21:18b), that it has one street which reaches all twelve gates (Rev. 21:21; 22:2), that the wall of the city is one hundred forty-four cubits high (21:17), and that the city itself is twelve thousand stadia high (21:16), we shall realize that the city proper must be a mountain. On top of this mountain is a throne, from which the street spirals down to the bottom to reach the twelve gates. On top of this golden mountain is the throne as the center. On the throne is Christ as the Lamb with God in

Him (22:1). This Lamb is the lamp with God in Him as the light (21:23; 22:5).

This golden mountain is a stand, and upon this stand is a lamp. Therefore, this golden mountain—the New Jerusalem—is a golden lampstand. As a golden lampstand, it has Christ as the lamp with God in Him as the light shining out for eternity. Thus, the New Jerusalem, the aggregate of all the lampstands, the totality of today's lampstands, is a consummate, universal golden lampstand to shine forth God's glory in the new heaven and new earth for eternity.]

C. Expressing the Processed Triune God in Eternity

[As the consummation of the golden lampstands, the New Jerusalem will express the processed Triune God in eternity. The New Jerusalem will be a mountain of gold with pearl gates and with a jasper wall built upon twelve layers of precious stones. Gold expresses God in His nature, pearls express Christ in His death and resurrection, and the precious stones express the Spirit in His work of transformation. Therefore, the New Jerusalem will be the triune expression of the processed Triune God—the expression of the Father as the source, the Son as the embodiment, and the Spirit as the realization and transmission.]

This is the final aspect of the status of the church. This aspect is very exciting because the same symbol was used for the Triune God, the children of Israel, and the church. We will be mingled with Him to such an extent that we will express Him in full. One of the symbols used for Him, the lampstand, is also used for the church. This is wonderful! What else can we say except "Hallelujah! To You, O Lord, be glory forever in the church. Your plan for the church is marvellous. I will give my whole life to You for Your church. I will spend my energy for the building up of Your church. I will dwell in Your church forever and ever. Amen!"

Questions

1. Write a short essay about how the symbol of lampstand reveals the Triune God.

2. Why is the lampstand an appropriate symbol for the church?

3. Explain in detail the final stage of the church as the lampstand?

Quoted Portions

1. Conclusion of the New Testament (Lee/LSM), pp. 2327-2328, 2337.

Further References

1. Basic Revelation in the Holy Scriptures (Lee/LSM), pp. 68, 106, 113-114.

2. The Church the Reprint of the Spirit (Lee/LSM), pp. 11-13, 22, 24-27.

3. Completing Ministry of Paul (Lee/LSM), pp. 9, 34, 74-75, 91.

4. Conclusion of the New Testament (Lee/LSM), pp. 2045-2100, 2329-2347.

5. The Divine Economy (Lee/LSM), pp. 122-125, 129-130.

6. The Economy of God and the Building Up of the Body of Christ (Lee/LSM), pp. 48-49.

7. On Home Meetings (Lee/LSM), pp. 44-46.

8. Life Study of Romans (Lee/LSM), pp. 235, 550.

9. Organism of the Triune God in the Organic Union of the Divine Trinity (Lee/LSM), p. 8.

10. The Practical Expression of the Church (Lee/LSM), pp. 10, 93.

11. Scriptural Way to Meet and Serve for the Building Up of the Body of Christ (Lee/LSM), p. 9.

12. The Spirit and the Body (Lee/LSM), pp. 77-78.

13. Vision of God's Building (Lee/LSM), pp. 74-76, 196-197.

THE TWO ASPECTS OF THE CHURCH— UNIVERSAL AND LOCAL

Scripture Reading

Matt. 16:16-18; Eph. 1:22-23; Matt. 18:17; Eph. 2:22; 4:4; Tit. 1:5; Acts 14:23; 13:1; Rev. 1:4a, 11; Acts 2:42; 1 Cor. 10:16-17.

Outline

I. The truth according to the Bible

II. The universal aspect
   A. Including all New Testament believers
   B. As revealed by the Lord in Matthew 16:18

III. The local aspect
   A. The believers living in the local churches
   B. The local churches being the local expressions of the Body of Christ
   C. All the local churches constituting the one Body of Christ

IV. The genuine ground
   A. The ground of locality—one city, one church
   B. The ground of the genuine oneness—one body universally

V. The local administration and the universal fellowship
   A. The administration being separate and equal locally
   B. The fellowship being one universally

Text

After seeing all the glorious details of the status of the church, we will address the two crucial aspects of the church—the universal and local aspects. The truths in the Bible always have two sides. Brother Govett called it "the twofoldness of the truth." A sheet of paper has two sides as it cannot exist with one side only; likewise, the church has two aspects. Most Christians do not see the two aspects of the church, and therefore have made many mistakes concerning this matter for centuries. In order not to make the same mistakes, we must pay close attention to this truth.

I. THE TRUTH ACCORDING TO THE BIBLE

[Most Christians would agree that they need the fellowship of a church. Actually, there are very few Christians who are not members of a church. Most Christians have a church, but the question is, do they have the proper church or an improper church? Today in every large city there are too many different so-called "churches." In the city of Seoul, Korea, the Roman Catholic Church is very prominent. However, it is wrong to associate the word Roman with the church. In the Bible there is no Roman Church. Colossians 3:11 tells us that in the new man there is neither Greek nor Jew. Thus, there is no such thing as the Jewish Church or the Greek Church in the Bible. Furthermore, there is no Anglican Church, no Chinese Church, no Korean Church, no Presbyterian Church, no Baptist Church, and no Pentecostal Church. All these "churches" are improper because they are not scriptural, not according to God's holy Word.

In order to know what is proper regarding the church, we need to study the Bible. I have been studying the Bible concerning the matter of the church since 1925. In this chapter I wish to present to you a brief outline of this matter. This brief, accurate, and clear outline is the cream of my nearly sixty years of study concerning the church. I am happy to present this outline to you. My desire is to impress you with the proper practice of the church life according to the Bible.

There is nothing wrong with the church itself, but the way Christians practice the church life might be wrong. Out of all the different ways of practicing the church life among Christians today, it is difficult to find one that is right. To be right in the practice of the church life is to be according to the Bible. The proper practice of the church life is not according to culture, not according to society, not according to any kind of religious background, and not according to our imagination; it must be absolutely according to the holy Word of God.]

II. THE UNIVERSAL ASPECT

A. Including all New Testament Believers

There is only one church in the universe; thus, the church is universal, comprising all the believers in Christ throughout time and in every place (Eph. 1:22). The universal church comprises all of God's redeemed saints in the New Testament age. The Old Testament saints, such as Abraham, Isaac, Jacob, Judah, Moses, David, and Isaiah, were not members of the New Testament church. The New Testament church began at the outpouring of the Holy Spirit in the book of Acts. John the Baptist was not in the New Testament church. The Lord Jesus said, "I tell you, among those born of women, there is no one greater than John; yet he who is littler in the kingdom of God is greater than he" (Luke 7:28). This shows that John was not a member of the New Testament church.

At His coming back, the Lord Jesus will close the church age, and many Jews will repent. Zechariah 12 gives us the details of their salvation. The Jews will be saved, but they will not be in the New Testament church. We are the most blessed people because we are in the most blessed age, the age of the church. The church has a universal aspect, it includes Peter, John, Paul, and all the believers through the centuries. It also includes us, and it includes those who will follow us in the future.

B. As Revealed by the Lord in Matthew 16:18

[In Matthew 16:18 we have the Lord's first mentioning of the church. In this verse He says, "On this rock I will build My church." What is revealed here is the universal church for the unique testimony of the Lord in the universe.

The universal church is to be built by Christ, the Son of the living God revealed by the Father. When Peter declared that Jesus is the Christ, the Son of the living God, the Lord said to Him, "You are blessed, Simon Bar-jona, because flesh and blood did not reveal this to you, but My Father who is in the heavens" (Matt. 16:17). Only the Father knows the Son (Matt. 11:27) and can reveal the Son to us. The Son revealed by the Father is now building the universal church, not the church in a nation or the church in a city.]

The universal church is to be built on the rock of the revelation concerning Christ, the Son of the living God. This revelation is the crucial factor, the central point of the building up of the universal church. The church is not to be built up according to any doctrine, creed, or so-called belief.

The gates of Hades, Satan's power of darkness, shall not prevail against the church. Rather, the church has the keys of the kingdom of heaven. That means the church has the authority to bind the devil and to loose all God's people for His church. Hallelujah! How glorious and powerful is the church.

III. THE LOCAL ASPECT

The other aspect of the church is the local aspect. It is important to see the universal aspect. It is equally important to see the local aspect. Many Christians see very little concerning the universal church. Others may see something concerning the universal aspect of the church, yet they do not regard the local aspect of the church to be important.

A. The Believers Living in the Local Churches

In order to live in the universal church practically, we have to live in the local churches. [Actually, we cannot live directly in the universal church. It is impossible for us to live in the universal church without living in a local church. The Lord is building up the universal church, and each of us is living practically in a local church. In Matthew 18:17 the Lord said that if, as a believer, you have a problem with another believer, you should tell it to the church. Surely the church mentioned in this verse is not the universal church; it must be the church in the place where you are. If you are in Seoul and you have any problem, you should tell the problem to the church in Seoul. If you are in Pusan, you should go to the church in Pusan; if you are in Hong Kong, you should go to the church in Hong Kong; and if you are in New York, you should go to the church in New York. The church to which you should tell your problem is the local church.]

B. The Local Churches
Being the Local Expressions of the Body of Christ

[The local churches are the local expressions of the Body of Christ (1 Cor. 12:27; Eph. 2:22). There is only one Body, but there are many expressions. Universally, all the churches are one Body, and locally, every local church is a local expression of that universal Body. A local church is not the Body; it is only a part of the Body. It is a local expression of the Body. The church in Seoul is not the entire Body; it is a part of the entire Body as the Body's local expression.]

C. All the Local Churches
Constituting the One Body of Christ

[All the local churches constitute the one Body of Christ (Eph. 4:4). In Matthew 16:18 the Lord said, "I will build My church." Here the church is in the singular number, indicating that it must be the universal church. But in the Acts and the Epistles, a number of times the Bible says "the churches"—the churches in Syria, the churches in Asia, the churches in Macedonia, and the churches in Galatia. How could the Bible refer first to one church and then to many churches? It is because the one church, the universal church, is the totality of all the churches, and all the churches are local constituents of the one universal church.]

IV. THE GENUINE GROUND

[Now we need to consider what the genuine ground of the church is. The ground denotes the site on which a building is built. Every building is built upon a certain piece of land, and this land is the ground on which the building is constructed. The church has spread to many nations in Europe, North and South America, Africa, and Asia. In all the different nations, the church is built upon the proper ground.]

A. The Ground of Locality—One City, One Church

[The proper ground for the building of the church is the ground of locality. When the church spread to Korea, it first came to Seoul. The church is now being built in Seoul. Thus, the city of Seoul has become its ground.

In the Bible the church does not bear any particular name. In this respect, the church is like the moon. The moon does not have a particular name; its name is simply the moon. We do not name the moon the American moon, the Chinese moon, the Korean moon, or the German moon. There is only one moon, not many moons. However, we may speak of the moon in Seoul, the moon in Osaka, or the moon in Shanghai. This does not denote many moons, but one moon appearing in different cities.

The city is the ground on which the church is built. Therefore, taking the city as the ground, we may denote the church according to the city (Rev. 1:11). For example, you may say that you are a member of the church in Seoul. Since my wife and I live in Anaheim, California, we are members of the church in Anaheim. Many of the saints attending this conference came from different cities. We use the names of these cities to denote the different local churches. Because of this, we may say that there are many churches. But actually, the many local churches are simply the one universal church appearing in many cities.

When the one moon is seen in Seoul, it is the moon in Seoul. When it appears in New York, it is the moon in New York. There is only one moon. The moon in America is the moon in Korea, and the moon in Korea is the moon in China. There is only one moon, but this one moon appears in different cities. Therefore, it is correct to speak of the moon in a certain city. It is the same with the church.

We may say that there are many churches, yet the many churches are still just one church. Are we all in different churches, or are we in just one church? The proper answer is that, locally speaking, we are in many churches, but, universally speaking, we are all in one church. Are you in the local churches, or are you in the universal church? It is wise to answer, "I am in the universal church by being in a local church." We are not in the Roman Church, the British Church, the American Church, or the Korean Church; we are in the universal church by being in the local churches. Since we are now in the city of Seoul, we should say that we are in the universal church by being in the church in Seoul. Although my wife and I reside in Anaheim, we should remember that during our stay with the saints in Seoul, we are not in the church in Anaheim, but in the church in Seoul.

Now let me ask, of what church are you a member? The best answer is that you are a member of the universal church which Jesus Christ is building, by being a member of a proper local church. While we are in Seoul, we are members of the universal church by being members of the church in Seoul. This is the proper practice of the church. We are members of the universal church by being members of one of the local churches. As long as we are members of a proper local church, we are members of the churches universally.

The ground of the church in Seoul is the city of Seoul. Therefore, in one city there can be only one church (Titus 1:5; cf. Acts 14:23). Furthermore, the city can never be divided; a city always remains one city. Thus, the ground of locality is permanently one. Just as the city cannot be divided, the church ground can never be divided. Since we do not have two cities in Seoul, we do not have two churches in Seoul. In Seoul there is only one city; hence, in Seoul there is only one church. This unique ground keeps the church in oneness.

Today, in a given city there may be many so-called churches. This may be likened to one city having many city halls. If a particular city has more than one city hall, this would mean that city is divided. In any city there is only one city hall. This preserves the oneness of the city. A local church is built on the ground of its locality. This unique ground may be termed the ground of locality. The ground of locality is a protection which ensures that a church in a particular locality will always be preserved in oneness.]

B. The Ground of the Genuine Oneness—
One Body Universally

[The ground of the church should not be merely local; it should also be universal. Locally, the ground of the church is the ground of locality; universally, the ground of the church is the genuine oneness. Christ has only one Body. The oneness of Christ's Body is the universal ground of the church.

Suppose all the local churches in Korea are one with each other, but are not one with the churches in other continents. If this were the case, the churches in Korea may have the local ground, the ground of locality, but they would not have the universal ground, the ground of the oneness of the Body. In the entire universe Christ has only one Body. All the local churches in the six continents—in North America, in South America, in Europe, in Africa, in Australia, and in Asia—are one Body. This is the universal ground of the genuine oneness.

The churches in England may say to the churches in Germany, "We are the churches in England and you are the churches in Germany; therefore, don't bother us." Locally they may be right, but universally they are wrong. They may keep the local oneness, but they destroy the universal oneness. Locally the ground of the church is the ground of locality, and universally the ground of the church is the oneness of the universal Body of Christ. Hence, there is the local aspect of oneness, and there is also the universal aspect of oneness.

I hope that the young sisters will be clear about this and that they will teach their children, "Children, from my youth I have learned that the church should be one in two aspects: one in its locality, and one in the universe." The church is one locally based upon its locality, the city, and it is one universally based upon the one Body of Christ. This local and universal oneness is the genuine ground of the church.]

IV. THE LOCAL ADMINISTRATION
AND THE UNIVERSAL FELLOWSHIP

[At this point we need to consider another two items related to the proper practice of the church life: the local administration and the universal fellowship. In the proper church life, the administration of the church is local, but the fellowship of the church is universal.]

A. The Administration
Being Separate and Equal Locally

[The administration of each local church is separate from the administrations of all other local churches. Furthermore, the administrations of all the local churches are on an equal level. In administration, no church is higher than another church, and no church is lower. In a country or nation there are different levels of government. The highest is the central government, and under the central government are the provincial, or state, governments and the city governments. This kind of government with different levels may be likened to a pyramid. The central government is the highest level, and the provincial and city governments are on lower levels.

But in the proper church life there is not such a thing. All the local churches are on one level. In the Roman Catholic Church, the highest level of administration is in the Vatican. The Pope is at the top, and around him are the cardinals. The Pope exercises control over Roman Catholics in all the nations. All over the earth he has a number of archbishops. Under the archbishops there are the bishops, and under the bishops are the priests. This kind of governmental organization is a religious hierarchy. Such a hierarchy should be condemned. In the proper practice of the church life, all the churches on the whole earth are on one level. On the top there is only one throne, the throne of the Head, Christ, in the heavens. Only the Head is on the throne. Under the Head, all the churches are on the same level.

Suppose the church in Seoul is the largest local church in Korea. Would it be right for the church in Seoul to control all the other churches in Korea? Suppose the church in Pusan is the second largest church in Korea. Would it be proper for the church in Pusan to be under the church in Seoul? Then, suppose there is a smaller church in the vicinity of Pusan. Would it be right for the church in Seoul, as the largest church, to control the church in Pusan, and for the church in Pusan to control the smaller church in the same vicinity? In answer to such questions, I must say strongly that this kind of hierarchy and control is absolutely wrong.

In reference to the administration of the local churches, I have used two adjectives: separate and equal. The administration of the church in Seoul is separate from the administrations in Pusan and Geochang. The administrations of these churches are separate and equal. Even the administration of the smallest local church in Korea is equal with the administration of the church in Seoul. If I were an elder in the church in Seoul, I might consider that, since the church in Seoul is the largest, I should exercise some control over the smaller churches. The elders of the smaller churches may also consider that, since the church in Seoul is the largest and the oldest, they should surely submit to the elders in Seoul. In human eyes this may seem right, but in the practice of the proper church life, it is absolutely wrong.

Every local church has its own administration, and this administration is separate from all the others. It is also equal with all the others. Although the church in Seoul has been in existence for a number of years, and a much smaller church may have come into existence only two days ago, the administrations of these two churches are separate and on the same level. The administration of the church is local. No church, regardless of how large and mature it may be, should control another church.]

B. The Fellowship Being One Universally

[Although the administration of the church is separate and equal locally, the fellowship of the church is one universally. In fellowship there is no separation. On this entire earth there is only one fellowship, and this fellowship is universally one. The fellowship of the church is one not merely in a particular nation, but in the entire universe. There is not one fellowship in England, another fellowship in the United States, another fellowship in Germany, another fellowship in China, and another fellowship in Japan. In these nations there are separate churches in many cities, but there is only one fellowship in the entire universe.

This fellowship is called the fellowship of the apostles. Acts 2:42 says that the three thousand who believed in the Lord Jesus and became the members of the church on the day of Pentecost continued steadfastly in the teaching and the fellowship of the apostles. In the church both the fellowship and the teaching should be one universally. In all the churches we should only teach one thing—Jesus Christ as the Spirit to be our life for the producing of the church. This is the teaching of the apostles. If a different teaching comes in, we must reject it (1 Tim. 1:3-4). We accept only one kind of teaching, the teaching of the apostles, and have only one fellowship, the apostles' fellowship.

In the early days all the believers continued in the apostles' teaching and fellowship. This fellowship of the apostles is with the Father and with the Son. First John 1:3 says, "That which we have seen and heard we report also to you, that you also may have fellowship with us, and indeed the fellowship which is ours is with the Father and with His Son Jesus Christ." The apostles' fellowship is with the Father and with the Son. This means that it is with the Triune God. Around the globe there is only one Christian fellowship—the fellowship of the apostles with the Triune God.

This fellowship is expressed at the Lord's table. When we eat the bread we participate in the fellowship of the body of Christ, and when we drink the cup we participate in the fellowship of the Lord's blood (1 Cor. 10:16). The Lord's body and blood are unique, and the fellowship of Christ's body and blood is also unique. By partaking of the one bread, we have become the mystical Body of Christ (1 Cor. 10:17). Therefore, this universal fellowship is the fellowship of the Body of Christ. It is the fellowship passed on to us by the apostles. Hence, it is the apostles' fellowship, and this fellowship is with the Triune God. Such a fellowship must be universal. In administration the churches are separate locally, but in fellowship they are united to be one universally.]

CONCLUSION

After seeing the two aspects of the church, we should give ourselves daily to live in a local church in order to build up the universal church. We should never join an improper church that 1) includes non-Christians; 2) excludes some genuine Christians in the city; 3) is administered other than locally; and 4) is not in fellowship with other proper local churches. It is right that a local church always remain in fellowship with the apostles who raised up that church. The Lord used the apostles to raise up the churches. The Lord certainly will continue to use them to lead the churches on to maturity.

We should always love the church in our locality. Never criticize the elders, the serving ones, or the saints. Wherever the Lord places us is the best place. Thank and praise the Lord that He has brought us into a local church among the many local churches.

Questions

1. How do you know that the church mentioned in Matt. 16:18 is the universal church?

2. How do you know that the church mentioned in Matt. 18:17 is the local church?

3. Write a prophesy (approx. 150 words) on how the words "fellowship" and "administration" show both the universal and local aspects of the church.

Quoted Portions

1. Vital Factors for the Recovery of the Church Life (Lee/LSM), p. 45.

2. Conclusion of the New Testament (Lee/LSM), p. 2140.

3. Vital Factors for the Recovery of the Church Life (Lee/LSM), pp. 48-56.

Further References

1. Basic Revelation in the Holy Scriptures (Lee/LSM), pp. 66-67.

2. Church Affairs (Nee/LSM), pp. 137, 146.

3. Completing Ministry of Paul (Lee/LSM), p. 45.

4. Conclusion of the New Testament (Lee/LSM), pp. 2139, 2149.

5. Further Talks on the Church Life (Nee/LSM), pp. 11, 19-20, 22, 25, 123, 132-133.

6. Life Study of Ephesians (Lee/LSM), p. 740.

7. Normal Christian Church Life (Nee/LSM), pp. 96-97, 105, 162.

8. The Organic Building Up of the Church as the Body of Christ (Lee/LSM), pp. 16, 18, 50, 64.

9. The Practical Expression of the Church (Lee/LSM), pp. 24, 26.

10. The Problem of the Unity of the Church (Nee/LSM), pp. 44-45.

11. The Spirit and the Body (Lee/LSM), pp. 13, 184.

12. Vital Factors for the Recovery of the Church Life (Lee/LSM), pp. 47, 49, 52-53, 55-57.

THE FORMATION OF THE CHURCH

Scripture Reading

Rom. 5:18-19; 1 Pet. 3:18; John 12:24; 1 Pet. 1:3;
1 Cor. 15:45; John 20:19-22; 7:39; Acts 1:8; Luke 1:35;
1 Cor. 12:13; Matt. 16:18;Eph. 1:22-23; Acts 2:33;
Acts 2:17; Luke 24:49; Acts 1:4; Luke 4:18.

Outline

I. Christ's crucifixion to redeem people for the church

II. Christ's resurrection to regenerate people to be living members of the church

III. Christ's ascension to pour out the Spirit on His people to form the church
   A. Being universal
   B. On the day of Pentecost and in the house of Cornelius
   C. By Christ the Head
   D. Through the outpouring of the Spirit
      1. The baptism in the Holy Spirit
      2. On the one hundred twenty believers
      3. On the believers in Cornelius' house

Text

After seeing the vision of the church, God's purpose for the church, the status of the church, and the universal and local aspects of the church, we need to see the formation of the universal church and the establishment of local churches in the next two lessons.

Many Christians prefer one "church" over another because it appeals to their personal preference, or they form their own church when they want to do something different. We must refer to the Bible to see who is qualified to form the church, and to see how the local churches are established.

[We need to realize that none of us is qualified to form the church. Only the Lord Jesus is qualified for this. In Matthew 16:18 He says, "I will build My church." He is the unique one who is qualified to form the church.]

I. CHRIST'S CRUCIFIXION TO REDEEM PEOPLE FOR THE CHURCH

In forming the church, we first need the material, the people of God. Where were the people and what was the condition of the people before Christ's crucifixion? Before Christ's crucifixion, no one was qualified to be members of the church. The church is glorious. The church is holy. The church is of life, of the Triune God. All the people were under the condemnation of God because of offenses (Rom. 5:18a). They were constituted sinners because of disobedience (Rom. 5:19a). They were alienated from the life of God (Eph. 4:18) and therefore could not express God. They were born in sin, they struggled in sin their entire life, and they will die in sin. They were neither glorious nor holy. Neither were they one with the Triune God, rather, they were enemies of God. They became the old man of the old creation. Ultimately, they were dead in their offenses and sins. How can anyone form the church with people in such a condition? It is impossible!

Who then could redeem these people back to God? Could you or I? No! No one in heaven or on earth throughout the history of mankind could save God's people out of this dilemma except Jesus Christ our Lord. He is the perfect and unique Savior, because He is the complete God and the perfect and genuine man. As the genuine man, He has blood to shed. As the perfect man, His death is not for His own sins, but for ours. As the complete God, He can release the life of God into us. There has been only one such person throughout the history of humanity qualified to be the Savior. Hallelujah! Since He alone is the Savior, He alone is qualified to form the church.

By His vicarious death (1 Pet. 3:18), we were saved from the judgment of God (Rom. 5:18b). He is more than our substitution. As a result of His crucifixion, not only were all the negative things terminated on the cross, but the divine life was released. The divine life was released from the one grain of wheat to produce many grains (John 12:24), the many sons of God. Now we are no longer sinners and no longer the old man. We no longer belong to the old creation, but we are now sons of God and members of Christ. Ultimately, we are the church, the Body of Christ.

II. CHRIST'S RESURRECTION TO REGENERATE PEOPLE TO BE LIVING MEMBERS OF THE CHURCH

We need the redemption of Christ to save us back to God. We need another life—the life of God to regenerate our spirit so that we may be sons of God and living members of the church. Otherwise, we are not qualified to be members of His Body and Christ can not form the church.

In order for Christ to form the church, it was necessary for Him to pass through death and enter into resurrection that He might impart the divine life into our being. He brought the Triune God into our being to cause us to be born of God (1 Pet. 1:3). [In resurrection He was transfigured from the flesh to the Spirit. First Corinthians 15:45b tells us that in His resurrection and through His resurrection Christ as the last Adam became a life-giving Spirit.

On the day of His resurrection, the Lord Jesus appeared to His disciples in a wonderful way. "When therefore it was evening on that day, the first day of the week, and when the doors were shut where the disciples were for fear of the Jews, Jesus came and stood in the midst and said to them, Peace be to you" (John 20:19). The disciples were "startled and became frightened and thought they beheld a spirit" (Luke 24:37), that is, a phantom, a ghost, a specter. The Lord said to them, "See My hands and My feet, that it is I Myself; handle Me and see, for a spirit does not have flesh and bones as you behold Me having" (Luke 24:39). The Lord had a physical body that could be seen and touched. After showing the disciples "both His hands and His side" (John 20:20), the Lord "breathed into them and said to them, Receive the Holy Spirit" (v. 22). This is the Spirit expected in John 7:39 and promised in 16:16-17,

26; 15:26; 16:7-8, 13. Hence, the Lord's breathing of the Holy Spirit into the disciples was the fulfillment of His promise of the Holy Spirit as the Comforter. Here the Spirit as the breath was breathed as life into the disciples for their life. By breathing the Spirit into the disciples, the Lord imparted Himself as life and everything into them.

The Lord Jesus came to His disciples on the day of His resurrection as the pneumatic Christ. The Greek word for "Spirit" in John 20:22 is pneuma, a word that also means breath or air. In John 1 Christ is the Lamb, but in John 20, after His death and in His resurrection, He is the pneumatic Christ. To say that Christ is the pneumatic Christ means that He is full of the divine breath. Whereas in John 1 Christ came as the Lamb, in John 20 He came as the pneuma. The fact that He breathed into the disciples and told them to receive the Holy Spirit indicates that He had come to them as the breath, the pneuma. The Lord became the pneumatic Christ through resurrection, and today, in resurrection, He still comes to us as the Spirit, the pneuma.

After the Lord Jesus came in John 20:19, there is no word or hint in John's record indicating that the Lord left the disciples. The reason for this is that He stayed with them, although they were not conscious of His presence. Instead of leaving them, He disappeared, becoming invisible. But to the surprise of the disciples, at various times and in different places He would appear, manifesting Himself to them. Acts 1:3 tells us that to the apostles "He presented Himself alive after His suffering by many convincing proofs, through a period of forty days, appearing to them." His appearing does not mean that He ever left them; it simply means that He made His presence visible to them.]

III. CHRIST'S ASCENSION TO POUR OUT THE SPIRIT ON HIS PEOPLE TO FORM THE CHURCH

[After appearing to His disciples for a period of forty days, the Lord Jesus ascended to the heavens. Ten days later, on the day of Pentecost, He, having again received the consummated Spirit, poured out this Spirit upon all His disciples.

At this point we need to consider the difference between the essential Spirit and the economical Spirit. The essential Spirit is for the believers' spiritual life, living, existence, and being, and the economical Spirit is for God's economy, work, and move. On the day of His resurrection the Lord Jesus breathed the Spirit into the disciples essentially as life for their spiritual existence. Then fifty days later, on the day of Pentecost, Christ, in His ascension, poured out the consummated Spirit upon His disciples economically as power for their work.

In the Lord's resurrection, the Spirit of resurrection life is likened to breath, breathed into the disciples for their spiritual being and living essentially. In the Lord's ascension, the Spirit of ascension power, poured out upon the disciples, is symbolized by wind for the disciples' ministry and move economically (Acts 2:2). The essential Spirit of resurrection life is for the believers to live Christ; the economical Spirit of ascension power is for them to carry out His commission.

We need to see clearly the difference between the breathing in John 20 and the blowing in Acts 2. The breathing in John 20 is for the imparting of the life-giving Spirit into the believers essentially for their spiritual being and for their spiritual living. But the blowing in Acts 2 is for the pouring out of the economical Spirit of power upon the believers, who have already received the essential Spirit into them. The pouring out of the Spirit of power is not for the believers' spiritual being or living; rather, the outpouring of the Spirit of power is for the believers' ministry and move. Therefore, the essential aspect of the Spirit is for living, and the economical aspect is for ministry.

The Lord Jesus Himself is the pattern for the believers' receiving the Spirit both essentially and economically. First, the Spirit came as the divine essence for the conceiving and birth of the Lord Jesus (Luke 1:35; Matt. 1:18, 20). This was the coming of the Spirit essentially for Christ's existence and being as the God-man.

The Holy Spirit also came to Jesus Christ as the divine power for the anointing of Christ (Matt. 3:16). This was economical and was for Christ's ministry and work, whereas the coming of the Spirit, (at His birth,) as the divine essence was essential and was for the Lord's being and living. When He came forth at the age of thirty to minister and work for God, He needed the Spirit as His power economically, even though He had already been born of the Spirit and had the Spirit within Him.

The believers also received the Spirit both essentially and economically. On the day of the Lord's resurrection, the essential Spirit for the disciples' spiritual existence and being was breathed into them. This is proved strongly by the record of Acts 1. According to this record, even before the day of Pentecost, Peter was changed. In the four Gospels Peter often behaved in a foolish, nonsensical manner. But in chapter one of Acts Peter is a very different person, able rightly to expound the Psalms.

Another indication that the disciples had received the Spirit essentially before the day of Pentecost was the fact, also recorded in Acts 1, that they were able to pray in one accord for ten days. Before the Lord's crucifixion, the disciples were striving with one another. But in Acts 1 there is praying instead of striving. What made it possible to pray in one accord for ten days? This was made possible by the indwelling Spirit.

Although the disciples had received the Spirit essentially and had this Spirit within them, they still needed the economical Spirit to descend upon them. Concerning this, the Lord Jesus said to them, "You shall receive power when the Holy Spirit has come upon you, and you shall be My witnesses both in Jerusalem, and in all Judea and Samaria, and unto the remotest part of the earth" (Acts 1:8). Then ten days after His ascension, the Lord Jesus poured out Himself as the consummated Spirit upon His disciples.

Now we can see that the church was formed by two steps. The first step was the Lord's breathing the Spirit into the believers for their spiritual existence and being. The second step was the Lord's pouring out Himself as the consummated Spirit upon the believers, baptizing them into one Body. By these two steps the believers were filled inwardly with the Spirit and were clothed outwardly with the Spirit. Inwardly they had the Spirit of essence, the essential Spirit, and outwardly they had the Spirit of economy, the economical Spirit. As a result, they were altogether wrapped up with the Spirit, and by being wrapped up with the Spirit they were formed into the Body of Christ. This was the formation of the church.

On the day of Pentecost Christ baptized the Jewish believers in the economical Spirit. Not too long afterward, in the house of Cornelius He baptized the Gentile believers in the economical Spirit. On the day of Pentecost in Jerusalem, the economical Spirit descended upon the Jewish believers, and in the house of Cornelius in Caesarea, the same economical Spirit descended upon the Gentile believers. By these two instances of the believers being baptized in the economical Spirit, Christ, as the Head in the heavens, baptized His entire Body—both the Jewish side and the Gentile side—in one Spirit into one Body, as fully revealed in 1 Corinthians 12:13. Therefore, the church was formed through Christ's baptizing all the believers, both Jews and Gentiles, in one Spirit into one Body.

A. Being Universal

Through the once-for-all baptism in the all-inclusive Spirit, the church, in the eyes of God, was once for all, universally formed to be the fullness of Christ for His universal expression. It is after this universal formation of the Body of Christ that, through the centuries, all God's chosen people were, are, and will be brought into not only the reality but also the practicality of the Body of Christ until the completion is reached.

B. On the Day of Pentecost and in the House of Cornelius

The formation of the church took place in two steps at two different times: on the day of Pentecost and when Peter was in the house of Cornelius (Acts 2:1; 10:24). What happened on the day of Pentecost with the Jewish believers and in the house of Cornelius with the Gentile believers was for the formation of the church, the Body of Christ.

C. By Christ the Head

The church has been formed directly by Christ the Head (Matt. 16:18). Ephesians 1:22 and 23 tell us that God gave Christ to be Head over all things to the church, which is His

Body. The important phrase "to the church" implies that whatever Christ the Head has attained and obtained is transmitted to the church. This transmission from the Head is the source of the Body.

D. Through the Outpouring of the Spirit

The formation of the church by Christ the Head took place through the outpouring of the Spirit (Acts 2:17-18, 33). The outpouring of the Spirit differs from the breathing of the Spirit into the disciples out of the mouth of Christ at His resurrection. The pouring out of God's Spirit was from the heavens at Christ's ascension. The former is the essential aspect of the Spirit breathed into the disciples as life for their living; the latter is the economical aspect of the Spirit poured upon them as power for their work. The same Spirit is both within them essentially and upon them economically.

The pouring out of the Spirit at Christ's ascension was the descension of the resurrected and ascended Christ as the all-inclusive Spirit to carry out His heavenly ministry on earth to build up the church as His Body for God's New Testament economy.

In Acts 2:33 Peter, speaking of the Lord Jesus, says, "Therefore having been exalted to the right hand of God, and having received the promise of the Holy Spirit from the Father, He poured out this which you both see and hear." This was not the promise given by the Holy Spirit but the promise given by the Father in Joel 2:29, quoted by Peter in Acts 2:17, and referred to by the Lord in Luke 24:49 and Acts 1:4, concerning the Holy Spirit. The exalted Christ's receiving of the promise of the Holy Spirit is actually the receiving of the Holy Spirit Himself. Christ was conceived of the Spirit essentially for His being in humanity (Luke 1:35; Matt. 1:18, 20) and was anointed with the Spirit economically for His ministry among men (Luke 4:18). After His resurrection and ascension, He still needed to receive the Spirit economically again that He might pour Himself out upon His Body to carry out on earth His heavenly ministry for the accomplishment of God's New Testament economy.

1. The Baptism in the Holy Spirit

The outpouring of the Spirit is the baptism in the Holy Spirit. To the Holy Spirit it is an outpouring, but to Christ the Head it is a baptism.

The Lord Jesus referred to the baptism in the Holy Spirit in Acts 1:5. "John indeed baptized in water, but you shall be baptized in the Holy Spirit not many days from now." This has been accomplished in two sections involving the Jewish believers and the Gentile believers. Therefore, in 1 Corinthians 12:13 Paul says, "In one Spirit we were all baptized into one body, whether Jews or Greeks." Since the Spirit is the sphere and element of our spiritual baptism and in the Spirit we were all baptized into one organic entity, the Body of Christ, so we should all, regardless of our races, nationalities, and social ranks, be this one Body. It is in the one Spirit that we were all baptized into the one living Body to express Christ.

2. On the One Hundred Twenty Believers

First, the outpouring of the Spirit was on the one hundred twenty believers (Acts 1:15; 2:1-4). On the day of Pentecost the Jewish believers, the first part of the Body, were baptized.

3. On the Believers in Cornelius's House

After the Jewish believers had been baptized in the Holy Spirit for the formation of the church, the Gentile believers were baptized in the Spirit in the same way (Acts 10:24, 44-47a). The Holy Spirit fell upon those who heard the word in the house of Cornelius outwardly and economically. In the case of the house of Cornelius, the Holy Spirit's entering into the believers essentially for life and falling upon them economically for power took place simultaneously when they believed in the Lord. However, only His falling upon them economically is noted in Acts 10:46, because it was outward and   could be realized by others by their speaking in tongues and praising God, whereas His entering into them took place silently and invisibly. They received both aspects of the Holy

Spirit directly from Christ the Head of the Body, without any mediatorial channel, before they were baptized in water by other members of the Body of Christ. This indicates emphatically that the Head of the Body baptized the Gentile believers into His Body directly. The Gentile believers in the house of Cornelius received the Holy Spirit economically, as the early apostles and the Jewish believers did on the day of Pentecost, directly from the ascended Head.

Peter's word in Acts 11 proves that what happened in the house of Cornelius was the second step in Christ's baptizing His Body in the Holy Spirit once for all. Peter said, "As I began to speak, the Holy Spirit fell on them just as also on us at the beginning. And I remembered the word of the Lord, how He said, John indeed baptized in water, but you shall be baptized in the Holy Spirit" (vv. 15-16). Therefore, the record in Acts strongly indicates that only two cases—that of the Jewish believers on the day of Pentecost and that of the Gentile believers in the house of Cornelius—are considered the baptism in the Holy Spirit. In these two instances the Head Himself did something directly on His Body for the formation of the church. By these two steps the Head of the Body baptized all His believers once for all, both Jewish and Gentile, into His one Body. Hence, the baptism in the Spirit is an accomplished fact carried out by Christ in His ascension both on the day of Pentecost and in the house of Cornelius for the formation of the universal church, His Body.]

This is how Christ formed His Body, the universal church. Do you think that anyone can form a church because he wants to or because he does not like the church he is in? No! The Bible clearly reveals that only Christ can form the church, because the formation of the church involves the redemption, the regeneration in our human spirit by the Spirit essentially, and the baptism of all the regenerated members into one Body by the Spirit economically. Can you or I or anyone else other than Christ form the church? We praise Him that He alone is qualified and worthy to form the church. Hallelujah! The universal Church has been formed.

In the next lesson we will see the establishment of the local churches.

Questions

1. Briefly describe why Christ is the only one capable of forming the church; and what steps were necessary for Him to do it.

2. List three references each for the essential and economical aspect of the Spirit.

3. Why were the believers able to receive the Spirit essentially before Christ's ascension; whereas, the receiving of the Spirit economically was not until after Christ's ascension?

Quoted Portions

1. Conclusion of the New Testament (Lee/LSM), p. 2102.

2. Vital Factors for the Recovery of the Church Life (Lee/LSM), p. 28.

3. Conclusion of the New Testament (Lee/LSM), pp. 2102-2109.

Further References

1. Basic Revelation in the Holy Scriptures (Lee/LSM), pp. 81-82.

2. Body of Christ (Lee/LSM), pp. 8, 11-12.

3. Conclusion of the New Testament (Lee/LSM), p. 2245.

4. The Economy of God and the Building Up of the Body of Christ (Lee/LSM), pp. 38-41.

5. The Exercise of the Kingdom for the Building of the Church (Lee/LSM), p. 15.

6. Experiencing Christ as the Offerings for the Church Meetings (Lee/LSM), p. 45.

7. God's Purpose for the Church (Lee/LSM), pp. 22-23.

8. Life Study of Ephesians (Lee/LSM), pp. 178, 180, 265, 598-600, 728-729.

9. The One New Man (Lee/LSM), pp. 44-50, 58-60.

10. Organism of the Triune God in the Organic Union of the Divine Trinity (Lee/LSM), pp. 31, 45-46.

11. Practical and Organic Building Up of the Church (Lee/LSM), p. 96.

12. Scriptural Way to Meet and Serve for the Building Up of the Body of Christ (Lee/LSM), pp. 12-13, 144, 152, 156-158, 172, 175-176, 203-204.

13. The Spirit and the Body (Lee/LSM), pp. 114-116.

14. Vital Factors for the Recovery of the Church Life (Lee/LSM), pp. 21, 36, 38.

THE ESTABLISHMENT OF LOCAL CHURCHES

Scripture Reading

Acts 1:8; 8:1; 13:1; 14:23; 1 Cor. 1:2; 2 Cor. 8:1; Rev. 1:4, 11;
1 Tim. 3:1; Tit. 1:5; Acts 20:28; Phil. 1:1; 1 Tim. 5:19-20.

Outline

I. The need for establishing churches

II. Being local

III. The pattern of the apostles in the New
Testament
  A. Starting from Jerusalem
  B. Spreading to Judea, Samaria, and Galilee
  C. Reaching Antioch in Syria
  D. Spreading in the provinces of Syria and Cilicia
  E. Turning to Asia Minor
  F. Spreading to the province of Asia
    in Asia Minor
  G. Reaching Europe—churches raised up
    in the province of Macedonia
  H. Spreading to the province of Achaia, next to
    Macedonia—churches raised up in
  I. Spreading to Italy

IV. The government of the established local
churches

Text

In the last lesson we talked about the formation of the
universal church. In this lesson we shall consider the
establishment of the local churches. What is the difference
between the formation and the establishment? [There is an
important difference between the formation of the universal
church and the establishment of the churches. The universal
church is not established; rather, it is formed with two
categories of elements: all the believers as the extrinsic

element and the all-inclusive Christ, the embodiment of the processed Triune God consummated as the all-inclusive, compound Spirit as the intrinsic element. Instead of being established, the universal church is formed by these two categories of elements.]

The formation is related to the universal church and was accomplished by the Triune God exclusively. He did the choosing, the redeeming, and the regenerating through His incarnation, human living, crucifixion, resurrection, and ascension. Only He is qualified to form the church. None of us can help Him in the formation of the universal church. The establishment of the churches, however, is different. It is a job that man can participate in by co-operating with the Triune God. Man not only can participate, man is needed to establish the churches.

I. THE NEED FOR ESTABLISHING CHURCHES

Why is there a need to establish the churches? The universal church has already been formed by the Triune God, but where can people see it? This glorious church must be practical and real to people. Local churches are needed so that people may see God's glory. Before the Lord ascended to heaven, He said in Acts 1:8, "But you shall receive power when the Holy Spirit has come upon you, and you shall be my witnesses both in Jerusalem, and in all Judea and Samaria, and unto the remotest part of the earth." He desires that man would express Him everywhere, from Jerusalem to the remotest part of the earth. Local churches are His practical expression and His testimony. Therefore, local churches must be established all over the inhabited earth for the sake of His testimony. The apostles, in Acts, began to establish the local churches and we are continuing this process until the Lord's return.

II. BEING LOCAL

[The local churches are established, not formed. Establishment is different from formation. We should not say that we are going to a certain place to form a local church there. On the contrary, we go to a certain city not to form a local church but to establish a local church. The church as a whole was altogether formed more than nineteen hundred years ago on the day of Pentecost and in the house of Cornelius. This means that, in the eyes of God, the universal church, the Body of Christ, has been formed. This is an accomplished fact. Now, after the formation of this universal church as a complete entity, there is the need for the spreading of the church. The way to spread the church is to bring it to a certain locality and plant it. This planting is the establishment of a local church.]

[No one is able to go to a place to form a local church. Assuming to do such a thing would be abominable in the sight of God, for it is presuming to do something that only God Himself can do. But although we cannot form the church, we have the position, the right, the opportunity, and even the commission to go to the uttermost parts of the earth to establish local churches.

The Lord has formed the church. Our burden is to bring the church as a tree to every city, town, and village and plant a church there. We all need to be faithful to carry out the burden to establish local churches by planting church trees. We should be burdened not just for the saving of sinners but for the establishing of churches. The married couples should be like Prisca and Aquilla who planted a church tree wherever they went. If we all have the desire to establish churches by planting church trees, the establishing of the churches will be very fast and prevailing.]

You may say, "I am only in high school, how can I go and establish churches?" Do not worry. Prepare yourselves for the Master's use by reading the word and by praying everyday, by being in the church meetings, by developing a good character, by studying hard, and by going to a good college. After you graduate from college you can attend the full-time training. By being trained, you will be made ready by the Lord. When the time comes, based on the sending of the Holy Spirit, you will have the opportunity, along with other saints, to plant church trees, that is, to establish local churches.

III. THE PATTERN OF THE APOSTLES
IN THE NEW TESTAMENT

In this section [we shall give a history of the planting of local churches recorded in the New Testament. According to this record, the planting of the churches began in Jerusalem on the day of Pentecost and went as far as Rome. Although Paul wanted to go to Spain, he was not able to do so. Therefore, during New Testament times, the planting of the churches went only as far as Italy.]

A. Starting from Jerusalem

[The establishment of the churches began from the day of Pentecost (Acts 2:1), and it started from the city of Jerusalem (Acts 2:5).]

1. The First Local Church—the Church in Jerusalem

[The first local church was the church in Jerusalem. The first mention of the church in Acts is in 5:11. "Great fear came upon the whole church." This was the church in Jerusalem.]

[Acts 8:1 clearly speaks of "the church in Jerusalem." This was the first church established in a locality within the jurisdiction of a city, the city of Jerusalem. It was a local church in its locality, as indicated by the Lord in Matthew 18:17. It was not the universal church, as revealed by the Lord in Matthew 16:18 but only a part of the universal church, which is the Body of Christ (Eph. 1:22-23). The record of the New Testament concerning the matter of the establishment of the church in its locality is consistent throughout (Acts 13:1; 14:23; Rom. 16:1; 1 Cor. 1:2; 2 Cor. 8:1; Gal. 1:2; Rev. 1:4, 11).]

2. Composed of:

a. The Elders

[The church in Jerusalem was composed of the elders, the serving ones, and the believers. Acts 11:30 speaks of a gift sent "to the elders through the hand of Barnabas and Saul."

This indicates that in the early days the finances of the church were under the management of the elders.

An elder is an overseer (1 Tim. 3:1). The two titles refer to the same person: elder, denoting a person of maturity; overseer, denoting the function of an elder.]

b. The Serving Ones

[Acts 6:3-6 speaks of seven serving ones in the church in Jerusalem. Acts 6:3 says, "Now brothers, select seven well-attested men from among you, full of the Spirit and of wisdom, whom we shall appoint over this need."] Seven brothers were chosen. [Since these seven were chosen to serve tables, they may be considered deacons, just as those whom Paul and his co-workers appointed later in the churches (Rom. 16:1; Phil. 1:1; 1 Tim. 3:8).

It is significant that in the appointment of the seven serving ones no leader was appointed. This indicates that no rank or position was regarded. All the serving ones are the servants to the saints. This is a good pattern for us to learn and follow that we may avoid leadership in rank and position in any form.]

c. The Believers

[Two verses that speak of the believers who composed the church in Jerusalem are Acts 2:44 and 5:14. Acts 2:44 says, "All those who believed were together and had all things common," and 5:14 says, "Believers were all the more being added to the Lord, multitudes both of men and of women." The designation "believers" denotes those who have believed in Christ as the Son of God according to God's New Testament economy. This designation, of course, indicates the matter of believing. Anyone who does not have faith in Christ, who does not believe in Christ, is certainly not a believer.

The believers are also those who have received Christ as their generating life for them to become the children of God.]

[Furthermore, the believers are those who have believed into Christ as the Son of God to have an organic union with Him.] The church is composed of such believers.

B. Spreading to Judea, Samaria, and Galilee

[The establishing of the churches spread quickly from Jerusalem to Judea, Samaria, and Galilee. Acts 9:31 says, "So the church throughout the whole of Judea and Galilee and Samaria had peace, being built up; and going on in the fear of the Lord and in the comfort of the Holy Spirit, it was multiplied." This verse speaks of Judea, Galilee, and Samaria, all of which were provinces in the Roman Empire. Judea was in the southern part of the Jewish land, Galilee was in the north, and Samaria was between the south and the north. There were churches in all three of these provinces.]

[The Jews considered Galilee a despised region and Samaria a region full of mixture. Nevertheless, 9:31 speaks of the church throughout the whole of Judea and Galilee and Samaria. This indicates that no matter how much Galilee was despised and Samaria was rejected by the Jews in Jerusalem, the churches raised up in those regions were all considered one church. In the local sense, they were the churches, but in the universal sense, all these churches are the church. Here we have a basic revelation concerning the oneness of the church universally.]

C. Reaching Antioch in Syria

[Acts 11:19-26 records the spread of the gospel to Phoenicia, Cyprus, and Antioch through the scattered disciples. Verse 26 refers to the church in Antioch. When Barnabas found Saul, "he brought him to Antioch. And it came about that for a whole year they were gathered in the church and taught a considerable number."]

1. The Church in Antioch

[Acts 13:1 opens with the words, "Now there were in Antioch, in the church that was there." This clearly refers to the local church established in Antioch.

Acts 14:26 and 27 say that Paul and Barnabas "sailed away to Antioch, from which they had been commended to the grace of God for the work which they had fulfilled. And having arrived and gathered the church together, they declared all that God had done with them." Verse 27 does not say that they gathered the believers but that they gathered the church. This indicates that the church in its essential meaning is a meeting, a congregation or assembly. There was such a church, such a congregation, in Antioch.]

2. Including Prophets and Teachers

[Acts 13:1 tells us that in the church in Antioch there were "prophets and teachers: Barnabas and Simeon who was called Niger, and Lucius the Cyrenian, and Manaen, foster brother of Herod the tetrarch, and Saul." Prophets are those who speak for God and speak forth God by God's revelation. They sometimes speak with inspired prediction (11:27-28). Teachers are those who teach the truths according to the apostles' teaching (2:42) and the prophets' revelation. Both prophets and teachers are universal as well as local (Eph. 4:11).

When the establishment of the local churches started with the one hundred twenty in Jerusalem, only typical Jews were involved. But according to the record in Acts 13:1, the prophets and teachers in the church in Antioch were from a number of different sources. Barnabas was a Levite, a Cyprian by birth (4:36). Niger, whose name means black and should denote a Negro, was probably of African origin. Lucius the Cyrenian was from Cyrene in North Africa. Manaen was the foster brother of Herod and was governmentally related to the Romans. Finally, there was Saul, a Jew born in Tarsus and taught by Gamaliel according to the law of Moses (22:3). The fact that the prophets and teachers here were composed of Jewish and Gentile peoples with different backgrounds, education, and status indicates that the church is composed of all races and classes of people regardless of their background, and that the spiritual gifts and functions given to the members of the Body of Christ are not based upon their natural status.

In 13:1 the Lord set up a pattern for the spreading of the churches. From Antioch the Lord's move turned to reach the Gentile world, and in the Gentile world there were many different kinds of people, people of different cultures, races, and statuses. Therefore, at the very beginning of this turn, the pattern was established to indicate that the churches are composed of all races and classes of people.]

In Antioch, the Holy Spirit set Barnabas and Paul apart to be sent out to establish more churches among the Gentiles (Acts 13:2-4).

D. Spreading in the Provinces of Syria and Cilicia

1. Churches Established

[The establishment of the churches spread to the provinces of Syria and Cilicia. In these two provinces of the Roman Empire churches were established. This is recorded in Acts 15:40 and 41. "Paul, having chosen Silas, went out, being commended to the grace of the Lord by the brothers. And he passed through Syria and Cilicia, establishing the churches."]

2. Strengthened by the Apostles Paul and Silas

[After the churches were established in Syria and Cilicia, Paul and Silas were sent by the apostles from Jerusalem to strengthen them. Such a strengthening implies a confirmation, recognition, by the apostles.]

E. Turning to Asia Minor

1. Churches Established in the Cities of Lystra, Iconium, and Antioch in the Province of Galatia— the Churches in Galatia

[Acts 14:21-23 refers to the churches established in the cities of Lystra, Iconium, and Antioch. After Paul and Barnabas brought the good news to the city of Derbe and made a considerable number of disciples (vv. 20-21a), "they returned to Lystra and to Iconium and to Antioch" (v. 21b). This is not the Antioch from which they were sent out on this journey of ministry (13:1); rather, it is the Antioch in Pisidia, the Antioch in Asia Minor.

The churches in these cities were "the churches of Galatia" (Gal. 1:2), a province of the ancient Roman Empire.

Through Paul's preaching ministry churches were established in a number of cities in that province. Hence, "churches," not "church," is used when Paul refers to them.]

2. Elders Appointed in Every One of These Churches

[Elders were appointed in every one of the churches in Galatia. Acts 14:23 says, "When they had appointed elders for them in every church, having prayed with fastings, they committed them to the Lord in whom they had believed." The Greek words rendered "in every church" contain the preposition kata with the distributive usage—according to church. The phrase "in every church" in 14:23 equals "in each city" in Titus 1:5. The comparison of these phrases indicates not only that the jurisdiction of a local church is that of the city in which it is located, but also that in one city there should be only one church. The eldership of a local church should cover the entire city where that church is. Such a unique eldership in a city preserves the unique oneness of the Body of Christ from damage. One city should only have one church with one eldership. This practice is illustrated, beyond any question and doubt, by the clear pattern in the New Testament (Acts 8:1; 13:1; Rom. 16:1; 1 Cor. 1:2; Rev. 1:11), and it is an absolute prerequisite for the maintenance of proper order in a local church.

All the churches in which the elders were appointed respectively by the apostles in Acts 14:23 were established within less than one year. Hence, the elders appointed in these churches could not have been well matured. They must have been considered elders because they were comparatively the most matured among the believers. They were not voted in by their congregation; they were appointed by the apostles according to their maturity in Christ. They were charged by the apostles to care for the leadership and shepherding in the churches.]

F. Spreading to the Province of Asia in Asia Minor

1. Churches Established in the Cities of Ephesus, Smyrna, Pergamos, Thyatira, Sardis, Philadelphia, and Laodicea

[Revelation 1:4 speaks of "the seven churches which are in Asia," and verse 11 says, "What you see write in a book and send it to the seven churches: to Ephesus, and to Smyrna, and to Pergamos, and to Thyatira, and to Sardis, and to Philadelphia, and to Laodicea." Asia was a province of the ancient Roman Empire in which were the seven cities mentioned in verse 11. The seven churches were in those seven cities respectively, not all in one city.]

2. Elders as Overseers Appointed in These Churches by the Spirit

[Elders as overseers were appointed in these churches by the Spirit (Acts 20:17, 28). To the elders of the church in Ephesus Paul said, "Take heed to yourselves and to all the flock, among whom the Holy Spirit has placed you as overseers" (Acts 20:28a). It was the apostles who appointed the elders in every church. But here Paul, the leading one who did the appointing, says that the Holy Spirit did it. This indicates that the Holy Spirit was one with the apostles in their appointing the elders and that the apostles had done this according to the leading of the Holy Spirit.]

[This reveals that a local church comes into existence only through the work of the Holy Spirit. In other words, the work of the apostles concerning the churches should be absolutely the work of the Holy Spirit. Because the Holy Spirit establishes the elders, it is the Holy Spirit who establishes the churches.

The overseers in Acts 20:28 are the elders in verse 17. This proves that overseers and elders are synonymous terms denoting the same persons.]

[The Greek word for "overseer" is episkopos, from epi, meaning over, and skopos, meaning seer; hence, overseer (bishop, from Latin episcopus). An overseer (1 Tim. 3:2) in a local church is an elder. The two titles refer to the same person: elder, denoting a person of maturity; overseer, denoting the function of an elder. It was Ignatius in the second century who taught that an overseer, a bishop, is higher than an elder. From this erroneous teaching came the hierarchy of bishops, archbishops, cardinals, and the pope. This teaching is also the source of the Episcopal system of ecclesiastical government. Both the hierarchy and the system are abominable in the sight of God.]

G. Reaching Europe—Churches Raised Up in the Province of Macedonia

[The spreading of the churches continued and eventually reached Europe. Churches were raised up in the province of Macedonia, and in 2 Corinthians 8:1 Paul speaks of "the grace of God which has been given in the churches of Macedonia." Macedonia is a province of the Roman Empire in southeastern Europe between Thrace and Achaia on the Aegean Sea.]

1. The Church in Philippi, Comprising the Saints with the Overseers and Deacons

[A church was established in Philippi, comprising the saints with the overseers and deacons. In Philippians 1:1 Paul says, "Paul and Timothy, slaves of Christ Jesus, to all the saints in Christ Jesus who are in Philippi, with the overseers and deacons." This verse indicates that the church in Philippi was established in good order. Notice that Paul speaks of the "saints ... with the overseers and deacons." This is the only place in the New Testament where such an expression is found. It is significant that Paul speaks of the saints with the overseers and deacons. In every local church the unique group consists of the saints. The saints are the components of a local church. Among the saints there are leading ones, which the New Testament describes as elders or overseers. Both titles refer to the same people. When an elder is carrying out his responsibility in the church, he is functioning as an overseer.

In 1:1 Paul also mentions the deacons. Deacons are the serving ones in a local church under the direction of the overseers (1 Tim. 3:8). The English word "deacons" is an anglicized form of the Greek word diakonos, which means a serving one.]

2. The Church in Thessalonica

[Thessalonica, like Philippi, was a city of the Roman Empire in the province of Macedonia, north of the province of Achaia. After the Macedonian call, which Paul received on his second journey of ministry, he and his co-worker Silvanus visited first Philippi and then Thessalonica (Acts 16:9-12; 17:1-4). The apostle stayed and worked there for only a short time, probably less than one month (Acts 17:2).

First Thessalonians 1:1 says, "Paul and Silvanus and Timothy to the church of the Thessalonians in God the Father and the Lord Jesus Christ." Both 1 and 2 Thessalonians were addressed to the local church in Thessalonica, composed of all the believers in Christ in that city. Such a local church is of the believers and is in God the Father and the Lord Jesus Christ. This indicates that such a local church is born of God the Father with His life and nature and is united with the Lord Jesus Christ organically in all He is and has done. Hence, it is of men (such as the Thessalonians), yet in God and in the Lord organically.]

H. Spreading to the Province of Achaia, next to Macedonia—Churches Raised Up in:

1. Corinth—the Church in Corinth

[The planting of the churches also spread to the province of Achaia. Achaia was south of Macedonia and was a province of the Roman Empire, a great part of today's Greece, in which is the city of Corinth.

In 1 Corinthians 1:2 and 2 Corinthians 1:1 Paul addresses "the church of God which is in Corinth." The expression "the church of God" is marvelous. It indicates that the church in Corinth was not the church of Cephas, of Apollos, of Paul, nor of any practice or doctrine, but of God. The church was constituted of the universal God, but it existed in Corinth, a definite locality on earth. In nature the church is universal in God, but in practice the church is local in a definite place.]

2. Cenchrea—the Church in Cenchrea, with a Deaconess

[Another church in the province of Achaia was the church in Cenchrea. In Romans 16:1 Paul says, "I commend to you our sister Phoebe, who is a deaconess of the church which is at Cenchrea." Phoebe was a deaconess, that is, a serving one. Paul held her in such high esteem that in the following verse he said that "she has been a patroness of many and of myself as well." The word "patroness" in Greek is a word of dignity, denoting one who helps, sustains, and supplies. Phoebe was a sister who served others at any price and at any cost. If we mean business with the Lord in the church life, we also need to serve the church and care for it regardless of the cost. The first requirement for the practice of the church life is that we serve the church.]

I. Spreading to Italy

1. The Church Raised Up in Rome—the Church in Rome

[Eventually, the establishing of the churches spread to Italy, and a church was raised up in Rome—the church in Rome. The fact that there was a church in Rome is indicated by Paul's words in Romans 1:7: "To all who are in Rome, beloved of God, called saints."]

2. Meeting in the House of Prisca and Aquila

[The church in Rome met in the house of Prisca and Aquila. In Romans 16:3-5a Paul says, "Greet Prisca and Aquila, my fellow workers in Christ Jesus, who risked their own necks for my life, to whom not only I give thanks, but also all the churches of the nations; and greet the church in their house." The church in their house was the church in Rome. There were not two churches in Rome, one called the church in Rome and another which met in the house of Aquila and Prisca. The church in Rome simply met in the house of this couple, so there was a church in their house.

On the one hand, this couple was for all the churches; on the other hand, they were for their local church in particular. When they were living in Ephesus (Acts 18:18-19), the church in Ephesus was in their house (1 Cor. 16:19). When they were in Rome, the church in Rome met in their house. Therefore, the church in Rome could be called the church in their house.]

IV. THE GOVERNMENT OF THE ESTABLISHED LOCAL CHURCHES

[The government of the church is very simple. The apostles go out and preach the gospel to establish the churches. Then they select the more mature believers and appoint them to be elders to shepherd, to take care of, a local church. The elders should take care of the churches according to the apostles' teaching. Because all the churches are established by the apostles, and the elders are selected and appointed in different localities by the apostles, in taking care of the churches all the elders should take the word of the apostles.]

The apostleship is universal and the eldership is local. Before Paul and Barnabas were sent out from the church in Antioch, they were teachers and prophets in that locality, being local (Acts 13:1). When they were set apart and sent out by the Holy Spirit, they became apostles, the sent ones for the universal church (Acts 13:2-4). Although their apostleship was universal, the churches they established were local.

[Since it is the apostles who appoint the elders, the apostles are above the elders (Acts 14:23). Because all the elders in the local churches are established and appointed by the apostles, the apostles are over the elders.]

[The eldership is local, and it is under the apostleship. First Timothy 5:19-20 indicates that an accusation against an elder should be made to the apostles. This shows that the elders are under the apostles.] It is not true that once the eldership is established, the elders are divorced from the apostles. This is illogical and impossible. They are still under the leading and guiding of the apostles who raised them up and appointed them to their office. They should always stay in fellowship with these apostles to ensure that the churches established by the apostles will stay healthy in the Lord.

Questions

1. What is the difference between forming the church and establishing churches? Who is responsible for each?
2. How is an elder appointed? What is his function? Use several verses to support your answer.

Quoted Portions

1. Conclusion of the New Testament (Lee/LSM), pp. 2121-2138.
2. Vital Factors for the Recovery of the Church Life (Lee/LSM), pp. 56-57.

Further References

1. Body of Christ (Lee/LSM), p. 23.
2. Church Affairs (Nee/LSM), pp. 139, 150.
3. Church Services One (Lee/LSM), p. 10.
4. Conclusion of the New Testament (Lee/LSM), p. 2074.
5. Further Talks on the Church Life (Nee/LSM), p. 160.
6. The God-ordained Way to Practice the New Testament Economy (Lee/LSM), pp. 37-38, 95-96, 159-162, 164, 167-172.
7. Normal Christian Church Life (Nee/LSM), pp.77-87, 123-125.
8. The Organic Building Up of the Church as the Body of Christ (Lee/LSM), p. 63.
9. The Practical Expression of the Church (Lee/LSM), pp. 152-153.
10. The Problem of the Unity of the Church (Nee/LSM), pp. 46-47.
11. The Spirit and the Body (Lee/LSM), pp. 187, 223-224.
12. A Timely Word (Lee/LSM), pp. 22-32.

Lesson Ten

THE FAILURES IN THE CHURCHES, THE DEGRADATION AND RECOVERY OF THE CHURCH

Scripture Reading

Acts 5:1-11; 6:1; 15:1-2; Col. 2:8, 16, 20-22; 2 Tim. 1:15; Ezra 1:3-11; 1 Tim. 1:3-4; John 5:17.

Outline

I. The failures in the churches

II. The degradation of the church
   A. During the New Testament
   B. After the New Testament

III. The recovery of the church
   A. Typified by the return of the children of Israel from their captivity
   B. Indicated in the later epistles of the New Testament
   C. To be recovered:
      1. From the divisive and apostate ground with its deviation from the truths concerning:
         a. The person of the Triune God
         b. The person and work of Christ
      2. Back to the unique and pure ground of the oneness of the Body of Christ with its truths concerning:
         a. The New Testament faith and God's economy
         b. The person and work of Christ
         c. The person and the dispensing of the Triune God
         d. The church, the Body of Christ, the Corporate Christ
         e. The universal and local aspects of the church
      3. To build the Body of Christ, the temple of God, the house of God

4. To establish the kingdom life

Text

In the previous lessons we have only considered the positive things of the church. In the Bible there is a record not only of the positive things, but also a record of the failures in the churches and the degradation of the churches. The Bible also covers the recovery of the church. The Bible is very balanced in all these aspects.

I. THE FAILURES IN THE CHURCHES

[There are no failures in the universal church; however, there are failures in the local churches. All the failures come out of one source, and this source in Satan, who instigates the weak saints to cause all kinds of local problems. The universal church is heavenly, holy, and even divine. But when the universal church reaches a certain locality to be expressed in a local church, the church in that locality may become contaminated and polluted by certain local customs, practices, and philosophies.]

Hypocrisy—[The first failure in the churches was that of hypocrisy seen in the case of Ananias and Sapphira (Acts 5:1-11). Hypocrisy is a matter of pretending to be somebody in order to get a name that we may have vainglory. This is altogether related to ambition.]

Racial Difference—The second failure was that of being overcome by racial differences (Acts 6:1). "There was a murmuring of the Hellenists against the Hebrews" because of eating. This caused the practice of having all things common to wane.

Legal Practices—Another failure was that of bringing in the legal practices of the Old Testament (Acts 15:1-2). Acts 15:1 says, "certain men came down from Judea and were teaching the brothers, Unless you are circumcised according to the custom of Moses, you cannot be saved." This type of saying is an annulling of the faith in God's New Testament economy, and is a real heresy. This failure annulled the believers freedom in Christ. This even caused Peter to be hypocritical and caused the rest of the Jewish believers who were with him to join him in hypocrisy. Even Barnabas was carried away by their hypocrisy.

Compromise—A very serious failure in the churches was the compromise with Judaism led by the Apostle James (Acts 21:20-26). This failure brought in the mixture of Judaism to contaminate God's pure grace, which spoiled the purity of the church life, and damaged the pure testimony of Jesus Christ as the embodiment of God's pure grace. This failure brought about the termination of the church when Jerusalem was destroyed by the Roman army (under Titus) in A.D. 70, as a result of God's judgment.

Other failures included: judging one another in the matters of eating and the observing of days, and not building one another up (Rom. 14); making divisions and causes of falling contrary to the teaching of the apostles (Rom. 16:17); being puffed up on behalf of one gifted person against another unto strife and divisions (1 Cor. 1:11-12); committing fornication (1 Cor. 5:1); having lawsuits one against another (1 Cor. 6:4-7); questioning the apostleship and charging the apostle with being crafty in making gain with guile (1 Cor. 9:1-3; 2 Cor. 12:16); partaking of the table of the Lord and of the table of the demons (1 Cor. 10:21); eating the bread and drinking the cup of the Lord in an unworthy manner and not discerning the Body (1 Cor. 11:27); abusing the gift of tongue-speaking (1 Cor. 14:19-20, 23); saying that there is no resurrection of the dead (1 Cor. 15:12); and finally, walking disorderly (2 Thes. 3:11).

[God's intention in recording these failures in the holy Word is to give us a warning concerning the possibility of such failures recurring in the church life. We need to learn from all these failures and do our best to avoid them. If the churches in the apostles' time could suffer all these failures, it is even more likely that today, if we are careless, we also shall suffer the same kind of failures. Therefore, we need to look to the Lord that we may be kept from these failures.]

II. THE DEGRADATION OF THE CHURCH

[There is a difference between the failures in the churches and the degradation of the church. The failures are not serious in a basic way. Whereas the failures in the churches are not that basic, the degradation of the church is more than basic, for it cuts the root of the life, living, and growth of the church. Unlike failure, degradation not only brings in wrongdoings but cuts the root of the church "tree."]

A. As Described in the New Testament

Gnostic Philosophy—[The first aspect of the degradation of the church was the church's being taken over by the Gnostic philosophy and the elements of the world—the rudimentary teachings of both Jews and Gentiles, consisting of ritualistic observances in such things as meats, drinks, washings, and asceticism (Col. 2:8, 16, 20-22; Titus 1:14-15). Gnosticism is a composition of Greek and Oriental philosophy and Jewish religion. When the church spread to the Gentile world, the church was contaminated by Gnosticism. This contamination became a root problem in the church; it nearly cut off the entire root of the church life. Therefore, Gnosticism was a serious threat to the existence of the church life.]

Different Teaching—[Another aspect of the degradation of the church was the teaching of things different from the economy of God taught by the apostle, resulting in turning away from the apostle's teaching. Acts 2:42 tells us that all the new believers continued steadfastly in the teaching of the apostles. What the apostles taught was according to God's New Testament economy. But at a certain time some teachers began to teach certain biblical things, yet those things were different from the economy of God, that is, different from the teaching of the apostles.] [To teach differently was to teach myths, unending genealogies, and the law (1 Tim. 1:7-8), all of which were vain talking (v. 6), differing from the apostles' teaching centered upon Christ and the church.] [Eventually this resulted in a turning away from Paul's teaching (2 Tim. 1:15).]

Base Gain—[In 1 Timothy 6:5b Paul speaks of those who suppose "godliness to be a means of gain." They make godliness a way of gain—material profit, a gain-making trade. The desire for material gain is another reason certain ones teach differently from the economy of God taught by the apostles. Thus, because of pride and the desire for profit, for riches, some are teaching differently. Pride is related to wanting a name and a good reputation, and gain is related to money and material profit.]

Turning Away from the Apostle—[Paul's Epistles are the completion of the divine revelation concerning God's eternal purpose and economy (Col. 1:25). His ministry completes the revelation concerning the all-inclusive Christ and His universal Body, the church as His fullness to express Him. Nevertheless, in the degradation of the church, many turned away from Paul's ministry. "This you know, that all who are in Asia turned away from me" (2 Tim. 1:15).] [Those who turned away from Paul's ministry deviated from God's complete revelation, the center of which is Christ as the mystery in the saints (Col. 1:27).]

Heresies—[Second Timothy 2:16-18 says, "Avoid profane, vain babblings, for they will advance to more ungodliness, and their word will spread as gangrene, of whom are Hymenaeus and Philetus, who concerning the truth have misaimed, saying that the resurrection has already taken place, and overthrow the faith of some." Here Paul refers to those who bring in heresies as gangrene.]

Factious—[Titus 3:10 and 11 say, "A factious man after a first and second admonition refuse, knowing that such a one has been perverted and sins, being self-condemned." A factious man is a heretical, sectarian man who causes divisions by forming parties in the church according to his own opinions. The Gnostic Judaism referred to in the preceding verse must be related to this. The divisiveness is based on differing teachings. This is the reason that verse 10 comes after verse 9. Certain believers may have insisted on the teaching of the law and in so doing became divisive.]

Backsliding to Judaism—[In Hebrews 10:25-29 Paul warns the Hebrew believers not to forsake the church to sin willfully, that is, to go back to Judaism to offer the sacrifice for sin which has been terminated.]

Denying the person of Christ—[First John 2:22 says, "Who is the liar if not he who is denying that Jesus is the Christ? This is the antichrist, who is denying the Father and the Son."] First John 4:2 says, "In this you know the Spirit of God: every spirit which confesses Jesus Christ having come in the flesh is out of God." These verses reveal to us that some did not believe that Jesus Christ is God Himself come in the flesh (Jn 1:1, 14; 10:30; 20:28; Acts 20:28; 1 Tim. 3:16; Heb. 1:8).

Not Abiding in the Teaching of Christ—[Second John 9 says, "Everyone who goes beyond and does not abide in the teaching of Christ, does not have God; he who abides in the teaching, this one has both the Father and the Son." Literally, the Greek word translated "goes beyond" means to lead forward (in a negative sense), that is, to go further than what is right, to advance beyond the limit of orthodox teaching concerning Christ. This is contrasted with abiding in the teaching of Christ. The Cerinthian Gnostics, who boasted of their supposedly advanced thinking concerning the teaching of Christ, had such a practice. They went beyond the teaching of the divine conception of Christ, thus denying the deity of Christ. Consequently they could not have God in salvation and in life.]

Forsaking the Faith—[In the degradation of the church some forsook the faith. This was the reason Jude wrote, "Beloved, using all diligence to write to you concerning our common salvation, I found it necessary to write to you, entreating you to contend for the faith once for all delivered to the saints" (Jude 3). The faith in this verse is not subjective; it is objective. It does not refer to our believing, but refers to our belief, to what we believe. The faith denotes the contents of the New Testament as our faith (Acts 6:7; 1 Tim. 1:19; 3:9; 4:1; 5:8; 6:10, 21; 2 Tim. 2:18; 3:8; 4:7; Titus 1:13), in which we believe for our common salvation. This faith, not any doctrine, has been delivered once for all to the saints. For this faith we should contend (1 Tim. 6:12).] There were more points of degradation in Revelation. We will consider those in the next lesson.

B. After the New Testament Time

The church further degraded after the completion of the New Testament. Satan tried his best to destroy the church because he knew that the builded church would destroy him. He used the Roman emperors to persecute the church in an attempt to terminate her. [Persecution, as we know, did not terminate the Christians; it rather helped them. Then Satan changed his strategy. Under the rule of Constantine the Great the Roman Empire made Christianity legal, and Christians had the full freedom of worship. Because of the favors he granted the Christians, thousands of pagans were baptized and became Christians in name. These were the tares spoken of in Matthew 13:24-30. That ruined Christianity.] Constantine [acted openly as head of the church, which in his reign was first called Catholic; at the same time he kept his title of high priest of the heathen.]

[This ruin progressed from the fourth to the sixth centuries, by which time the papal system was fully established. With this the Roman Catholic Church reached its full development; it claimed to be the one, universal church (catholic means universal) and exercised worldly power over people and nations. No protest or dissent was tolerated. Over the centuries when it held sway, the Roman Catholic Church killed more genuine Christians than the pagan Roman Empire had killed. Under such a dark church, the so-called Dark Ages were produced, lasting about ten centuries, from about A.D. 500 to 1500.] Shortly thereafter, the Lord began to recover the church. Hallelujah!

III. THE RECOVERY OF THE CHURCH

[When we speak of the recovery of the church, we mean that something was there originally, that it became lost or damaged, and that now there is the need to bring that thing back to its original state. Because the church has become degraded through the many centuries of its history, it needs to be restored according to God's original intention. Concerning the church, our vision should be governed not by the present situation nor by traditional practice but by God's original intention and standard as revealed in the Scriptures.]

[First, God purposed and then He came in to accomplish His purpose. Furthermore, the New Testament also gives us a clear record of how God's enemy came in to destroy what God had accomplished.] [Nevertheless, God is a God with an eternal purpose. He is a purposeful God, and once He has made up His mind to do something, nothing can change His mind or stop Him. Therefore, after Satan's destruction, God comes in to redo the things that He had done before. This redoing is His recovery. This is to bring back whatever has been lost and destroyed by God's enemy, Satan.]

A. Typified by the Return of the Children of Israel from Their Captivity

[The recovery of the church is typified by the return of the children of Israel from their captivity (Ezra 1:3-11). In order to understand the recovery of the church, we need to consider the history of the people of Israel in the Old Testament.]

[The entire history of the nation of Israel is a full type, an all-inclusive type, of the church. The nation of Israel began with the exodus. The children of Israel were in slavery in Egypt, but through the lamb of the Passover they were redeemed out from Pharaoh's usurpation. They made their exodus from Egypt, crossed the Red Sea, entered the wilderness, and came to Mount Sinai, and there they built the tabernacle as God's dwelling place on earth. Eventually, the people of Israel crossed the Jordan and entered into Canaan, the good land. After conquering the people and gaining the land, they built the temple. The time immediately after the building of the temple was a golden time. However, that golden time did not last very long. Mainly due to the failure of Solomon, the temple was destroyed, and the children of Israel were taken to Babylon as captives. The Babylonian army not only destroyed Jerusalem with its temple but also brought the utensils of the temple to Babylon and put them into idol temples. What a shame! The people of Israel remained in Babylon for seventy years.]

[As typified by the latter part of the history of the children of Israel, the recovery is from Babylon—the capturing and divisive ground (Ezra 1:11). For the children of Israel to be recovered meant for them to be brought back to Jerusalem from Babylon. Negatively, to be recovered means to be brought out of Babylon; positively, it means to be brought up to Jerusalem,] [the God-ordained unique ground. Jerusalem was the place the Lord had chosen (Deut. 12:5). Jerusalem, therefore, was the center for God's people to worship Him, and this unique center preserved the unity of the people of God. Without such a center, after the children of Israel had entered the good land, they would have been divided.] [The recovery of the church is also typified by the rebuilding of the temple of God, the house of God, in Jerusalem after the return of God's people from Babylon] (Ezra 1:3). [Finally, the recovery of the church is typified in the Old Testament by the rebuilding of the city of Jerusalem (Neh. 2:11, 17). After the recovery of the building of the temple, there was still the need to build up the city. Without the city, there would have been no protection for the temple. The temple, the place of the Lord's presence, needed protection. The wall of the city was the defense to the temple.]

[Spiritually speaking, the church, due to its degradation, has been in captivity. God's people have been divided, scattered, and carried away from the proper ground of unity to a wrong ground. In the Old Testament type, the children of Israel were centered around Jerusalem, but later they were scattered and carried away to many places, in particular, to Babylon. This portrays the situation among many of today's Christians. In a very real sense, the believers today are more scattered than the children of Israel were. Therefore, we need to be recovered. We need not only revival but also recovery.]

B. Indicated in the Later Epistles
of the New Testament

[The recovery of the church is fully revealed in the New Testament even though the word "recovery" is not used. This recovery is revealed mainly in the later Epistles of the New Testament. We do not find the recovery of the church in such Epistles as Romans or 1 Corinthians, but we do find it in Titus, 2 Timothy, 2 John, and Revelation. In these later writings of the New Testament the recovery is fully unveiled.]

[For the recovery of the church, we need to be separated from the factious—the sects and denominations. This is indicated by Paul's word in Titus 3:10. "A factious man after a first and second admonition refuse." A factious man is a sectarian man who causes divisions by forming parties in the church according to his own opinions. A factious, divisive person, after a first and second admonition, should be refused, rejected. This is to stop intercourse with a contagiously divisive person for the church's benefit.

Nearly all believers today are factious. They honor, respect, and uplift their denominations. Furthermore, they nourish and build their denominations. Hence, they are builders of sects and denominations. Millions of Christians today are members of these sects. Because they are members of sects, we cannot join them, even though they may be genuine brothers in Christ. We surely love our brothers in Christ, but they are in the denominations and the sects, where we cannot be. It is not that we separate ourselves from other believers; it is that the sects and denominations separate us from the church life. If we are to share in the recovery of the church, we need to be separated from all the sects and denominations. Like Ezra, Nehemiah, and other faithful ones in the Old Testament, we need to leave Babylon and come back to Jerusalem.]

C. To Be Recovered:

1. From the Divisive and Apostate Ground with Its Deviation from the Truths concerning:

a. The Person of the Triune God

[We need to be recovered from the divisive and apostate ground with its deviation from the truth concerning the person of the Triune God. During the centuries, three main schools of teaching concerning the Trinity have emerged: modalism, tritheism, and the pure revelation according to the Bible. Modalism teaches that the Father, the Son, and the Spirit are not all eternal and do not all exist at the same time, but are merely three temporary manifestations of the one God. Tritheism teaches that the Father, the Son, and the Spirit are three Gods. We should have nothing to do with modalism, for that extreme view of the Trinity is a heresy. It is also a great heresy to teach that there are three Gods.]

[The truth concerning the person of the Triune God is twofold.] [The twofoldness of the truth concerning the Trinity is embodied in the word "triune." This adjective is actually a Latin word composed of two parts: tri-, meaning three, and -uno, meaning one. The word triune, therefore, means three-one. On the one hand, our God is uniquely one; on the other hand, He is three. In the aspect of God's being one, there is no separation between the Father, the Son, and the Spirit. However, in the aspect of God's being three, there is a distinction between the Father, the Son, and the Spirit. The Lord Jesus said, "I am in the Father, and the Father is in Me" (John 14:10). Because the Father and the Son are mutually in each other, They cannot be separated. Nevertheless, there is still a distinction between the Father and the Son.]

b. The Person and Work of Christ

We also need to be recovered from the divisive and apostate ground with its deviation from the truth concerning the person and work of Christ. Some deny that Jesus is the Christ (1 John 2:22-23). These people deny the deity of Christ, not confessing that the Man Jesus is God becoming a man. In turn, these also reject Christ's redemption, insisting that His death was a martyrdom rather than for our redemption. According to 1 Cor. 15:12-17, some do not believe that Christ resurrected. If He did not resurrect, then we have no proof of our justification (Rom. 4:25), and He would not be the life-giving Spirit to regenerate and transform us. Therefore, the church needs to be recovered from this apostate condition also.

2. Back to the Unique and Pure Ground of the Oneness
of the Body of Christ with Its Truths concerning:

a. The New Testament Faith and God's Economy

[In 1 Timothy 1:3 and 4 Paul says, "Even as I urged you, when I was going into Macedonia, to remain in Ephesus in order that you might charge certain ones not to teach differently, nor to occupy themselves with myths and unending genealogies, which give occasion for questionings rather than God's dispensation which is in faith." The Greek words translated "God's dispensation" may also be rendered "God's household economy" (Eph. 1:10; 3:9). This is God's household administration to dispense Himself in Christ into His chosen people, that He may have a house, a household, to express Himself, which household is the church, the Body of Christ (1 Tim. 3:15). The apostle's ministry was centered upon this economy of God (Col. 1:25; 1 Cor. 9:17), whereas the differing teachings of the dissenting ones were used by God's enemy to distract His people from this.]

[In 1 Timothy 1:4 Paul tells us that God's dispensation is in faith. The dispensing of the processed Triune God into us is altogether by faith. The dispensation of God is a matter in faith, that is, in the sphere and element of faith, in God through Christ. God's economy to dispense Himself into His chosen people is not in the natural realm, nor in the realm of the law, but in the spiritual sphere of the new creation through regeneration by faith in Christ (Gal. 3:23-26). By faith we are born of God to be His sons, partaking of His life and nature to express Him. By faith we are put into Christ to become the members of His Body, sharing all that He is for His expression. This is God's dispensation according to His New Testament economy, carried out in faith.] We need to be recovered back to this item.

b. The Person and Work of Christ

[Concerning the person and work of Christ, we must preach that Christ is God incarnated to be a God-man, that He is both divine and human. We must also preach His redemptive death. In His redemptive work He died on the cross for our sins and for us sinners. Then He was resurrected so that He could impart Himself into us as the divine life. Therefore, the gospel we preach is that Christ, the God-man, died for our sins and was resurrected.] He is the complete God and the perfect and genuine man. He alone is qualified to be our Savior. The matter of His person and work is covered in the second year of summer school of the truth.

c. The Person and the Dispensing of the Triune God

[The recovery of the church also requires that we be recovered to the truth concerning the person and the dispensing of the Triune God. This matter of God's dispensing is something that is altogether missed by many Christians today. By the Lord's mercy we have been enlightened to see that in the New Testament economy of God there is the divine, triune Person for the dispensing of Himself into His chosen people to be their life, life supply, and everything. Because this has been neglected by many today, we need to be recovered to the proper understanding and apprehension of the divine dispensing of the riches of the processed Triune God into our being.]

[God's New Testament economy is His plan to dispense Himself into His chosen people in His trinity. This dispensing has three steps. First, it is of God the Father, who is the source, the origin. Second, this dispensing is through God the Son, who is the course. Third, God's dispensing is in God the Spirit, who is the instrument and sphere. Through these steps of God the Father, through God the Son, and in God the Spirit the processed Triune God dispenses Himself into His chosen people.]

d. The Church, the Body of Christ, the Corporate Christ

[Ephesians 1:22-23 speaks of "the church, which is His Body, the fullness of the One who fills all in all." The Body of Christ is an organism constituted of all the believers, who have been regenerated and have God's life, for the expression of the Head. The Body is the fullness of the Head, and the fullness is the expression of the Head.

Because the church is the Body of Christ and Christ is the Head of the church (Col. 1:18), the church and Christ are one Body, the mysterious, universal great man, having the same life and nature and sharing the same position and authority. Just as Christ is far above all and sits in the heavenlies (Eph. 1:20-21), so also the church sits together with Him in the heavenlies (Eph. 2:6). Just as Christ has received all authority in heaven and on earth (Matt. 28:18), so also the church participates in His authority (Luke 10:19). Today the life of the church is hidden with Christ in God, and in the future the church will be manifested with Christ in glory (Col. 3:3-4). What Christ is, what Christ has, where Christ is, and what Christ does are what the church is, what the church has, where the church is, and what the church does. Christ is the life and content of the church, and the church is the organism and expression of Christ. The church receives everything from Christ, and everything of Christ is expressed through the church. The two, Christ and the church, are thus mingled and joined as one, with Christ being the inward content and the church, the outward expression.]

e. The Universal and Local Aspects of the Church

[The truth concerning the universal and local aspects of the church also needs to be recovered. In a very real sense, these matters have been lost, even annulled. Therefore, we need to be recovered to the truth concerning these two aspects of the church.

In the universal aspect the church is uniquely one. This aspect of the church is revealed by the Lord Jesus in Matthew 16:18, where He says, "On this rock I will build My church." What is revealed here is the universal church for the unique testimony of the Lord in the universe.]

[In the local aspect the church is expressed in many localities as many local churches. The one universal church expressed in many places on earth becomes the many local churches. The expression of the church in a locality is the local church in that particular locality. Without the local churches there would be no practicality and actuality of the universal church. The universal church is realized in the local churches.]

3. To Build the Body of Christ,
the Temple of God, the House of God

[In the recovery of the church, we are building the Body of Christ, the temple of God, the house of God. This was typified by the rebuilding of the temple under the leadership of Ezra in Old Testament times. Today we are rebuilding the church life as God's temple, the Body of Christ.

Ephesians 4:12-17 has much to say about the building up of the Body of Christ. Verse 12 says, "For the perfecting of the saints unto the work of ministry, unto the building up of the Body of Christ." In this verse "unto" means for the purpose of, for, with a view to. The many gifted persons in verse 11 have only one ministry, that of ministering Christ for the building up of the Body of Christ, the church. This is the unique ministry in the New Testament economy (2 Cor. 4:1; 1 Tim. 1:12). Furthermore, according to the grammatical construction of verse 12, "the building up of the Body of Christ" is "the work of ministry." Whatever the gifted persons in verse 11 do as the work of ministry must be for the building up of the Body of Christ.

The four special gifts in verse 11—the apostles, the prophets, the evangelists, and the shepherd-teachers—do not build the Body of Christ directly. Instead, these special gifts perfect the saints that they may build the Body of Christ directly. First, the apostles, prophets, evangelists, and shepherd-teachers perfect, equip, the saints. This means that they build up the saints. Then the perfected saints become the building members to build the Body of Christ directly. From this we see that the Body is not built directly by the special gifts but by all the members of the Body. If we realize this, we shall avoid the great heresy of the clergy-laity system. In the church there is no clergy or laity. On the contrary, in the church every member of the Body functions to build up the Body of Christ directly.]

4. To Establish the Kingdom Life

[Finally, the recovery of the church involves the establishing of the kingdom life. This is indicated by Paul's word in Romans 14:17. "The kingdom of God is not eating and drinking, but righteousness and peace and joy in the Holy Spirit." This verse reveals that the kingdom of God is the living of the church. According to the context of Romans 14, the kingdom is today's church life. The reality of the church life is the kingdom. Romans 12 speaks of the Body life and Romans 14, of the kingdom life. This indicates that, according to Romans, the kingdom life is the reality of the Body life.

The kingdom of God as the living of the church is righteousness, peace, and joy in the Holy Spirit. When the authority of God's kingdom operates in us, righteousness, peace, and joy will characterize our daily life. To have such a living is to establish the kingdom life as typified in the book of Nehemiah by the rebuilding of the city of Jerusalem. Therefore, in the recovery of the church, we are building up the church as God's house and city.]

CONCLUSION

Although there were and still are many failures in the churches as well as the degradation of the church, the Lord is always recovering. He is never defeated or discouraged. He has an eternal plan. He will not change His mind because of problems. He will not stop until He finishes His work. Jesus said, "My Father is working until now, and I am working"

(John 5:17). But He needs people to cooperate with Him for His recovery. Many Christians do not see what God is doing. Some have heard about His recovery, yet without the proper vision they have come and gone. May the Lord be merciful to us, to open our eyes to see His eternal purpose, the degradation of the church, and the failures in the churches, that we may remain in His recovery and not repeat history.

Pray like this, "O Lord! I see Your eternal purpose for the church. I see Your economy for the building up of Your church. I see Your recovery of the degraded church. I give myself to You for the recovering and building up of Your church until You come back for her. O Lord, keep me faithful until the end."

Questions

1. Explain the difference between the failures of the church and the degradation of the church?

2. What are the items of degradation of the church revealed in the New Testament? Make a list and use verse references.

3. What are the major items we need to be recovered from and recovered to?

Quoted Portions

1. Conclusion of the New Testament (Lee/LSM), pp. 2349-2397.

2. The World Situation and God's Move (Lee/LSM), p. 12.

3. Conclusion of the New Testament (Lee/LSM), pp. 2447-2496.

Further References

1. The Economy of God and the Building Up of the Body of Christ (Lee/LSM), p. 50.

2. The Glorious Church (Nee/LSM), p. 61.

3. The One New Man (Lee/LSM), pp. 7-8.

4. The Speciality, Generality, and Practicality of the Church Life (Lee/LSM), pp. 15-16.

THE SEVEN CHURCHES IN REVELATION SIGNIFYING THE SEVEN STAGES OF THE CHURCH

Scripture Reading

Rev. 1:3; 22:7; 2:1-29; 3:1-22.

Outline

I. The church in Ephesus depicts the end of the stage of the initial church during the last part of the first century

II. The church in Smyrna prefigures the suffering church under the persecution of the Roman Empire from the last part of the first century to the early part of the fourth century

III. The church in Pergamos pre-symbolizes the worldly church, the church married to the world

IV. The church in Thyatira pre-symbolizes the apostate church from the ordination of the papal system in the latter part of the sixth century to the end of the church age

V. The church in Sardis prefigures the protestant church, from the reformation in the early part of the sixteenth century to Christ's coming back

VI. The church in Philadelphia prefigures the church of brotherly love, the recovery of the proper church life, from the early part of the nineteenth century to the second appearing of the Lord

VII. The church in Laodicea foreshadows the degraded church life of the brothers from

the latter part of the nineteenth century to
the Lord's return

Text

[Revelation is a book of prophecy (Rev. 1:3; 22:7), for the revelation it contains is in the nature of prophecy. Most of the visions refer to things to come. Even the seven epistles to the seven churches in chapters two and three, in the sense of signs, are prophecies regarding the church on earth until the Lord's coming back.]

The seven churches signify [prophetically the progress of the church in seven stages. The first epistle, to the church in Ephesus, affords a picture of the church at the end of the first stage, during the last part of the first century. The second epistle, to the church in Smyrna, prefigures the suffering church under the persecution of the Roman Empire, from the last part of the first century to the early part of the fourth century, when Constantine the Great brought the church into imperial favor. The third epistle, to the church in Pergamos, pre-symbolizes the worldly church, the church married to the world, from the time Constantine accepted Christianity to the time the papal system was established in the latter part of the sixth century. The epistle to the church in Thyatira depicts prophetically the apostate church, from the ordination of the papal system in the latter part of the sixth century to the end of this age, when Christ comes back. The fifth epistle, to the church in Sardis, prefigures the Protestant church, from the Reformation in the early part of the sixteenth century to Christ's coming back. The sixth epistle, to the church in Philadelphia, predicts the church of brotherly love, the recovery of the proper church life, from the early part of the nineteenth century, when the brothers were raised up in England to practice the church life outside all denominational and divisive systems, to the second appearing of the Lord. The seventh epistle, to the church in Laodicea, foreshadows the degraded church life of the brothers in the nineteenth century, from the latter part of the nineteenth century until the Lord's return.]

I. THE CHURCH IN EPHESUS

[The church in Ephesus depicts the end of the stage of the initial church during the last part of the first century. "Ephesus" in Greek means desirable. This signifies that the initial church at its end was still desirable to the Lord; the Lord still had much expectation in her.]

A. The Condition of the Church at This Stage

[The crucial words in the Lord's epistle to the church in Ephesus are love, life, and light. The basic requirement for having the church life is our love toward the Lord. There is no problem, of course, with the Lord's love toward us. He has loved us and He continues to love us. The problem is with our love toward Him. Although we have loved Him in the past and may love Him now, there is the danger that our love for the Lord Jesus might fade. The epistle to the church in Ephesus warns us of this. This epistle also gives us a clear revelation of the source of the degradation of the church life—the fading of the first love. Love gives us the position, the ground, the right, and the privilege to eat of the tree of life. Love gives us the supply of life. If we love the Lord, we shall have the full right to enjoy Him as the tree of life, as our life supply. Light always follows life, issuing out of the abundant supply of life. Life, therefore, gives us light. It is vitally important that we love the Lord. If we have love, then we shall have the life symbolized by the tree of life and the light signified by the lampstand.]

B. The Lord's Promise to the Overcomers of This Stage

[In Revelation 2:7 the Lord says that to him who overcomes He will give to eat of the tree of life. For the proper church life and the recovery of the church life, that is, for the proper growth in the Christian life, what we need is not merely the mental apprehension of teachings but the eating in our spirit of the Lord as the bread of life (John 6:57). Even the words of the Scripture should not be considered merely doctrines to teach our mind but food to nourish our spirit (Matt. 4:4; Heb. 5:12-14).]

[The matter of eating the tree of life brings us back to the beginning, because at the beginning there was the tree of life (Gen. 2:9, 16). The tree of life always brings us back to the beginning where there is nothing but God Himself. In the church life, again and again we need to be brought back to the beginning, forgetting all other things and enjoying Christ Himself as the tree of life.]

[But to enjoy Christ requires us to love Him with the first love. We must love Him above all things, above our work for Him and whatever we have for Him. By simply loving Him we shall be brought back to the beginning where we care for nothing except the Triune God Himself as our life supply in the tree of life. This is the proper way to maintain the church life and to be kept in the church life.]

II. THE CHURCH IN SMYRNA

[In Greek "Smyrna" means myrrh, a sweet spice which, in figure, signifies suffering. In typology, myrrh signifies the sweet suffering of Christ. Thus, the church in Smyrna was a suffering church, prefiguring the church under the persecution of the Roman Empire from the latter part of the first century to the early part of the fourth century.]

A. The Condition of the Church at This Stage

The church suffered the slander of the Jews. [In Revelation 2:9 the Lord Jesus said that He knew "the slander of those who call themselves Jews and are not, but are a synagogue of Satan." This indicates that persecution came from religion, from the unbelieving Jews of the synagogue of Satan. The slander of the Judaizers toward the suffering church was their evil criticism of her.]

The church also suffered the persecution of the Roman Empire. [In 2:10 the Lord speaks of the church in Smyrna having tribulation "ten days." As a sign, these ten days indicate prophetically the ten periods of persecution which the church suffered under the Roman Emperors.]

B. The Lord's Promise to the Overcomers of This Stage

To overcome in this epistle means to overcome persecution by being faithful unto death. The Lord said, ["Be faithful unto death, and I will give you the crown of life" (2:10b). Here, as elsewhere in the New Testament, the crown denotes a prize in addition to salvation. The crown of life as a prize to those who are faithful unto death in overcoming persecution denotes the overcoming strength, which is the power of the resurrection life (Phil. 3:10).]

["He who overcomes shall by no means be hurt of the second death" (Rev. 2:11b). The second death is God's dealing with man after man's death and resurrection. It is, therefore, the final settlement (Rev. 20:11-15). Because the overcomers have overcome death through their faithfulness unto death under persecution and have left nothing requiring further dealing by God, after their resurrection they will not be "hurt," touched, by the second death, the death after resurrection. This indicates that those who do not overcome persecution will be hurt by the second death. This is for a believer to suffer some dealing from the Lord after he has been resurrected.]

III. THE CHURCH IN PERGAMOS

[In Greek "Pergamos" means "marriage," implying union, and "fortified tower." As a sign, the church in Pergamos prefigures the church which entered into a marriage union with the world and became a high fortified tower, the equivalent of the great tree prophesied by the Lord in the parable of the mustard seed (Matt. 13:31-32). When Satan failed to destroy the church through the persecution of the Roman Empire in the first three centuries, he changed his strategy. He sought instead to corrupt her through Constantine's welcoming her as the state religion in the first part of the fourth century. Through Constantine's encouragement and political influence, multitudes of unbelieving ones were baptized into the "church," and the "church" became monstrously great. The church has been called out of the world and has been separated from the world to God for the fulfillment of His purpose. However, by being welcomed by the Roman Empire, the church went back to the world and, in the eyes of God, even married the world.] [Because the church, as a chaste bride, is the spouse to Christ, her union with the world is considered spiritual fornication in the eyes of God.]

Now you can see why the leading ones in your locality always speak against the world and the worldly things. We must only have eyes for Christ and forsake the world.

A. The Condition of the Church at This Stage

[In Revelation 2:13 the Lord Jesus said to the church in Pergamos, "I know where you dwell, where Satan's throne is." Satan's dwelling place is the world. Because the church entered into union with the world and became worldly herself, she began to dwell where Satan dwells—in the world.]

[In 2:14 the Lord said, "I have a few things against you, because you have some there who hold the teaching of Balaam, who taught Balak to put a stumbling block before the sons of Israel, to eat idol sacrifices and to commit fornication." Balaam was a Gentile prophet who caused God's people to stumble. For the sake of reward (2 Pet. 2:15; Jude 11), he brought fornication and idolatry to God's people (Num. 25:1-3; 31:16). In the worldly church some began to teach the same things. When the worldly church disregarded the name, the person, of the Lord, she turned to idolatry, which issued in fornication.]

[In Revelation 2:15 the Lord went on to say, "You also have those who hold in like manner the teaching of the Nicolaitans." "Nicolaitans" is an equivalent of the Greek word nikolaitai, the root of which is nikolaos, composed of two words: niko, meaning "conquer" or "above others" and laos, meaning "common people," "secular people," or "laity." Hence, nikolaos means "conquering the common people," "climbing above the laity." The Nicolaitans, then, must refer to a group of people who esteemed themselves higher than the common believers. In the church in Pergamos their works (Rev. 2:6)

progressed into a teaching. They not only practiced the
hierarchy but also taught it. This hierarchy destroys the
function of the believers as members of the Body of Christ,
thus annulling the Lord's Body in expressing Him.]

B. The Lord's Promise to the Overcomers of This Stage

[In 2:17 we have the Lord's promise to the overcomers of
this stage. To overcome here means specifically to overcome
the church's union with the world, the teaching of idolatry
and fornication, and the teaching of the hierarchy.]

[In 2:17b the Lord says, "To him who overcomes, to him I
will give of the hidden manna." Manna is a type of Christ as
the heavenly food enabling God's people to go His way. A
portion of that manna was preserved in a golden pot
concealed in the ark (Exo. 16:32-34; Heb. 9:4). The open
manna was for the enjoyment of the Lord's people in a public
way; the hidden manna, signifying the hidden Christ, is a
special portion reserved for His overcoming seekers who
overcome the degradation of the worldly church. While the
church goes the way of the world, these overcomers come
forward to abide in the presence of God in the Holy of Holies,
where they enjoy the hidden Christ as a special portion for
their daily supply. This promise is fulfilled today in the
proper church life and will be fulfilled in full in the coming
kingdom.]

[The Lord also promised the overcomer in Revelation
2:17 that He "will give him a white stone, and on the stone a
new name written, which no one knows but he who receives
it." A stone in the Bible signifies material for God's building
(Matt. 16:18; 1 Pet. 2:5; 1 Cor. 3:12). In our natural being we
are not stones but clay. Because we have received the divine
life with its divine nature through regeneration, we can be
transformed into stones, even precious stones, by enjoying
Christ as our life supply (2 Cor. 3:18). Those who do not follow
the worldly church but enjoy the Lord in the proper church
life will be transformed into stones for the building of God. As
indicated by the color white, these stones will be justified and
approved by the Lord. The overcomers will be justified by God

and approved by the Lord. Therefore, they will be the materials for the building up of God's temple according to God's New Testament economy.]

IV. THE CHURCH IN THYATIRA

[The church in Thyatira is the church in apostasy. "Thyatira" in Greek means "sacrifice of perfume" or "unceasing sacrifice." As a sign, the church in Thyatira prefigures the Roman Catholic Church, which was fully formed as the apostate church by the establishment of the universal papal system in the latter part of the sixth century. This apostate church is full of sacrifices, as demonstrated in her unceasing mass. This apostate church will remain until the Lord's coming back.]

A. The Condition of the Church at This Stage

[The church in Thyatira is a continuation of the worldly church, pre-symbolized by the church in Pergamos. The church in Pergamos had the teaching of the Gentile prophet Balaam and the teaching of the Nicolaitans, that is, the teaching of a clerical system. The Catholic Church continues these teachings, the teaching of Balaam to bring people into idol worship and fornication and the teaching of the Nicolaitans to build up the hierarchy. In the Catholic Church today there is a strong teaching concerning the building up of a religious organization with its hierarchy.]

[One of the crucial points in the epistle to the church in Thyatira concerns the woman Jezebel. The Lord refers to her in Revelation 3:20. "I have this against you, that you tolerate the woman Jezebel, who calls herself a prophetess, and she teaches and leads My slaves astray to commit fornication and to eat idol sacrifices." This is the very woman prophesied by the Lord in Matthew 13:33, the woman who added leaven (signifying evil, heretical, and pagan things) into the fine flour (signifying Christ as the meal offering for the satisfaction of God and man). This woman is also the great prostitute of Revelation 17, who mixes abominations with the divine things. The pagan wife of Ahab, Jezebel, was a type of this apostate church.]

B. The Lord's Promise to the Overcomers of This Stage

[In verse 26 the Lord says that to the one who overcomes He will give authority over the nations. This is a prize to the overcomers of reigning with Christ over the nations in the millennial kingdom (20:4, 6). This promise of the Lord strongly implies that those who do not answer His call to overcome the apostate church will not participate in the reign of the millennial kingdom.]

[In 2:28 we have another aspect of the Lord's promise to the overcomer in this stage. He says, "I will give him the morning star." The morning star here refers to the coming Christ. At Christ's first coming, the wise men, not the Jewish religionists, saw His star (Matt. 2:2, 9-10). At His second coming, He will be the morning star to His overcomers, who watch for His coming. To all the others, He will appear only as the sun (Mal. 4:2). Only the hidden overcomers, those who enjoy Christ as the hidden manna, will see the hidden Christ appearing as the morning star to those who love Him.]

V. THE CHURCH IN SARDIS

["Sardis" in Greek means "the remains," "the remainder," or "the restoration." As a sign, the church in Sardis prefigures the Protestant Church from the time of the Reformation to the second coming of Christ. The Reformation was God's reaction to the apostate Roman Catholic Church, signified by the degraded church in Thyatira. The Reformation was accomplished by a minority of the believers, the remainder. Hence, it was the restoration by the remainder.]

A. The Condition of the Church at This Stage

[To the messenger of the church in Sardis the Lord says, "I know your works, that you have a name that you are living, and you are dead" (Rev. 3:1). The reformed Protestant Church has been considered by many to be living, but the Lord says that she is dead. Hence, in her dead condition, she needs the seven living Spirits and the shining stars.]

[In verse 2 the Lord says to "establish the things which remain, which were about to die." "The things which remain" are the things lost and restored by the Reformation, such as justification by faith and the open Bible. Although these things were restored, they "were about to die." Hence, the Protestant Church needs revivals to keep things alive.

In verse 2 the Lord also says, "I have not found your works completed before My God." Nothing begun in the Reformation has been completed by the Protestant churches. Therefore, the church in Philadelphia (3:7-13), signifying the church in recovery, is needed for the completion. In the eyes of God, there are no completed works in the so-called reformed churches.]

B. The Lord's Promise to the Overcomers of This Stage

[In 3:5 we have the Lord's promise to the overcomers of this stage. To overcome here means to overcome the deadness of the Protestant churches, that is, to overcome dead Protestantism. The whole of verse 5 is the Lord's promise to the overcomers. It will be fulfilled in the millennial kingdom after He comes back.]

[In 3:4 the Lord says, "But you have a few names in Sardis who have not defiled their garments, and they shall walk with Me in white, for they are worthy." Garments in the Bible signify what we are in our walk and living. To defile the garments means particularly to stain them with deadness. Death is more defiling before God than sin (Lev. 11:24-25; Num. 6:6, 7, 9). In this verse the defilement denotes anything of the death nature. The defilement in Sardis was not the defilement of sin but the defilement of death.

Speaking of those who have not defiled their garments, the Lord says, "They shall walk with Me in white, for they are worthy." White not only signifies purity but also approvedness. White garments here signify the walk and living which are unspotted by death and which will be approved by the Lord. It is a qualification for walking with the Lord, especially in the coming kingdom.]

[The Lord says in 3:5b, "I will by no means erase his name out of the book of life, and I will confess his name before My Father and before His angels." The book of life is a divine record of the names of those who partake of the blessings God has prepared for them. These blessings are in three stages: the church, the millennial kingdom, and eternity. All the believers will share in the blessings of the first and third stages, but only the overcomers will share in the blessings of the second stage, that is, the blessings in the millennial kingdom. Those who cooperate with God's supplying grace and mature in life in the church age will be given the prize of the entrance into the millennial kingdom and the participation in the divine blessings in that stage. This means that their names will not be erased out of the book of life during the millennium.]

VI. THE CHURCH IN PHILADELPHIA

[In Greek, "Philadelphia" means brotherly love. As a sign, the church in Philadelphia prefigures the proper church life recovered by the brothers who were raised up by the Lord in England in the early part of the nineteenth century. Just as the reformed church, prefigured by the church in Sardis, was a reaction to the apostate Catholic Church, prefigured by the church in Thyatira, so the church of brotherly love is a reaction to the dead reformed church. This reaction will continue as an anti-testimony to both apostate Catholicism and degraded Protestantism until the Lord comes back.]

A. The Condition of the Church at This Stage

The church is keeping the Lord's word. [In Revelation 3:8b the Lord Jesus says, "You have a little power and have kept My word." One outstanding feature of the church in Philadelphia is that she kept the Lord's word. According to history, no other Christians have kept the Lord's word as strictly as those in the church in Philadelphia. The church in Philadelphia, the recovered church, does not care for tradition; she cares for the word of God.]

[In 3:8 the Lord also says that the church in Philadelphia has not denied His name. The brothers who were raised up by the Lord in England in the early part of the nineteenth century did not take any name other than the name of the Lord. The word is the Lord's expression, and the name is the Lord Himself. The apostate church has deviated from the Lord's word and has become heretical. The reformed church, though recovered to the Lord's word to some extent, has denied the Lord's name by denominating herself with many other names. The recovered church has not only returned to the Lord's word in a full way but has also abandoned all names other than that of the Lord Jesus Christ. The recovered church belongs to the Lord absolutely, having nothing to do with any denominations (any names). To deviate from the Lord's word is apostasy, and to denominate the church with any name other than the Lord's is spiritual fornication. The church as the chaste virgin betrothed to Christ (2 Cor. 11:2) should not have any name other than her Husband's. All other names are an abomination in the eyes of God.]

[In 3:8a the Lord says, "I know your works; behold, I have put before you an open door which no one can shut." As the One who has the key of David and who opens and no one shall shut (v. 7), the Lord has given the recovered church "an open door which no one can shut." Since the recovery of the proper church life began, in the early part of the nineteenth century, until now, a door has always been wide open to the Lord's recovery.]

["Because you have kept the word of My endurance, I also will keep you out of the hour of trial which is about to come on the whole inhabited earth, to try them who dwell on the earth" (3:10). This promise actually refers to the rapture of the overcomers before the great tribulation. "Trial" in 3:10 undoubtedly denotes the great tribulation (Matt. 24:21) "which is about to come on the whole inhabited earth," as indicated by the fifth, sixth, and seventh trumpets with the seven bowls (Rev. 8:13-9:21; 11:14-15; 15:1; 16:1-2). The "trial" may also include the supernatural calamities of the sixth seal and the first four trumpets. The Lord promises the recovered church that He will keep her "out of the hour of trial" (not only out of the trial but out of the hour of trial) because she has kept the word of His endurance. This promise of the Lord, like that in Luke 21:36, indicates that the saints who have kept the word of the Lord's endurance will be raptured before the great trial.]

B. The Lord's Promise to the Overcomers of This Stage

[In Revelation 3:11 and 12 we have the Lord's promise to the overcomers in Philadelphia. To overcome in this epistle means to hold fast what we have in the recovered church.]

[In verse 11 the Lord says, "I come quickly; hold fast what you have that no one take your crown." The recovered church has gained the crown already. However, if she does not hold fast what she has in the Lord's recovery until the Lord comes back, her crown may be taken away by someone. Being a reward from the Lord, this crown needs to be kept until He comes back.]

[In 3:12a the Lord says, "He who overcomes, I will make him a pillar in the temple of My God, and he shall by no means go out anymore." In 2:17 the overcomer becomes a transformed stone for God's building. Here the overcomer will be made a pillar built into the temple of God. Because he is built into God's building, "he shall by no means go out anymore." This promise will be fulfilled in the millennial kingdom as a prize to the overcomer.]

[In 3:12b the Lord goes on to say concerning the overcomer, "I will write upon him the name of My God and the name of the city of My God, the New Jerusalem, which descends out of heaven from My God, and My new name." Here the Lord speaks of the New Jerusalem. The New Jerusalem is not a physical city but a composition of the believers. This composition will appear first in the millennium as the totality of all the overcomers. These overcomers will bear the name of God because they have God's nature in them; and they will bear the name of God's city because they are God's city. This means that the overcomers will be the New Jerusalem.]

VII. THE CHURCH IN LAODICEA

[In Greek, "Laodicea" means the opinion, the judgment, of the people or of the laymen. The church in Laodicea as a sign prefigures the degraded recovered church. Less than a century after the Lord recovered the proper church in the early part of the nineteenth century, some of the recovered churches ("assemblies") became degraded. This degraded recovered church differs from the reformed church signified by the church in Sardis; it also differs from the proper recovered church signified by the church in Philadelphia. The degraded recovered church, signified by Laodicea, will exist until the Lord comes back.]

A. The Condition of the Church at This Stage

["I know your works, that you are neither cold nor hot; I wish you were cold or hot. So because you are lukewarm and neither hot nor cold, I am about to vomit you out of My mouth" (Rev. 3:15-16). Once the recovered church becomes degraded, it is lukewarm—neither cold nor hot.]

[According to verse 16b, the Lord is about to vomit the lukewarm ones out of His mouth. Once we become lukewarm, we are not fitting for the Lord's move and shall be vomited out of His mouth. When the recovered church becomes degraded, she is in danger, unless she repents to be hot in seeking the rich experiences of the Lord, of being vomited out of the Lord's mouth. To be vomited out of the Lord's mouth is to lose the enjoyment of all that the Lord is to His church.]

[In verse 17 the Lord continues, "Because you say, I am rich and have become rich and have need of nothing, and do not know that you are wretched and miserable and poor and blind and naked." The degraded recovered church ("assembly") boasts of her riches (mainly in the knowledge of doctrines). She does not realize that she is poor in life, blind in sight, and naked in conduct.]

[In verse 18 the Lord goes on to say, "I counsel you to buy from Me gold refined by fire that you may be rich, and white garments that you may be clothed and that the shame of your nakedness may not be manifested, and eyesalve to anoint your eyes that you may see." To buy requires the paying of a price. The degraded recovered church needs to pay a price for the gold, the white garments, and the eyesalve, which she desperately needs.]

[In Revelation 3:20a the Lord says, "Behold, I stand at the door and knock." The door here is not the door of individuals but the door of the church. The church in Laodicea has knowledge, but she does not have the presence of the Lord. The Lord, the Head of the church, is actually standing outside the degraded church, knocking at her door. This means that, in a very practical way, the degraded recovered church is Christless. This church has Christ in name but not in presence. In actuality, the Lord is outside her door.]

B. The Lord's Promise to the Overcomers of This Stage

[In 3:20b and 21 we have the Lord's promise to the overcomers of this stage. To overcome here means to overcome the lukewarmness and pride of the degraded recovered church, to buy the needed items, and to open the door for the Lord to come in.]

[In verse 20b the Lord says, "If anyone hears My voice and opens the door, I will come in to him and dine with him and he with Me." According to the Greek, the word "dine" signifies the principal meal of the day at evening. To dine is not merely to eat one item of food but to partake of the riches of a meal. This may imply the fulfillment of the type of the children of Israel eating the rich produce of the good land of Canaan (Josh. 5:10-12).

The dining promised in Revelation 3:20b is not only for the future but also for today. If we are overcomers, when the Lord comes in the kingdom we shall have the special privilege of eating with Him. Before that day, however, we may enjoy His dining with us.]

[In verse 21 the Lord says, "He who overcomes, to him I will give to sit with Me on My throne, as I also overcame and sat down with My Father on His throne." To sit with the Lord on His throne will be a prize to the overcomer that he may participate in the Lord's authority in the coming millennial kingdom. This means that the overcomers will be co-kings with Christ ruling over the whole earth.]

CONCLUSION

[The seven churches in Revelation 2 and 3 not only signify prophetically the progress of the church in seven stages but also symbolize the seven kinds of churches in church history: the initial church, the suffering church, the worldly church, the apostate church, the reformed church, the recovered church, and the degraded recovered church. The initial church had its continuation in the suffering church; the suffering church turned into the worldly church; and the worldly church became the apostate church. Hence, the first four churches eventually issued in one kind of church, that is, the apostate church, the Roman Catholic Church. Then, as a reaction to the apostate church, the reformed church came into existence as another kind of church, a church not fully recovered. Following this, the recovered church was raised up as a full recovery of the church life. By the degradation of the recovered church, the degraded recovered church came into being. These four kinds of churches—the Roman Catholic Church, the reformed church, the recovered church, and the degraded recovered church—will remain until the Lord comes back. Undoubtedly, only the recovered church can fulfill God's eternal purpose, and only she is what the Lord is after.]

Questions

1. Write a prophecy, listing for each church, the time period it covers, the significance of its name, how their condition can be applied to us today, and what is the reward for each and how it relates to their condition.

Quoted Portions

1. Conclusion of the New Testament (Lee/LSM), pp. 2497-2535.

Further References

1. Conclusion of the New Testament (Lee/LSM), pp. 2497-2535.

2. The Orthodoxy of the Church (Nee/LSM), pp. 9-109.

Lesson Twelve

THE CONSUMMATION OF THE CHURCH

Scripture Reading

Eph. 2:8; Rev. 5:9; Eph. 1:22-23; 2 Cor. 3:18; Rev. 12:5; 14:4; Matt. 25:21; Heb. 12:6; Rev. 21:14.

Outline

I. All the members of the church are produced in the church age

II. The New Testament overcomers are also perfected in the church age
   A. The perfection of the New Testament overcomers in the church age
   B. The reward of the New Testament overcomers
      1. At the end of the church age
      2. In the age of the millennium

III. The immature believers will be perfected in the age of the millennium
   A. Through the Lord's dispensational and governmental discipline
   B. As illustrated by the case of the unfaithful slave
   C. As illustrated by the case of the slothful slave

IV. All the regenerated and perfected believers of the New Testament will be the components of the New Jerusalem, which is the church's ultimate consummation
   A. Consummated in enjoying the eternal and divine life of the processed and consummated Triune God
   B. Consummated in experiencing the mingling of humanity with divinity
   C. Consummated in expressing the Triune God in His ultimate manifestation for eternity

Text

This is the last lesson on the vision concerning the church. The last twelve lessons will cover how to build up the church. The topic of this lesson is concerning the consummation of the church. Everything has a beginning and a consummation. Without a good consummation, nothing is properly concluded. Such a wonderful and marvellous church must have a matching consummation.

[The consummation of the church will be the New Jerusalem. Today the church is a miniature of the New Jerusalem. The proper church life in its genuineness is a small model of the New Jerusalem. The crucial matter here, however, is that the New Jerusalem will be the consummation of all of God's chosen, redeemed, regenerated, sanctified, transformed, perfected, and glorified people.

The New Jerusalem will be the totality of God's work in both the old creation and in the new creation. First, God created the old creation. Although the old creation became fallen, God was prepared to deal with that situation. He came to be a man, a God-man, a man with divinity mingled with humanity, to accomplish redemption. This God-man could redeem sinners, dying for them, because He had the blood to shed for them. This blood is called "His own blood" (Acts 20:28) and "the blood of Jesus His Son" (1 John 1:7). Through His all-inclusive death, the Lord released His resurrection life, and with this life He produced, sanctified, transformed, built, and glorified the people whom He had predestinated. The totality of this work, its ultimate consummation, will be the New Jerusalem. Instead of being a material city, the New Jerusalem is a symbol of the totality of God's work.]

I. ALL THE MEMBERS OF THE CHURCH ARE PRODUCED IN THE CHURCH AGE

[All the members of the church are produced in the church age, that is, in the age between Christ's first coming and His coming back. The members of the church are those who were fallen sinners and who have been saved by the grace of God (Eph. 2:8) through their God-given and

God-allotted faith (2 Pet. 1:1), which has brought them into an organic union with the Triune God in Christ (1 Cor. 6:17). These members of the church have been forgiven of their sins (Acts 10:43). They have been justified by God in Christ (Acts 13:39; 1 Cor. 6:11), and they have been reconciled to God (Rom. 5:10), so they have been redeemed back to God (Rev. 5:9). Based upon this, the members of the church have been regenerated in their spirit by the Spirit of God (John 3:6) to be the children of God unto the divine sonship (John 1:12-13; Rom. 8:16) and to be the members of Christ (Eph. 5:30) unto His stature (Eph. 4:13) to be His fullness (Eph. 1:23).]

II. THE NEW TESTAMENT OVERCOMERS ARE ALSO PERFECTED IN THE CHURCH AGE

A. The Perfection of the New Testament Overcomers in the Church Age

[The New Testament overcomers are not only produced in the church age but are also perfected in the church age. The perfecting of the New Testament overcomers is a matter of transformation through the subjective experience and enjoyment of Christ. Second Corinthians 3:18 says, "We all with unveiled face, beholding and reflecting as a mirror the glory of the Lord, are being transformed into the same image from glory to glory, even as from the Lord Spirit." To be transformed is to have Christ added into our being to replace what we are so that Christ may increase and our natural life may decrease. As the process of transformation takes place within us, the old element of our natural being is carried away, and the glory, the resurrected Christ as the life-giving Spirit, is added into us to replace the natural element. It is through such a process that the New Testament overcomers are perfected in this age.]

B. The Reward of the New Testament Overcomers

1. At the End of the Church Age

The believers may be overcomers either as the man-child (the dead overcomers—Rev. 12:5) or as the firstfruits (the living overcomers—Rev. 14:4). The dead overcomers of both the Old Testament and the New Testament will resurrect and be raptured to God and to His throne to fight and defeat Satan before the period of the great tribulation. The living overcomers, comprised only of the New Testament overcomers, will be the firstfruit of God's harvest on the earth. They will be raptured to Mount Zion in the heavens for God and Christ's satisfaction before the great tribulation.

All the overcomers, both the dead and the living, will be the bride at the marriage feast of Christ and in the millennium (Rev. 19:7-9; 21:2). The overcomers will also be the armies in heaven fighting with the coming Christ against the Antichrist and his armies (Rev. 17:12-14; 19:11-21).

2. In the Age of the Millennium

In the coming kingdom the overcoming believers will reign with Christ as co-kings (Rev. 20:4). This includes being crowned with many crowns such as the crown of righteousness (2 Tim. 4:8), the unfading crown of glory (1 Pet. 5:4), the crown of life (Rev. 2:10), and an incorruptible crown (1 Cor. 9:25). This also means that they will sit with Christ on His throne (Rev. 3:21) having authority over the nations to shepherd them (Rev. 2:26-27; 12:5), and to participate in the joy of the Lord (Matt. 25:21, 23).

They also will inherit the kingdom of Christ and of God to enter the manifestation of the kingdom of the heavens (Eph. 5:5), to be glorified with Christ (Rom. 8:17), to inherit eternal life in the Millennium (Matt. 19:29), to have their names remain in the book of life (Rev. 3:5), to not be hurt of the second death (Rev. 2:11), to have the right to the tree of life (Rev. 2:7), to shine forth as the sun in the kingdom of their Father (Matt. 13:43), to participate in the feast of the kingdom of the heavens (Matt. 8:11), and to enjoy the reward (Matt. 5:11). Finally, they will become the New Jerusalem—the paradise of God- in the millennium (Rev. 3:12; 2:7). This list of rewards should give all of us much aspiration and encouragement to be overcomers in the age of the church.

III. THE IMMATURE BELIEVERS WILL BE PERFECTED IN THE AGE OF THE MILLENNIUM

[The need for transformation is neglected by many Christians today. As a result, many have been kept from being transformed and perfected by the genuine experience and enjoyment of the all-inclusive Christ with His unsearchable riches. As a result, there is no way for God to perfect these immature believers in the church age. However, because they are God's chosen, redeemed, called, and regenerated people, God will not let them go. Rather, He will perfect them in the coming age of the millennium.]

A. Through the Lord's Dispensational and Governmental Discipline

[The perfecting of the immature believers in the age of the millennium will be through the Lord's dispensational and governmental discipline. Hebrews 12:6 tells us, "Whom the Lord loves He disciplines and scourges every son whom He receives." The Lord's discipline of the believers is not only in this age but also in the coming age. Because the age of the millennium will still belong to the old heaven and the old earth, the coming age will still be a time for the Father to deal with His children so that they may be perfected. Those believers who are not perfected in the church age will be perfected in the age of the millennium. The means of their perfection will be the Lord's dispensational and governmental discipline. This discipline will be for those who were slothful in the church age, in the dispensation of grace, and did not apply the Lord's sufficient grace and enjoy it, taking this grace as their portion. Such believers will need the Lord's loving discipline in the coming age for their perfection.]

B. As Illustrated by the Case of the Unfaithful Slave

[The Lord's dispensational and governmental discipline of the immature believers in the age of the millennium is illustrated by the cases of the unfaithful slave and the slothful slave in Matthew 24:48-51 and 25:24-30. Matthew 24:48 and 49 speak of an evil slave who says in his heart, "My master is delaying his coming," and who begins to "beat his fellow slaves, and eat and drink with the drunken." Verses 50 and 51 say, "The master of that slave shall come on a day when he does not expect him, and in an hour which he does not know, and shall cut him asunder and appoint his portion with the hypocrites; there shall be the weeping and the gnashing of teeth." The problem with the evil slave is not that he does not know that the Lord is coming but that he does not expect Him. He does not like to live the kind of life that is prepared for the Lord's coming. Moreover, the evil slave beats his fellow slaves, that is, mistreats the fellow believers, and eats and drinks with the drunken, that is, keeps company with worldly people, who are drunk with worldly things. Therefore, when the Lord comes back, He will cut asunder the evil slave and appoint his portion with the hypocrites.

To "cut him asunder" means to cut him off, not to cut him to pieces. This signifies a separation from the Lord in His coming glory. The Lord will not cut the evil slave in pieces; rather, He will cast him off from the glory in which He Himself will be. The issue here is not salvation but the discipline of an immature believer in the coming age. Such a believer will miss the enjoyment of the kingdom and instead suffer punishment and discipline where there will be weeping and gnashing of teeth.

For a believer to be cut asunder is for him to be cut asunder from the organic union with the Lord. Whenever a person believes in the Lord, he is put into an organic union with the Triune God so that he may enjoy Him. According to Matthew 28:19, the believers are to be baptized into the name of the Triune God, that is, into an organic union with the Triune God, so that they may participate in Him, partake of Him, and enjoy Him. By enjoying the Triune God in the organic union we are transformed and perfected, made ready for the Lord to come back to take us into His enjoyment in the millennium. However, Matthew 24 tells us clearly that in the coming age certain ones will be cut asunder from the organic union. This means that they will be cut off from the enjoyment of the Lord. This cutting off from the organic union corresponds to the taking away of the branches in John 15. For a branch to be cut off from the vine means that it is cut off from the union with the vine. Those branches that are in union with the vine enjoy and participate in all the riches of the vine, but those branches that are cut off from the vine lose this enjoyment. This is the correct understanding of the cutting asunder in Matthew 24.

After the immature believers have been cut asunder, cut off from the organic union with the Lord, they will be put into the outer darkness, the darkness outside the bright glory in the manifestation of the kingdom of the heavens. This is different from being cast into the lake of fire after the millennium for eternity (Rev. 20:15). The overcomers will be called into the Lord's enjoyment, which will be in the glory, but the defeated ones will be put outside this glory. They will be outside the glory in which the Lord and His overcomers will be during the coming age. To be in the glory will be a reward, but to be put outside the glory will be a kind of punishment. Those who are put into the outer darkness will weep and gnash their teeth. The weeping will indicate regret, and the gnashing of teeth, self-blame. Both the weeping and the gnashing of teeth will be a sign of suffering the Lord's dispensational and governmental discipline.]

C. As Illustrated by the Case of the Slothful Slave

[The Lord's dispensational and governmental discipline is also illustrated by the case of the slothful slave in Matthew 25:24-30. In verses 26 through 30 we see that the one-talented one who was not faithful in using his gift is rebuked by the Lord and punished. Verse 30 says, "Cast out the useless slave into the outer darkness; there shall be the weeping and the gnashing of teeth." Whoever is cast into outer darkness will be cut off from the Lord, from His presence, from His fellowship, and from the glorious sphere in which the Lord will be. This is not to perish eternally but to be chastened dispensationally during the coming age of the kingdom. This chastening, this punishment, has a goal, and this goal is the believers' perfection.

In this dispensation of grace, the Lord is supporting us and supplying us with rich grace so that we may enjoy this grace, be edified, and be transformed for our perfection. If we are faithful, we shall enter into His joy in the coming age. But if we are not faithful, we shall be disciplined by Him in the coming age so that we may be perfected. Those who are faithful in this age of grace will be rewarded by the Lord in the coming age. They will be with Him in glory and even reign with Him. But for those who are not perfected in the church age, the age of the millennium will be a time of discipline. In order to be fitting to enter into the New Jerusalem in the new heaven and the new earth, the immature believers will need to be perfected through discipline during the coming age.]

IV. ALL THE REGENERATED AND PERFECTED BELIEVERS OF THE NEW TESTAMENT WILL BE THE COMPONENTS OF THE NEW JERUSALEM, WHICH IS THE CHURCH'S ULTIMATE CONSUMMATION

[God's intention is that the church will consummate in the New Jerusalem. All the regenerated and perfected believers as members of the church, represented by the twelve apostles (Rev. 21:14), will be the components of the New Jerusalem. After the dispensation of grace, there will be the dispensation of the kingdom. During this dispensation, all the perfected ones, including the overcomers of the Old Testament and the overcomers of the New Testament, will be the totality of overcomers to be the New Jerusalem. They will be the New Jerusalem in its first stage, the stage of the millennium. During this stage, the New Jerusalem will be Christ's bride. Also during the millennium, the defeated, slothful, immature believers will be perfected through their suffering of the Lord's dispensational and governmental discipline. Therefore, after the millennium, they also will be components of the New Jerusalem in the second stage, that is, in the new heaven and the new earth. In this second stage the New Jerusalem will be enlarged to be the New Jerusalem in Revelation 21. This enlarged New Jerusalem will be the consummation of the church. From this we can see that the ultimate consummation of the church life will be the New Jerusalem, first in a smaller scale in the millennium composed only of the overcomers and then in an enlarged scale in the new heaven and the new earth composed of all the believers of the New Testament.]

A. Consummated in Enjoying the Eternal and Divine Life of the Processed and Consummated Triune God

[The proper church life today is the enjoyment of the eternal and divine life of the processed and consummated Triune God. This enjoyment is just a foretaste; the full taste will be in New Jerusalem in the new heaven and new earth, which will be the consummation of our enjoyment of our processed and consummated Triune God in its fullest without limitation for eternity.]

B. Consummated in Experiencing the Mingling of Humanity with Divinity

[Our Christian life today is the experience of the mingling of divinity with humanity in the dispensing of the unsearchable riches of the processed and consummated divine Trinity. This is also a foretaste, and its full taste as its consummation will be also in the New Jerusalem in the new heaven and new earth eternally.]

C. Consummated in Expressing the Triune God in His Ultimate Manifestation for Eternity

[Both our Christian life and church life are the expression of the processed and consummated Triune God in His ultimate manifestation for eternity. Today this is just in the initial stage. Its consummation will be also in the New Jerusalem as the ultimate manifestation of the processed and consummated Triune God for eternity.

The church today should grow and be built up in the three matters of enjoying the eternal and divine life of the processed and consummated Triune God, of experiencing the mingling of humanity with divinity in the dispensing of the unsearchable riches of the processed and consummated divine

Trinity, and of expressing the processed and consummated Triune God in His ultimate manifestation. This means that the church must grow and be built up in the enjoyment of the eternal, divine life, the life of the processed and consummated Triune God; that the church must grow and be built up in experiencing the mingling of the believers with the Triune God in the way of His dispensing of the unsearchable riches of the processed and consummated divine Trinity; and that the church must grow and be built up in the expression of the processed and consummated Triune God in His manifestation. This is the church life.

In some of the foregoing messages we covered the various aspects of the status of the church: the assembly, the house of God, the kingdom of God, the Body of Christ, the counterpart of Christ, the new man, and the golden lampstands. Now we need to see that all these matters can be realized by us in the local churches only as we enjoy the life of the processed and consummated Triune God, experience the mingling of humanity with divinity in the dispensing of the unsearchable riches of the processed and consummated divine Trinity, and express the processed and consummated Triune God in His manifestation.]

The Lord loves us very much. His mercy upon us is immeasurable. We left God, offended God, and were under the righteous judgment of God. We were void of the life of God needed to fulfill His purpose. Rather, we were filled with Satan's life and nature to cause us to struggle in sin all our life. Yet, God is full of love and mercy. He became a man to die for us to meet God's righteous demand so that we do not have to die. He destroyed the devil and left our flesh of sin on the cross so that we may be free from the law of sin and of death. Then He released His life on the cross, and as the life-giving Spirit, through resurrection, He brought the life of God into us. He, as the Spirit, is now mingled with us, supplying us daily with His life to transform us. He also brought us into the church to be with all the saints that we may go on together and be built-up together to fulfill God's purpose. This is our foretaste in this age.

If we enjoy the foretaste properly by exercising our spirit everyday all the day long, then we will receive a reward which is the enjoyment of the full-taste, the New Jerusalem, a thousand years earlier. Even if some miss this foretaste period due to sin and the world, He will be merciful to give them another opportunity to be perfected in the next age. Ultimately, those who are perfected in the next age will join those who are perfected in this age to be the New Jerusalem, enjoying the full-taste for eternity. Hallelujah! What a loving and merciful God we have. We all must give ourselves diligently to enjoy the Lord by praying in spirit and reading His Word. We must also exercise to live in the local church life by preaching the gospel and meeting with the saints to increase the church and to be built up. We should not hesitate. Now is the time. This is the age. We can be the ones to overcome and bring this age to a conclusion.

Questions

1. What are the items (concerning the perfecting the members of the church) that can only be accomplished in this age—the age of grace?

2. What will be the reward or punishment of the church members during the millennium?

3. What determines whether you will receive a reward or punishment?

4. How can you experience the New Jerusalem today? Give several examples.

Quoted Portions

1. Conclusion of the New Testament (Lee/LSM), pp. 2537-2544.

Further References

1. Basic Revelation in the Holy Scriptures (Lee/LSM), pp. 94-96, 100-101, 123-124.

2. Basic Revelation in the Holy Scriptures (Lee/LSM), p. 36.

3. Conclusion of the New Testament (Lee/LSM), pp. 2226-2227, 2345-2347, 2418-2446.

4. The Divine Economy (Lee/LSM), pp. 133, 136.

5. The Economy of God and the Building Up of the Body of Christ (Lee/LSM), p. 51.

6. The Exercise of the Kingdom for the Building of the Church (Lee/LSM), pp. 42, 78.

7. The Glorious Church (Nee/LSM), pp. 128-129.

8. Life Study of Ephesians (Lee/LSM), p. 148.

Lesson Thirteen

THE INDIRECT BUILDING UP OF THE BODY OF CHRIST BY THE GIFTS TO THE BODY

Scripture Reading

Matt. 16:16-18; Eph. 4:8-14.

Outline

I. Christ's prophecy on building the church
  A. Building the church on this rock
  B. The gates of Hades not being able to prevail against the church

II. The way Christ builds up the church
  A. By the gifted persons and the perfected saints
  B. By the ascended Head giving the gifts to His Body
  C. The gifts to the church—some apostles
  D. The gifts to the church—some prophets
  E. The gifts to the church—some evangelists
  F. The gifts to the church—some shepherds and teachers
  G. For the perfecting of the saints unto the work of ministry unto the building up of the Body of Christ

Text

In the first twelve lessons, we have seen the vision concerning the church. In the next twelve lessons, we will see the building up of the church and our participation in her building up. We not only want to show you a heavenly vision of the church, we also want you to know how this vision can be accomplished. This lesson is concerning the first subject—the building up of the universal church, the Body of Christ, not the local churches. [The local churches are local—they are in the different localities and are plural in number. Today, on the whole earth, over the six continents, there are about eleven hundred churches in the Lord's recovery. But the Body of Christ is unique in the whole universe. There is only one Body. All the local churches in all times and places are part of this unique Body of Christ.]

I. CHRIST'S PROPHECY ON BUILDING THE CHURCH

A. Building the Church on This Rock

[The Lord prophesied in Matthew 16 that He would build His church, which is His Body, upon this rock. On the one hand, this rock signifies Christ; on the other hand, it signifies the revelation seen by the apostles. The Bible shows us that, on the one hand, the Body of Christ is built upon Christ Himself, with Him as the foundation (1 Cor. 3:11). On the other hand, it is built upon the foundation of the apostles and the prophets (Eph. 2:20). The foundation of the apostles and the prophets is the revelation they have seen, which is the whole New Testament, from Matthew to Revelation.

The church is mentioned for the first time in the whole Bible in Matthew 16. Although there are several types in the Old Testament typifying the church, the word "church" is not found in the Old Testament. Therefore, in the Old Testament the church is a mystery hidden in God. None of the ones such as Adam, Noah, Abraham, Moses, David, or Isaiah knew about this. The Old Testament saints did not know why they were fearing and worshipping God and why God was caring for them; they only knew that the Messiah, the Christ, would come. They earnestly expected Him to come to establish the kingdom of the heavens on earth. They did not know that God wanted to obtain a church as the Body of Christ. In the New Testament, John the Baptist appeared, calling people to repent and to believe in the gospel. The Lord Jesus continued what John had preached, and as a result, Peter, James, John, and many others received it. Of these, the Lord appointed twelve as apostles and sent them out to preach the gospel, but none of them knew that all this was for the church. I believe by the time they came to Matthew 16, the disciples had been following the Lord for about two to three years. At that time the Lord brought them out of Jerusalem and the land of Judea, away from the holy city, the holy temple, the sacrifice, the incense, and the places full of religious atmosphere, to the region of Caesarea Philippi in the north, at the foot of a mountain by the border of the land of Judea. There the Lord asked them, "Who do you say that I am?" Peter answered and said, "You are the Christ, the Son of the living God" (v. 16). This time he did not say foolish things; his sky was clear, without clouds. He received the revelation and saw that according to His ministry, the Lord Jesus is God's Anointed for the fulfillment of God's purpose, and that according to His person, He is the Son of God, the embodiment of God. Here Peter uttered some stunning words. Immediately the Lord told him that this was not revealed to him by man but by God the Father. Furthermore, the Lord said, "On this rock I will build My church" (v. 18). In this word the Lord showed Peter that it is not enough just to know Him as the Christ; Peter must also know that upon Him He will build the church. Christ is only the Head; He needs a Body, which is the church, to be His match. The Head and the Body cannot be divided; Christ and the church is a great mystery (Eph. 5:32). Not only must we know Christ; we must know the church as well.

It has now been nearly two thousand years since the time of Christ's ascension. The greatest thing that has happened during this time is the producing of the church. What we are doing here today is to "stir up" churches. To say that we are building up the church means that we are "stirring up" churches. What were Peter and Paul doing? They were stirring up churches! What were the Western missionaries doing when they left their countries and kinsmen and crossed the ocean? They were stirring up churches! At present, Christ on the throne in heaven is sending His seven Spirits to enliven us. For what purpose? For the purpose of stirring up churches everywhere, until the whole world is so stirred up that it is filled with churches! The Lord said that the gospel of the kingdom shall be preached in the whole inhabited earth and then the end shall come. Today the end has not yet come, because the gospel has not yet been preached in the whole inhabited earth, and the whole earth has not yet been filled with churches.]

B. The Gates of Hades
Not Being Able to Prevail Against the Church

[In Matthew 16:18 the Lord continued by saying, "the gates of Hades shall not prevail against it (the church)." The gates of Hades is the authority of Satan's darkness; it is also the authority of death. However, it cannot prevail against the church, for the church is the Body of Christ, the Head, who sits on the throne in heaven. All authority in heaven and on earth is given to Christ. Since the church is His Body, the gates of Hades cannot prevail against the church. This ascended Head has already been crowned with glory and honor on the throne (Heb. 2:9). He has also received authority from God the Father and has been made Lord and Christ (Acts 2:36) and the Ruler of the kings of the earth (Rev. 1:5). Now He operates by His Spirit, which is the sevenfold intensified Spirit (Rev. 4:5; 5:6), to apply all that He has accomplished and obtained to us for the building up of His Body. This is the work of Christ in heaven. Heaven, where He is, is joined to our spirit. The spirit within us is linked to heaven. The book of Genesis in the Old Testament records the story of Jacob when he dreamed of a heavenly ladder in the wilderness. On the ladder there were angels of God ascending and descending (Gen. 28:12). The heavenly ladder is a type of the ascended Christ. The place where the ladder was set up was called Bethel, and it was the gate of heaven (Gen. 28:18-19). Hebrews 4:16 tells us that we can come boldly to the throne of grace. We are now living on earth. How then can we come to God's throne in heaven? The key is the spirit mentioned in verse 12 of Hebrews 4. The Christ who is sitting on the throne in heaven is now also in us (Rom. 8:10), that is, in our spirit (2 Tim. 4:22). God's dwelling place is this spirit. Bethel is the house of God, the habitation of God, and the gate of heaven. There Christ is the ladder, linking earth to heaven and bringing heaven down to earth. Since our spirit now is God's dwelling place, this spirit is the gate of heaven. Here Christ is the ladder, joining us, the people on earth, to heaven and bringing heaven to us.

Sometimes when you wake up in the morning, you feel very weak. But when you call "O Lord Jesus," immediately the ascended Christ will be transmitted into you like electricity, and you will be strengthened within. Sometimes you feel tired and do not want to come to the meetings. But as soon as you say softly within, "Lord!" something will start moving within you, and you will end up coming to the meeting. The more you come to the meetings, the more you will be joined to heaven, and the stronger you will become. All the tiredness will be gone. This is Christ bringing heaven to us within, enabling us to overcome Satan's might of death.]

II. THE WAY CHRIST BUILDS UP THE CHURCH

A. By the Gifted Persons and the Perfected Saints

[There are two kinds of building up—one is by the gifted persons and the other is by the perfected saints. The building up of the Body of Christ by the gifted persons is under the Head's supply and is done indirectly. The gifted persons do not build up the Body of Christ directly. Even Christ as the Head of the church does not build the church directly. In Matthew 16:18 the Lord told us that He would build His church, but He builds His church indirectly through His giving of the gifts to His Body. Then these gifts perfect the saints, and the perfected saints do the building work directly. The building up of the Body of Christ by the perfected saints is under the gifted persons' perfecting and is done directly. Ephesians 4:16 says that the Body will build itself up in love because all the members build up the Body of Christ. They build up the Body of Christ by growing into the Head in all things (Eph. 4:15). The growth in life of each member of the Body added together equals the building up of the Body. The perfected saints also build up the Body by functioning out from the Head, causing the growth of the Body that the Body may be built up directly by itself (4:16).]

B. By the Ascended Head Giving the Gifts to His Body

[The intrinsic building up of the church is by the ascended Head giving the gifts (Eph. 4:8-11). Ephesians 4:8 says, "Wherefore He says, Having ascended to the height, He led captive those taken captive and gave gifts to men." We may appreciate the Lord's coming down from the heavens, but we also need an uplifted appreciation of His ascension. In Ephesians 4:8, Paul points out that it is the ascended Christ who is able to give the gifts.

When Paul said that Christ "ascended to the height," he quoted from Psalm 68:18. "Height" in this verse refers to Mount Zion (Psa. 68:15-16), symbolizing the third heaven, where God dwells (1 Kings 8:30). Psalm 68 implies that it was in the ark that God ascended to Mount Zion after the ark had won the victory. Verse 1 of Psalm 68 is a quotation of Numbers 10:35. It indicates that the background of Psalm 68 is God's move in the tabernacle with the ark as its center. Wherever the ark, a type of Christ, went, the victory was won. Eventually, this ark ascended triumphantly to the top of Mount Zion. This portrays how Christ has won the victory and ascended triumphantly to the heavens.

In His ascension, Christ "led captive those taken captive." The redeemed saints had been taken captive by Satan before being saved by Christ's death and resurrection. We were captives under Satan's hand through sin and death. But Christ defeated Satan, solved the problem of sin and death, and rescued us out of the hand of Satan. Then He led us to the heavens as His captives. He took these captives and made them gifts to men.

One of these gifts was Saul of Tarsus, who later became Paul, the apostle. He had been a captive of Satan and a top sinner. In First Timothy 1:15 Paul said that he was "the foremost" sinner. He was a big captive of Satan under sin and death, but one day Christ rescued him. He was on the way to Damascus to arrest those who called on the Lord's name (Acts 9:1-2, 14). Then the Lord Jesus seized him and rescued him out of the hand of Satan. Saul was Satan's captive, but he became Christ's captive.

Saul of Tarsus had been opposing Christ and devastating the church. Suddenly he became a gift. Christ took this one and made him a gift by the name of Paul. He became a gift who could expound the Old Testament, who could preach the gospel, teach the saints, and prophesy. How could Paul become such a gift? He himself tells us with a parenthetical word in Ephesians 4:9-10: "Now this, He ascended, what is it except that He also descended into the lower parts of the earth? He who descended is the same who also ascended far above all the heavens that He might fill all things."

Paul was a wonderful writer. He wrote this portion in describing Christ's death and resurrection to accomplish His full redemption and impart life to us. Christ first descended to the earth from the heavenly throne in the third heavens. He did this through the process of incarnation. He lived on the earth for thirty-three and a half years. Then He entered into death, and in death He descended further. In the second step of His descension, He descended into the lower parts of the earth. This refers to Hades, underneath the earth, where Christ went after His death (Acts 2:27). The first step of Christ's descension was for His incarnation. The second step was for His redemption. His descension was the means to accomplish His all-inclusive, full redemption, which has saved us from sin, death, Satan, and the lake of fire. In the first step of His ascension, He ascended from Hades to the earth in resurrection. In His resurrection, He imparted life into us. His descension accomplished redemption, and His ascension accomplished the impartation of life. In the second step of His ascension, He brought us to the Father in the third heavens.

When He ascended before His disciples into heaven (Luke 24:51; Acts 1:9-11), they did not fully understand what was going on. They only saw Jesus ascending. But the Scriptures reveal that when Jesus was ascending, He was ascending with a train of vanquished foes. The Amplified New Testament renders "He led a train of vanquished foes" for "He led captive those taken captive." When He was ascending, He was a returning General who had won the victory over Satan, sin, and death. He defeated all of His enemies, and He had many captives. He brought these captives with Him in a procession to celebrate His victory.

Peter and John did not see this when the Lord ascended before their eyes, but the angels saw a tremendous and great train of vanquished foes as a procession for the celebration of Christ's victory. We were there in that procession; Satan was there; and death was also there. What a procession that was! The Lord then presented us, the redeemed saints, His defeated and vanquished foes, as a present to the Father. It is as though He said, "Father, here are the persons You have given to Me. They were dead captives of Satan. Now I have captured them; I rescued them out of the hand of Satan, out from under sin and death. I have also imparted My life into them through My resurrection, the first step of My ascension from Hades to the earth. Now they are not dead, but living presents. I give them all to You as a big, corporate present."

This present included all of the redeemed saints. It included Peter, Paul, Martin Luther, John Nelson Darby, and Watchman Nee. I am honored to be included in this present. We were all included there in Christ's ascension as a big, living present to the Father. The Father, no doubt, was so happy. He could have said, "I am so happy for My redeemed people. They were dead and captured by Satan. But My Son, through His death and resurrection, rescued them and imparted life into them, making them living."

We all must realize that we have already been to the heavens. We were there with Christ, because He brought us, as His present, to the Father. He did not go empty-handed. He went to the Father with all His redeemed ones, including you and me, as a corporate present to the Father. The Father then gave us back to the Son as gifts for His Body (Psa. 68:18). Thus, through His descension and ascension, Christ rescued us, enlivened us, and made us gifts with His resurrection life.

Paul was such a gift. Sometimes I have wondered how Paul received such great revelations, such as the revelation in Ephesians 4. Undoubtedly, Christ spent some particular time with Paul. After he was saved, Paul went to Arabia and stayed there for a period of time (Gal. 1:17). No one knows what he did there, but, no doubt, during this time there was much contact between him and Christ. I believe the Lord used this time to constitute Paul into a big gift to His Body. When Paul returned from Arabia, he was able to preach and to speak wonderful things. That means he became a big gift to the church in the category of the gifted persons mentioned in Ephesians 4:11. This is why he was able to describe Christ's death and resurrection in the marvelous way of verses 8 through 10.

We all should learn to preach the gospel in such a rich way as that portrayed in Ephesians 4. We may speak in this way to our unbelieving contacts: "I would like to tell you that our Savior descended in two steps. He descended from the heavens to the earth and then from the earth to Hades. In the first step of His descension, He accomplished incarnation; He became a man. In the second step of His descension, He entered into death and even went into Hades, dying for us to save us from sin, death, and Satan. As sinners, we were captives of Satan, but through the death of Christ we were forgiven and even rescued from Satan. Then the Lord ascended from Hades to the earth in resurrection. In His resurrection He imparted Himself into us as life. He accomplished redemption through His death and life-impartation through His resurrection. Then we were made alive. In the second step of His ascension, He led us as a train of vanquished foes to the third heaven to give us as a present to His Father." Sometimes we should preach the gospel in this way when we go out to visit people.

During the time of the Roman Empire, when a general gained a victory, all his captives became a procession in the celebration of his victory. Eventually, some of these captives were put to death, and some were given life (2 Cor. 2:15-16). The ones in this procession who were put to death were Satan and his fallen angels, and the ones who were made alive were we, the redeemed saints. After we were presented to the Father as a present and the Father gave us back to the Son as gifts, the Son gave us all as gifts to His Body for its building up.]

[In 1977 I encouraged all of our young people to do their best to get a proper education. One young brother among us took my fellowship and went back to school. Eventually, he graduated with a Ph.D. in linguistics and specialized in Greek. In these past few years, he has rendered a great amount of help to me in helping us to improve, to revise, our present Recovery Version. I was bearing a heavy burden to revise our version, but my knowledge of Greek is inadequate for this task. This young brother, who took my fellowship twelve years ago to go back to school, has become a great gift to me. He has been like an arm or a shoulder to me. We all can be such gifts. Thank the Lord for the gifts given by the ascended Head to His Body for its intrinsic building up.]

C. The Gifts to the Church—Some Apostles

[The ascended Head gave four kinds of gifts. The first class is the apostles (Eph. 4:11). These apostles receive the revelation of God's New Testament economy concerning Christ and the church (Matt. 16:16-18; Gal. 1:11-12, 15-16; Eph. 3:3-4, 8-11; 5:32). First, they receive the revelation, and the revelation makes their spirits burning and causes them to forget about themselves. They then go out to preach the revelation that others may also be burned. These apostles also preach the gospel of Christ to save the sinners chosen and called by God, bringing them to Christ (Gal. 1:16a; Eph. 3:8; 2 Cor. 11:2). They do not preach the superficial gospel, one that tells people about going to heaven instead of hell; rather, they preach to others the all-inclusive Christ as the gospel. Furthermore, the apostles are able to establish local churches and to appoint in them the elders for leading, shepherding, teaching, and overseeing (Acts 14:23; 1 Tim. 5:17; 1 Pet. 5:2). They are also able to determine doctrines, to release the truth, to perfect the saints, and to build up the Body of Christ (1 Tim. 2:7; Eph. 4:11-12). These are the four things that an apostle should do.]

D. The Gifts to the Church—Some Prophets

[The prophets are the second class of gifts given by the ascended Christ (Eph. 4:11). The prophets are those who through the Lord's revelation, speak for the Lord, speak forth the Lord, and speak the Lord into others. Sometimes they are also moved to utter some predictions. For the perfecting of the saints and the building up of the Body of Christ, they are second only to the apostles and are a very important class of people.]

E. The Gifts to the Church—Some Evangelists

[The evangelists are the third class of persons given by the ascended Head. They can preach Christ and the unsearchable riches of Christ as the gospel to save the desolate sinners, bringing them to Christ.]

F. The Gifts to the Church—
Some Shepherds and Teachers

[The shepherds and teachers are the fourth class of persons given by the ascended Head. According to the grammatical structure in Greek, the shepherds and teachers here refer to one class of gifted persons. The shepherds should know how to teach others, and the teachers should also know how to feed others. They are able to shepherd and teach the believers and are also able to feed the new ones in the same way that a mother feeds, shepherds, leads, and teaches her children.]

G. For the Perfecting of the Saints Unto the Work of Ministry Unto the Building Up of the Body of Christ

[The four classes of persons—the apostles, the prophets, the evangelists, and the shepherds and teachers—preach the gospel to save others on the one hand. On the other hand, they raise up churches in the localities. Then they also feed, shepherd, and teach the saints. Furthermore, among these saints they speak for the Lord and speak the Lord into them. In this way all the saints are perfected. The meaning of perfecting can be illustrated by university students being taught by professors of different subjects. After four years of studying, they graduate and are able to do the same things that the professors do; they have all been perfected. Christ as the Head gave these four kinds of gifts to the church for the purpose of perfecting the saints that the latter may also be the apostles, the prophets, the evangelists, and the shepherds and teachers. Unfortunately this is not the case in the existing system of Christianity. It only trains some preachers to gather a congregation on Sunday for a service where one speaks and the rest listen. Most of them after listening for decades still have not received much perfecting.

In the Lord's recovery, all the gifts such as the apostles, the prophets, the evangelists, and the shepherds and teachers should do the work of perfecting. In other words, they should all do the work of training. They should be like the professors perfecting the students. In this way, after a few years, the saints will be perfected and will be able to do the work that they do. At present, the publications among us are very rich and numerous. There are at least four thousand different messages. If you would spend the time, these materials are very good to help you be perfected.] [If you would spend two hours every day for two years to read these Life-study Messages, you will be equipped. In four years' time you will be able to finish all of these messages.

At the same time, you are in the church seeing how the apostles raise up churches, how they appoint elders, how they preach the high gospel, how they bring people into Christ to enjoy the riches of Christ, and how they determine doctrines. For example, someone asked me this morning about the difference between the denominations and the church. In a simple word, first, the denominations are denominated; they have divided the Body of Christ. The church is not denominated; it is one. All the believers, whether they are sprinkled or immersed, are in the church as long as they are saved. Second, the denominations do not have a definite ground. The church, however, has a definite ground which is also the unique ground. Here we stand on the ground of oneness in the different localities to worship God together and to build up the Body of Christ together. I believe that after five years many of you will be able to be apostles, preaching the gospel from city to city and from village to village, establishing churches, releasing the truth, and building up the Body of Christ.

Next are the prophets. The present atmosphere in the church meetings is that you are being trained to speak for the Lord. For example, the sharings after a message are mostly repetitions of words that you just heard. After speaking this way for a while, you will be able to speak for the Lord. Perhaps the first time you stand up you are afraid to speak, and you are scared. But as long as you keep practicing, your boldness will increase, and your voice will get stronger. Gradually you will not only be able to speak for the Lord, but you will also be able to speak forth the Lord and to speak the Lord into others. After the meetings, people may not remember much about the messages they heard. But they will feel that there is One following them all the time. The reason for this is that you have spoken the Lord into them. After you return home, do not only chat with your family; instead you must learn to speak the Lord's word to your family, to speak forth the Lord, and to speak the Lord into them. In this way they will discover that you have changed, and they will also change through your speaking. This is to prophesy. Paul said in 1 Corinthians 14 that you can all prophesy one by one (v. 31).

The evangelists' perfecting of the saints makes every saint burdened with a spirit for the gospel. It cheers and warms up the gospel atmosphere for the saints that they would become burning to preach the gospel. In preaching the gospel it also helps them to speak to the point, not deviating from the subject. While they speak, the listeners' hearts, mouths, and spirits will all be open and they will receive the Lord to be saved. The shepherds and teachers' perfecting is like perfecting people to be mothers. Many brothers and sisters cannot feed people after they have been brought to salvation. They are like the mother who cannot nurse her child; thus the new ones do not receive much supply and teaching. Hence, we all have to be shepherds perfecting others, and we all have to learn. The more we do these things, the more we will improve, and the better we will become at doing them.

In the end, after this kind of perfecting, the saints will be able to be the apostles, the prophets, the evangelists, and the shepherds and teachers. Every member will be able to function and will participate in the work of the New Testament ministry, which is the building up of the Body of Christ, until we all arrive at the oneness of the faith and of the full knowledge of the Son of God, at a full-grown man, and at the measure of the stature of the fullness of Christ. In this way we will no longer be babes tossed by waves and carried about by the winds of teachings. The whole church will grow into a mature man with the stature of Christ. This is the building up of the Body of Christ.]

Questions

1. How is it possible for Christ to build up the church?
2. How does the church receive the gifts?
3. Describe what each of the following do.
   a. The apostles.
   b. The prophets.
   c. The evangelists.
   d. The shepherds and teachers.

Quoted Portions

1. Building Up of the Body of Christ (Lee/LSM), pp. 55-58.
2. Further Light Concerning the Building Up of the Body of Christ (Lee/LSM), p. 45.
3. The Organic Building Up of the Church as the Body of Christ (Lee/LSM), pp. 40-45.
4. Building Up of the Body of Christ (Lee/LSM), pp. 59-63.

Further References

1. Body of Christ (Lee/LSM), p. 41.
2. Building Up of the Body of Christ (Lee/LSM), pp. 13-20, 37.
3. Church Affairs (Nee/LSM), pp. 137, 139, 148.

4. The Economy of God and the Building Up of the Body of Christ (Lee/LSM), pp. 38, 41, 59-60.

5. The Excelling Gift for the Building Up of the Church (Lee/LSM), pp. 48, 68-70.

6. Further Light Concerning the Building Up of the Body of Christ (Lee/LSM), pp. 22, 38, 43.

THE DIRECT BUILDING UP OF THE BODY OF CHRIST BY THE PERFECTED SAINTS

Scripture Reading

Eph. 4:12-13, 15-16; 2 Cor. 4:1; 3:8-9; Rom. 5:18b; Jude 3b; Eph. 2:15b; 4:24; 4:13.

Outline

I. Being willing and ready to be perfected

II. The saints being perfected by the perfecting gifts with the life supply as the nourishment for the growth in life

III. Unto the work of the ministry—unto the building up of the Body of Christ

IV. Until we (the gifted persons and the saints) all arrive
   A. The oneness of the faith and of the full knowledge of the Son of God
   B. A full-grown and mature man
   C. The measure of the stature of the fullness of Christ

Text

[We have seen that God's intention is to give the gifted persons—the apostles, prophets, evangelists, shepherds and teachers—to perfect the saints that all the saints may participate in the work of the building up of the Body of Christ. These gifted persons perfect the saints to be what they are. This is similar to the professors in a teachers' college who perfect their students to become teachers like they are. A local church may be likened to a teachers' college, and the gifted persons are like professors teaching different courses. They perfect the saints to be what they are—apostles, prophets, evangelists, and shepherds and teachers. The gifts' perfecting of the saints results in a proper local church.]

I. BEING WILLING AND READY TO BE PERFECTED

[The Lord desires all the saints to be perfected (Eph. 4:13), but the Bible shows us that the Lord is calling for overcomers. In the seven epistles to the seven churches in Revelation 2 and 3, the Lord is sounding the trumpet for overcomers. His call for the overcomers indicates that not all the saints will be perfected. Just some of them will be perfected. The ones who are willing to be perfected will be the overcomers. These overcomers will eventually constitute the bride of Christ, and this bride will be the fighting army, following Christ to fight against and defeat the Antichrist (Rev. 19:11-21). According to Revelation 17:14 the army of overcomers that follow the Lamb are "called and chosen and faithful." The choosing of the Father in eternity past was for salvation, but the choosing in Revelation 17 at the end of this age is for overcoming. Thank God that we have been chosen by Him in eternity for salvation, but now we are under the test to be approved. If we are faithful to follow the New Testament teaching to run the course, to pass the test to be approved, we will be chosen to be the overcomers who constitute the army and the bride of Christ. The army is formed in Revelation 17. These chosen ones constitute a ready-to-fight army. Then these ready-to-fight chosen overcomers will be the bride in Revelation 19 to attend the wedding feast of the Lamb (vv. 7-9). After the marriage feast, Antichrist will fight directly against the descending Christ. Christ will fight him with His bride, who is the chosen army.

I am concerned for some of the saints because they are still not willing or ready to be perfected. By the Lord's mercy and under the covering of His blood, I would ask you as you are reading this book—are you willing and ready to be perfected? If you are not willing and ready, you will make yourself a dropout. The door is open for everyone to be perfected. I hope that we all would have a hearing ear to hear the calling of the Lord. Everyone who is contented with the present situation of the church life is not ready to be perfected, to go on with the Lord. This means that they are in the risky situation of becoming a dropout. In these days, I believe that the Lord has given me a vision with a burden for His churches, His recovery. Our present situation is not something with which we should be contented. We should feel sorry for our present situation. The recovery has been in the United States for over twenty-five years. During this period of time, we may have heard many messages, yet our situation is not up to a level with which we can be satisfied. We have to realize that we are far off from the goal. We need to say, "Lord, I am ready and willing to be perfected by You. I will take the perfecting word through Your gifted persons."

All the members of the Body of Christ are parts of the one organism. What a privilege, what a mercy, and what an all-sufficient grace that we are now in the one organism of the Triune God! As living members of this organism, we need the organic perfecting. We need to be perfected to do what the apostles, prophets, evangelists, and shepherds and teachers do. We have to be perfected so that the entire Body of Christ functions in the same way that the gifted members do.

There is much hope that we can be perfected to do what the gifted members do. In a local church, some can do the apostles' work to preach the gospel, teach the truth, establish churches, and appoint elders. The Lord needs many apostles, not just one or two. God's intention is to perfect every saint to do what the apostles, prophets, evangelists, and shepherds and teachers do. Some saints will do the apostles' work. Some will be perfected to do the prophets' work to speak God, speak for God, and speak forth God, ministering Christ to all the people. They will be perfected not merely to give a testimony but to give a living word of revelation. Some of the saints who were not evangelists may be perfected to be evangelists. They will be those who are on fire and burdened for the preaching of the gospel. They will have the ability and the knowledge to talk to people about sin, the fall of man, the love of God, the person of Christ, redemption, forgiveness, and regeneration. Then there will be no need for the saints to bring their unbelieving contacts to a gifted person because the saints will have been perfected to do the work of an evangelist. Some of the saints also need to be perfected to shepherd. Today very few of the ones that we baptize are under the proper care because of a lack of shepherding. This is why we lose many of the ones that we baptize. But if the saints are perfected to be shepherds, every baptized one will have a nursing mother (1 Thes. 2:7). Immediately after the new ones are baptized, the saints will pick up the burden to care for them. They will care for the new ones as they would care for newborn babes, nourishing and cherishing them.

The saints in a local church must be perfected to do the same work that the apostles, prophets, evangelists, and shepherds and teachers do. Because the situation is not like this today, we have to strive and to struggle by fighting. There are many resistances that we have to fight through. We all should pray, "Lord, make me willing and ready to be perfected. I will receive the perfection from the apostles, the prophets, the evangelists, and the shepherds and teachers. I am not content with my present situation." This is my intimate fellowship with you all. I hope that you are willing to accept my fellowship.]

II. THE SAINTS BEING PERFECTED BY THE PERFECTING GIFTS WITH THE LIFE SUPPLY AS THE NOURISHMENT FOR THE GROWTH IN LIFE

[The saints are perfected by the perfecting gifts with the life supply as the nourishment for the growth in life. Proper mothers feed their babes nourishing food. We have to perfect the saints with some solid food supply that they may be nourished. This food supply actually is the life supply. Christ Himself is not only our life but also our life supply.] The gifted persons must perfect the saints that they may know how to minister Christ as life to sinners and then know how to minister life to supply the saved ones. The gifted persons help the saints by feeding them with solid food. The gifted persons not only teach people, but feed people.

The gifted persons perfect the saints, not by Bible teaching, but by nourishing them. [Bible teaching has been going on for centuries with very few of the Lord's children being perfected. What is needed today is the nourishment of

Christ. Do not tell people what is right and what is wrong. Even if something is right, that does not mean anything in the sight of God. Only life means something. Only life counts.] The saints need to be perfected not by something, but with something, that is, with the very life of God, with the very Christ whom the gifted persons enjoy. This is what nourishes the saints to perfect them.

III. UNTO THE WORK OF THE MINISTRY— UNTO THE BUILDING UP OF THE BODY OF CHRIST

[Ephesians 4:12 says that the gifted persons are "for the perfecting of the saints unto the work of ministry, unto the building up of the Body of Christ." According to the grammatical construction, the work of the ministry is the building up of the Body of Christ. The perfecting is unto the work of the ministry, which is the building up of the Body of Christ. The word "unto" in Greek in Ephesians 4:12 means in view of, for the purpose of, resulting in, issuing in. The perfecting of the saints is in view of the work of the ministry, which is the unique ministry in the New Testament. Thousands of believers may be doing a work of a thousand parts, but every part should be for the unique work of the unique ministry to build up the Body of Christ. Paul referred to the building up of the Body of Christ, not to the building up of the church. Paul's stress was not on the building up of the church as a congregation but on the building up of the Body as an organism. The saints are perfected unto the work of the ministry for the building up of the Body of Christ as an organism. The New Testament ministry builds up an organism not an organization.]

[All the members of the Body of Christ who do the work of the ministry participate in the unique ministry of God's New Testament economy (2 Cor. 4:1; 3:8-9). This unique ministry is the ministry of the Spirit, who gives life (2 Cor. 3:8). The unique ministry of the Old Testament was the ministry of death because that was the ministry of the law which condemns and kills us (2 Cor. 3:7a, 9a). But the unique ministry of the New Testament is altogether a life-giving, organic ministry. This ministry is the ministry of righteousness, which brings in justification unto life (2 Cor. 3:9; Rom. 5:18b). The ministry of the law was the ministry of condemnation unto death, while the ministry of the faith, the New Testament, is the ministry of justification unto life, so it is altogether organic. The work of the ministry to build up the Body of Christ is directly by the perfected saints in the growth in life (Eph. 4:15-16). The saints grow up by being nourished, and this growing up is the building up.]

IV. UNTIL WE (THE GIFTED PERSONS AND THE SAINTS) ALL ARRIVE

[The saints are perfected unto the work of the ministry, the building up of the Body of Christ, until we (the gifted persons and the saints) all arrive at the oneness of the faith and of the full knowledge of the Son of God, at a full-grown man, at the measure of the stature of the fullness of Christ. The building up of the Body is a continuous matter. We are under the process of building and we are on the way of building until we arrive at the practical oneness.]

A. The Oneness of the Faith and of the Full Knowledge of the Son of God

[We need to arrive at the oneness of the faith and of the full knowledge of the Son of God. The faith refers to the full redemptive work of Christ as the object of our believing (Jude 3b). The Old Testament ministry was a ministry of the law, whereas the New Testament ministry is the ministry of the faith. The law was the very center of all the teachings in the Old Testament. When the New Testament came, the faith replaced the law. The entire teaching of the New Testament is centered on the faith. Galatians 3 tells us that the law was there in the Old Testament but faith came (vv. 23-25). Now we are not under the law but in the faith. As the law is the center and reality of the Old Testament, so the faith is the center and reality of the New Testament.

The faith implies the entire teaching of the New Testament. The New Testament record is a record of the full redemptive work of Christ. The New Testament begins with the incarnation of Christ and continues with His death, resurrection, and second coming. His death and resurrection with His second coming issue in the New Jerusalem, which is the ultimate consummation of the church. We believe in Christ's full redemptive work that is recorded in the entire New Testament. This full redemptive work is of Christ as a person.

We need to arrive at the oneness of the faith and of the full knowledge of the Son of God, which is the full knowledge of the person of Christ. The person of Christ is so marvelous and all-inclusive. This person is the embodiment of the Triune God and the perfect, transformed, tripartite man. He is also the processed Triune God as the all-inclusive, compound, life-giving, sevenfold, indwelling Spirit. He is the reality of every positive thing in the universe. We need to know in full the all-inclusive person of Christ.

When we arrive at the oneness of the faith and of the full knowledge of this all-inclusive person, we will not care for minor things. In Romans 14 Paul was very general in his attitude toward doctrinal matters that did not concern the faith or Christ's all-inclusive person. Things such as whether to observe the Sabbath and whether to eat meat or vegetables did not matter to Paul. As long as a person believed in Christ, Paul recognized him as a brother in Christ and received him. When I was a young Christian, I was so much for the truth of baptism by immersion that it affected the way I received the believers. If a believer was sprinkled instead of being immersed, I did not care that much for him. Baptism by immersion was my first "Christian toy." Children like to play with toys. Some Christians receive other believers on the basis of what they believe concerning the Lord's second coming and the rapture. They will not receive those who have a different view than they do regarding the rapture. This is another "toy" that Christians like. Humanly speaking, an older person does not like to play with toys. Only the children like to play with toys. If we are still playing with minor doctrinal matters and practices other than the faith and the person of Christ, this is a strong sign that we are still babes. A grown-up person does not care for minor things. He only cares for the marvelous, full redemptive work of Christ and the all-inclusive person of Christ.

We have to learn the aspects of Christ's person in His death on the cross and the things that He terminated and took away on the cross. We have to know Christ as the very embodiment of the processed Triune God, the complete God and the perfect, tripartite man. We also have to know how this wonderful One is being dispensed into His chosen and redeemed people for their full salvation and for His glorious expression. His chosen and redeemed ones are regenerated, they are being transformed, and eventually they will be glorified. Matters such as these should occupy us and be the subjects of our talk at home and with the saints. Anything other than these things are toys that divide us.]

B. A Full-grown and Mature Man

[Ephesians 4:13 tells us that we need to arrive at a full-grown and mature man. All of us need to grow up to reach this state. This full-grown and mature man is the church as the new man (Eph. 2:15b; 4:24). We are growing up in full measure through the direct building of all the saints perfected in the growth of life by the gifts. This means that each member's growth is a part of the building. The growth of all the saints equals the building up of the Body.]

C. The Measure of the Stature of the Fullness of Christ

[Ephesians 4:13 also says that we need to arrive at the measure of the stature of the fullness of Christ. The measure is the size, and this measure is of the stature. The stature is of the fullness of Christ. The fullness of Christ is the very expression of the Triune God, which is the Body of Christ (1:23). This Body has a stature, and the stature has a measure. We can arrive at the measure of the stature of the fullness of Christ by the growth in life.]

CONCLUSION

Christ, the Head of the Body, prophesied in Matthew 16 that He will build the church. But He cannot build the church directly. The way He builds the church is to recapture many men from Satan's usurpation by the power of His crucifixion and resurrection. Then He brings these men to the heavens in ascension to offer them to God the Father. God the Father in turn gives them back to Christ to be constituted as gifts for the Body. These gifts include apostles, prophets, evangelists, and shepherds and teachers. These gifts are not for the direct building up of the Body. They are given to the Body to perfect all the saints, not to replace the saints. Every saint perfected by the gifts directly builds up the Body of Christ. Therefore, all the young ones need to be willing to be perfected, trained, and equipped by the gifts to the Body so that they may participate in the great work of building up the Body of Christ.

Questions

1. Why do we say that those willing to be perfected are overcomers?

2. What does it mean to be willing to be perfected? Are you willing to be perfected?

3. How are the saints perfected?

Quoted Portions

1. Building Up of the Body of Christ (Lee/LSM), pp. 21-35.

Further References

1. Basic Revelation in the Holy Scriptures (Lee/LSM), p. 42.

2. Body of Christ (Lee/LSM), p. 30.

3. Building Up of the Body of Christ (Lee/LSM), pp. 12-13, 21-35, 46-50, 55.

THE BUILDING UP OF THE BODY OF CHRIST IN ONENESS

Scripture Reading

1 Cor. 8:4; Isa. 45:5; John 17:20-23; Eph. 2:15;
Rom. 15:7; Phil. 2:2; 1 Cor. 12:25; Psa. 133:1-3

Outline

I. God being one
   A. In His essence
   B. In His purpose
   C. In His economy
   D. In His acts

II. The unique God having a unique expression

III. The Lord's aspiration and prayer concerning the oneness of the Body

IV. The Lord's accomplishment of the oneness of the Body

V. The fulfillment of the oneness of the Body

VI. The practice of the oneness of the Body universally
   A. Receiving the teaching and fellowship of the Apostles
   B. Staying in fellowship with all the churches

VII. The practice of the oneness of the Body locally
   A. On the ground of oneness
   B. Being one with all the saints
   C. Submitting to the authority of the elders

Text

Oneness is crucial for Christ, the perfecting gifts, and the perfected saints to build up the Body of Christ. If there is no oneness, it is impossible to build up the Body of Christ. Christ is not divided. He has only one Body; therefore, everyone who is related to the building up of the one Body of Christ must be in oneness. Oneness is different from unity. Unity is outward. Different people with different purposes and opinions may try to unite themselves in organizations like the United Nations or labor unions. But they are not one. Oneness is inward, it is of the same essence and nature. Out of this inward oneness comes the outward one accord expressed in the way people act and move. By the intrinsic oneness and the outward practice of the one accord, Christ the Head, the perfecting gifts, and the perfected saints will build up the Body of Christ.

I. GOD BEING ONE

A. In His Essence

There is only one God (1 Cor. 8:4; Isa. 45:5; Psa. 86:10). He has three aspects—the Father, the Son, and the Holy Spirit (Matt. 28:19; 2 Cor. 13:14). Though He has the aspect of three, nevertheless, He is one God. The Father, Son, and Spirit may be distinct yet never separate. Though they coexist from eternity to eternity, they coinhere, living within one another. You can never find the Father without the Son in Him, neither can you find the Son without the Father in Him, nor can you find the Spirit without the Father and the Son. All three are one; thus, God is called the Triune God. God is one in essence and cannot be divided.

B. In His Purpose

God is one in His purpose. God, the Triune God—Father, Son, and Spirit—has one purpose. The purpose of God is to build up the church to express Him and to satisfy Him.

C. In His Economy

God is also one in His economy. God's economy is to work Himself—Father, Son, and Spirit—into His chosen, created, redeemed, and regenerated people so that they may be filled with Him, be transformed, and be built up into the one Body of Christ.

D. In His Acts

The one God accomplished many things to work out His economy. You can see the principle of oneness, which is according to God's nature of oneness, in everything He did. He created one universe. He created one earth for His purpose out of hundreds of billions of galaxies and stars. God needs billions of people for His purpose, yet He created only one man. He did not create a woman. Out of this one man, He built a woman. From this one couple came billions of people.

During the flood, He saved one family, Noah's family. He selected and called one man, Abraham, to be the head of one chosen race. He used one man, Moses, to bring His one people out of Egypt at one time. He desired one tabernacle for the children of Israel to worship Him. He brought them into one good land at one time and required them to fight together in oneness. He required His people to worship Him at one place—the one temple in one city, Jerusalem.

In order to have a new creation, He was first incarnated as one man, Jesus. Out of the death and resurrection of this one Man, He created one new man, the church. Ultimately, the church will become the one and only New Jerusalem for eternity.

You can see that our God is one in Himself, in His purpose, in His economy, and in His acts. Because He is in oneness, His operating principle is oneness, His actions are in oneness, and His finished work is in oneness; therefore, the way to build up the church must be in oneness.

II. THE UNIQUE GOD HAVING
A UNIQUE EXPRESSION

God is one in every respect. His expression must also be in oneness. Since there is one God, there can only be one house of God to be the one dwelling place of God. Since there is one Head, there can only be one Body. As with one husband there is one wife, so also, there is only one church as the full expression of the one God. Any division is disallowed because division does not build up the church. It is impossible to build up the Body of Christ when there is division.

III. THE LORD'S ASPIRATION AND PRAYER CONCERNING THE ONENESS OF THE BODY

The Lord's prayer in John chapter 17 shows His aspiration for the oneness of His Body. The organic oneness of the Body of Christ is the organic oneness in the Triune God. [Verse 20 says, "And I do not ask concerning these only, but concerning those also who believe in Me through their word." This verse tells us that the Lord's prayer here includes us, all the ones who believe in Him. Verse 21 says, "That they all may be one; even as You, Father, are in Me and I in You..." This shows that the oneness of all the believers should be like the oneness in the Triune God. The Triune God is three yet one. The Father is in the Son, and the Son is in the Father. The oneness in the Godhead is not a mere unification. That is the oneness of men. The oneness of the Three of the Godhead is that They mutually indwell one another. What is the oneness among the believers? No word can adequately explain it, but there is the example of the divine oneness among the Three in the Godhead.]

[Verse 21 goes on to say, "Even as You, Father, are in Me and I in You, that they also may be in Us, that the world may believe that You have sent Me." As the Father is in the Son and the Son in the Father, we also are in the Father and the Son. Before we believed in the Lord Jesus, we were separate from the coinhering Triune God, but now we are in the Triune God. God the Father's being in the Son, God the Son's being in the Father, the Father and the Son's being in the Spirit, and the Spirit's being in the Father and the Son has an issue, an outcome. This issue, this outcome, is that all the believers may also be in the Three of the Godhead. In the entire universe there is such a oneness, and this oneness is that the believers are mingled and wrapped up with the Triune God.]

[Verse 22 says, "And the glory which You have given Me I have given to them, that they may be one, even as We are one." What is the glory in this verse? The Father has given His divine life to the Son that the Son may express the Father. This expression is the glory. Now the Son has given us His life by which we can express Him. This expression is also glory. This indicates that the oneness we have with the Triune God is the divine life, and by this divine life we can express the Triune God. The divine life has been given to us and is within us. When we express the Triune God by this divine life, that is the oneness. The oneness is the very expression of the Triune God in and by His divine life.]

[Verse 23 says, "I in them, and You in Me, that they may be perfected into one, that the world may know that You have sent Me and have loved them even as You have loved Me." The Son is in the believers, the Father is in the Son, and by this the believers may be perfected into one. On the one hand, we are in the divine oneness. On the other hand, we still need to be perfected. This means that we may be in the oneness only to a small degree. This is why we need to be perfected into one. To be perfected is for us to have the growth in the divine life every day. The divine life has been given to us, and we need to live by this divine life. Then our expression will be the divine oneness. At the start of our Christian life, we have just a little of the divine life, so we need to be perfected. This means that the divine life within us is continually increasing, and that we are growing in this increasing of the divine life. The more we grow in the increasing of the divine life, the more we are perfected and the more oneness we live out. I hope that we all can realize that the very Christian oneness is the mingling of the Triune God with the believers in an increasing way. Last year the divine oneness expressed among us might have only been fifty percent. This year our expression of the divine oneness may increase to sixty percent. Later we may go up to seventy percent. This increasing of the divine life and its expression is our being perfected into one.

The prayer of the Lord in John 17 is a unique prayer made by the Son to the Father. We may be accustomed to calling the prayer in Matthew 6 the Lord's prayer, but the prayer in John 17 is also the Lord's prayer. Actually, the prayer in John 17 is much higher than the one in Matthew 6. As we have seen, the Lord's prayer in John 17 is that we, all the believers in the Son, may be one; even as the Father is in the Son and the Son is in the Father, that we also may be in the Triune God (v. 21). The oneness among us is a oneness of coinherence. The Three of the Godhead mutually indwell each other as one, we are one with the Triune God, mutually indwelling each other as one, and we believers all are one in the coinhering Triune God. We believers and the Triune God are all one. Although the believers in Christ come from many different countries and cultures, they all have the same unique divine life. The same life that is in you is also in me. Through this life we are one with each other and with the Triune God.]

IV. THE LORD'S ACCOMPLISHMENT OF THE ONENESS OF THE BODY

Immediately after the Lord's prayer in John 17, He went to the cross. On the cross, He accomplished redemption for us. He also "abolished in His flesh the law of the commandments in ordinances, that He might create the two (both Jews and gentiles) in Himself into one new man, making peace" (Eph. 2:15). In His resurrection and ascension, He became the Spirit. As the life-giving Spirit, He breathed the Spirit into His disciples (John 20:22). Before His crucifixion, His disciples were arguing to see who would be greater in the kingdom. They were afraid of the Jews and the soldiers who sought to seize Jesus and therefore ran away when Christ was captured. They were divisive and cowardly, but after receiving the Spirit they were able to pray in one accord (Acts 1:14). This indicates that they received the Spirit of oneness. Later, on the day of Pentecost (Acts 2) and in the house of Cornelius (Acts 10), the Spirit was poured out upon them to form the one Body of Christ. In one Spirit, they were all baptized into one Body (1 Cor. 12:13). These are all accomplished facts.

V. THE FULFILLMENT OF THE ONENESS OF THE BODY

The oneness of the Body was accomplished by the Triune God and we began to experience this oneness when we believed and were baptized. [Matthew 28:19 refers to a marvelous fact in the universe: we believers have been baptized into the Triune God. This verse says that we have been baptized into the name of the Father, of the Son, and of the Spirit. The name of the Triune God denotes the person of the Triune God. To be baptized into the Triune God is to be baptized into the divine person of the divine Trinity. Our baptism brought us into a mystical and organic union with the processed Triune God so that all of us, the believers in the Son, may be one in this organic union. The proper oneness among us Christians is a oneness in the organic union among one another and a oneness between us and the Triune God. The Lord prayed in John 17 based upon the fact that we all have to be one in the Triune God.]

VI. THE PRACTICE OF THE ONENESS OF THE BODY UNIVERSALLY

A. Receiving the Teaching and Fellowship of the Apostles

As we have pointed out in earlier lessons, the Lord sent the apostles out to raise up churches by their gospel, teaching, and fellowship. The saints in these local churches were once sinners under God's righteous condemnation, but due to the apostles preaching of the truth of the gospel they became obedient to the faith. They repented, believed, and were baptized into the Triune God, Christ, Christ's death, and His Body. Then they continued in the teaching and fellowship of the apostles that they might grow in the Lord and be perfected to build up the church. Because they were begotten of the apostles and were shepherded by the apostles, they should always receive the apostles, their teaching, and their fellowship. Local churches should never be divided from the apostles who raised them up. This type of division causes a local church to lose its supply of life.

On the negative side, a church must not be separated from the fellowship of the apostles. On the positive side, it is the apostles who raised up the church, and therefore can and must continue to nourish the church and perfect the saints. They have the authority to resolve problems in the church, as was the case in the church in Corinth and the churches in Galatia. As a result of the care of the apostles, the church will be built up. This is God's very sweet and effective ordained way to care for the church. Any deviation from His ordained way will cause the building up of the church to slow down and possibly stop. This is very practical.

Some may have a [different opinion concerning the apostles' relationship with the churches that they have established. Some have said that once the apostles establish churches and appoint elders, they should keep their hands off the churches. To their feeling, the churches should be absolutely independent from the apostles. But according to the Bible, after the apostles established churches and appointed elders in them, they still took care of the churches.

The Apostle Paul's relationship with the church in Ephesus is a strong evidence of this. According to Acts 20, Paul established the church in Ephesus and appointed elders in that church, but after this he did not leave the church and the elders alone. Instead, he once stayed with the church in Ephesus for three years (v. 31). While Paul was on his way to Jerusalem, he sent some from Miletus to call the elders in Ephesus to come to him (v. 17). When they came to him, Paul reminded them of how he behaved, worked, and labored among them for three years, admonishing the saints with tears (v. 31) and teaching them publicly and from house to house (v. 20). He charged them to take heed to themselves and to the flock committed to them (v. 28). He warned them that after he would leave, wolves would come in among them, not sparing the flock (v. 29). He told them that some would rise up from among them, speaking perverted things to draw away disciples after themselves (v. 30). This portion of the Word in Acts 20 shows that Paul did not leave the church in Ephesus alone. On the contrary, he was always caring for them.]

B. Staying in fellowship with all the churches

All the local churches should remain in fellowship with one another. No church is a separate entity. All the local churches constitute the one Body of Christ. Each local church may have different practical needs locally, but its main need is to be filled up with the one Triune God. Each local church may have a different administration (eldership), but one universal fellowship. No local church should be secretive. There should be no particular fellowship between local churches. Any saint can fellowship with any local church at any time. The spiritual and financial surplus as well as the needs of a local church should not be restricted to one particular locality. The churches should fellowship with each other regarding their surplus and lack. In this way, all the churches will maintain the proper relationship for the building up of the Body of Christ.

VII. THE PRACTICE OF THE ONENESS
OF THE BODY LOCALLY

A. On the Ground of Oneness

In order to practice the oneness of the Body locally, we must stand on the ground of oneness. Many groups of Christians call themselves churches. But what ground are they standing on when they call themselves churches? Many take the ground of nationality, for example, the Church of England, Chinese for Christ, etc. Many take the ground according to a person, such as the Lutheran Church. Some take the ground of practice, for example, the Baptist church. Some say that unless a person is baptized their way, he is not saved. Some say that unless a person rests on Saturday (Sabbath), he is going to hell. All these are divisive grounds. What ground should we take? The genuine ground of oneness. Since the Triune God is one, we should receive all those He has received (Rom. 15:7). We are one with all the ones God the Father created and begot, with the ones Christ redeemed and loved, and with the ones the Spirit regenerated and is transforming.

Christians always like to ask, "What church do you go to?" We should never ask this question. There is only one church. All the saved ones are in the church. All are one in

Christ. Christ is not divided; there cannot be more than one church. We do not go to church because we are the church. We do not join any denominations because they are built on divisive ground. Joining a denomination will cause us to be divided from other Christians. We fellowship with all the believers, yet we should never join a divisive group. We stand on the ground of oneness, one with the Triune God, accepting all the believers in Christ.

Some say they are interdenominational—accepting people from all denominations. The problem is that they all return to their denominations. They are not truly standing on the ground of oneness. They are shaking hands over a fence.

Some call themselves non-denominational churches. These are like those in 1 Corinthian 1:12 who said that they were of Christ. They still separate themselves from all other believers. They are "free groups" not standing on the genuine ground of oneness.

The Biblical principle is one church in one city. It is not many churches in one city or one church over many cities. Denominational, interdenominational, and non-denominational churches are not built on the genuine ground of oneness. The genuine ground of oneness is in the Triune God, accepting all believers, and having one church in one city, yet fellowshipping with the apostles and the other local churches. Without such a genuine ground of oneness, it is impossible to build up the church.

B. Being One With All the Saints

In order to build up a proper local church, we need to be one with all the saints in the church. We should never criticize or backbite. Neither should we have a particular love for some and not for others (Phil 2:2). Since we need to build one another up, we must be one with one another without any division. "There should be no division in the body, but that the members should have the same care for one another" (1 Cor. 12:25).

C. Submitting to the Authority of the Elders

Submitting to the authority of the elders is essential to keep the oneness for the building up of the Body. The elders are the more mature brothers in each locality appointed by the apostles to shepherd and perfect the church. Not being one with the elders and not submitting to their authority leads to spiritual suicide. A local church not in fellowship with the apostles cannot go on. Likewise, saints that do not submit to the authority of the elders cannot be built up. Our God is not a God of confusion. He has established the proper order in the Body. Elders do not have authority of themselves, but they are the deputy authority of the Lord to care for the churches. The saints should not fear the elders but should fellowship with them continually and be open to receive their fellowship, realizing that the elders have been appointed by the Lord to shepherd the church. By submitting to the authority of the elders, all the saints will be shepherded into life and be perfected to build up the church.

CONCLUSION

Psalm 133 is a psalm on building up the church. The key is the oneness among the brothers. Because of the oneness, the anointing oil and the watering dew flow from the Head to the Body. There is also the commanded blessing of life for evermore. Division kills. Oneness brings in life and building. We all must live in our spirit to keep the oneness of the Spirit to build up the Body of Christ.

Questions

1. Why must God's expression be in oneness?

2. How do we practice the oneness with the church universally?

3. How do we practice the oneness with the local church where we meet?

Quoted Portions

1. Practical and Organic Building Up of the Church (Lee/LSM), pp. 16-22.

Further References

1. Practical and Organic Building Up of the Church (Lee/LSM), pp. 15-24.

Lesson Sixteen

THE INCREASE AND THE SPREAD
OF THE CHURCH

Scripture Reading

John 15:4-5, 7-8; Phil. 1:27; Matt. 28:18-20; Acts 1:8; 8:1.

Outline

I. The increase of the church
  A. The need to increase
  B. The wrong concepts
  C. The normal way
  D. The God-ordained way to increase the church

II. The spread of the church

Text

After seeing the vision of the church and how the church may be built up, we must proceed to see the matter of the increase and spread of the church. Many Christians think that after they are saved initially, they simply wait to go to heaven. They have no idea that they were saved as members of the Body to build up the church. Some among us may think that we have nothing to worry about, because by His mercy, we are in the church. It is true that all of our sins have been forgiven. It is also true that we are in the practical local church life. Yet, we must labor diligently in building up the church. In this lesson we will address two of the most crucial matters concerning building up the church—increase and spread.

I. THE INCREASE OF THE CHURCH

A. The Need to Increase

[The increase of the church is to impart Christ to others and make them a part of Christ. The branches of the Vine bear fruit by imparting the life of the Vine to others and making them a part of the Vine. If the branches of a vine do not bear fruit, there will be no increase of the vine. The fruit-bearing of the branches is the increase of the vine tree. So the increase of the church is by the fruit-bearing of all the members. All the members must bear fruit; otherwise, there will be no increase of the local church.

Today in Christianity, nearly everything is abnormal, even the preaching of the Gospel. Christianity today depends upon the giant preachers with huge Gospel campaigns, but this is not so in the Bible. In the Bible, especially in the Gospel of John, the real Gospel preaching is the fruit-bearing of every member.] [It is just like the Tree of Life in the New Jerusalem: it bears new fruits every month. This is the proper preaching of the Gospel, and this is the increase of the church. It does not depend upon great preachers and large Gospel campaigns. The normal daily life of the members of the church is simply to bear fruit; then there is the increase of the church.

The proper way to preach the Gospel is to impart Christ into others as life. We should not trust in the great preachers; we have to trust in ourselves. Every member of the church is a branch to bear fruit. Consider the fruit tree. Every kind of fruit tree bears fruit at least once a year—this is a natural law. I do believe that as living members of the local church, we must bring at least one new convert a year to the Lord. Suppose a branch of the vine does not bear fruit year after year. What do they do with it? They prune it or cut it off. Every local church must encourage every member to bring at least one new convert to the Lord every year. Even to bring in ten or twelve a year is not too many, for that is simply like a cluster of grapes.

In the local church, we should be fruitful. Whenever we come to the church meeting, we must come with some new ones. Do not come to the meetings alone—that is not a glory; that is a shame! We need to come to the meetings with others for the increase of the local church.]

B. The Wrong Concepts

[In the Gospel preaching, there are some wrong concepts that I must point out to you. In some of the denominational churches there is much activity in the outreach of the Gospel. This is good, but the problem is that there is too much human effort and struggle. This is wrong, but this does not mean that we should retire from fruit-bearing and not bear fruit. We should not be old in bearing fruit; we should always be renewed. There is no retirement in the spiritual life.

Another kind of concept in Christianity is that we must wait and pray for a great revival—then the Lord will send a giant speaker, and we will come together to have a Gospel campaign. This is abnormal.]

[There is a third concept—at the other extreme—which is also wrong. Some say, "Look at those people! All their Gospel campaigns are just in the energy of the flesh!" Of course, we must realize that all our Gospel preaching must be the overflow of the inner life. But those who criticize in this way have been criticizing others for years, yet they themselves have not brought in any new ones. It seems that there is no overflow of life with them. So they have gone to the other extreme.]

C. The Normal Way

[What is the normal way? The normal way is not to use our human effort; nor is it to depend upon a revival campaign with a giant preacher. Fruit-bearing is the outflow of life; so we must grow in life and also take the responsibility of fruit-bearing. The church should encourage every member to pray for the bringing in of new converts to the church. We should spend at least two or three hours weekly to take care of some new ones. It is not right for a church to remain the same in number year after year. Suppose that after five years we still have the same number. This is absolutely wrong. This means that we do not have the exercise of the flow of life.

What do I mean by the flow of life? I mean that we must abide in the Lord and enjoy the riches of His life. Then we must be burdened for fruit-bearing. We must pray, "Lord, my daily life is to bear fruit." Then the Lord will give us a deep realization for two or three persons for whom we should care. We may know 50 persons, but at that time the Lord will burden us with only two or three. We will pray for them, mentioning their names to the Lord. Then we need to seek the Lord's guidance regarding how to contact them. Perhaps we will invite them to dinner along with some of the brothers and sisters; then there will be others to help in ministering life to them. The brothers and sisters in the church should help one another in a mutual way in the matter of fruit-bearing. We should not do this just once in a while, but constantly. This is our daily life. We should spend at least two or three hours weekly in this matter. Do not expect a quick job. It is by doing it steadily and constantly that we will see the results.

If every year each one would bring in one new convert, within a year's time the church would be doubled. And after another year, it would be doubled again. The young people should bring in one new one every six months. It is not too much to bring in one new convert in one hundred and eighty days. In fact, it is too little. If each one could bring in two a year, by the end of the year, the church would be doubled twice. This is the increase.

Some may say that this is too much. Suppose then that each one brings in one every two years, or that two brothers bring in one each year. In six years, the church will have doubled three times. That is not bad. And you cannot say that it is too much for each one to bring in one every two years. What an increase there would be!

We must not trust in the big Gospel campaigns, we must trust in the increase of the church. The increase of the church is the fruit-bearing, not a great campaign. As a branch we must bear fruit, and one fruit every two years is so easy.]

D. The God-ordained Way to Increase the Church

[Going out to visit people is the most effective way to spread the gospel for the kingdom of God. Actually, visiting people by knocking on their doors is not a new way but an ancient way. This way began from the garden in Genesis 3. Every Christian should knock on people's doors to bring others the gospel. To knock on people's doors means to visit people. To visit people by knocking on their doors is actually the God-ordained, Christian way to spread the gospel that has been picked up by the Mormons and Jehovah's Witnesses to spread their heretical teaching. It is regrettable that the proper people, the Christians, have nearly given up the God-ordained way to spread the gospel. But now the Lord is leading us back to this way.

We have to take the way of going out to visit people by learning how to do it and by being trained. The greatest hindrance to our being trained to go out to visit people is our concept. We may be holding on to our past practice of preaching the gospel. Our past practice may have been good, but it is not nearly as effective as our present practice of going out to visit people. The first requirement of our being trained in the new way is to drop our concept. We must drop our concepts and pick up the instructions of the training. We cannot be trained by the Lord if we hold on to our old practice. If we would forget about our old way and pick up the Lord's new way, we will see the positive results.

In the Lord's new way we must be believing, assured, bold, and aggressive. We have been sent to visit people by the ascended Christ, and while we are talking to people we are linked to Christ. We have the position and the authority of the ascended Christ to direct people to believe and be baptized. Because we have been entrusted with the authority of the ascended Christ to preach the gospel, we should not ask people questions. We should not ask, "Will you believe?" We need to direct them to believe. We should not ask others if they want to be baptized, but we need to direct them to be baptized. We need to be like John the Baptist who told people, "Repent, for the kingdom of the heavens has drawn near" (Matt. 3:2). John the Baptist preached with an imperative, not with questions.

In our natural man we always want to be nice, good, and humble. We like to ask others, "Would you please believe in the Lord Jesus?" But if we ask others questions in this way, we will be rejected most of the time. Our asking of questions opens the door for rejection. We need to speak everything in the way of a command. We are the Lord's heavenly ambassadors who have been committed with all the authority in heaven and on earth to baptize people into the Triune God. We need to direct people to repent and confess their sins. We need to lead them to pray. After a little prayer we need to tell them that they are now ready to be baptized. If we would exercise this divine authority, many of the people we visit will be like lambs. We will be able to lead them out of the kingdom of Satan into the kingdom of God. The most effective way to preach the gospel is not to ask questions but to direct people to repent, pray, and be baptized. When we baptize a person into the Triune God, he will become another person. Baptism changes people because we are baptizing them into the name of the Triune God, which is the sum total of the divine Being.]

II. THE SPREAD OF THE CHURCH

The church increases locally and spreads universally. As a local church increases in life and number, we call it the increase. When a local church spreads to other cities to have more local churches, we call it the spreading of the churches. It is wrong for a church to exist in an area for 10 years without spreading to other cities. We need to spread the church life from city to city, from country to country, and from continent to continent until there are local churches everywhere on earth.

[If we read the Book of Acts carefully, we will see that the spreading of the Gospel had two lines. The first line was the migration of the saints—not the going out of the apostles. Acts 8:1 says very plainly that all the saints were scattered abroad, except the apostles. We have always thought that the apostles had to go out and the saints had to stay. But the Lord scattered all the saints and kept the apostles in Jerusalem. The sent ones stayed, and all the others were sent out. This was the first spreading of the Gospel. It was not by the apostles going, but by the scattering of the believers. This is what we call migration. The spreading of God's kingdom really does not only depend on the apostles, but also on the believers migrating from city to city.

According to Luke 21:24, Jerusalem has been returned to the people of Israel. This is the strongest fact that the time of the Lord's return is very near. Therefore, locally we must have the increase, and universally we must have the spreading. As a local expression, we must have many saints going out. We are not here for our interest; we are here for the Lord's recovery. And the time is near; the Lord is coming back. We must take care of His interest. We must look to the Lord that some will be burdened to go, and all of us should be willing to be burdened to go. We are the descendants of Abraham. Abraham was a stranger who continually sojourned on the earth. It is not right for us to be so settled in one place. We have to move from one place to another. We must be here for the Lord's interest. If we are here as a local expression of the Lord's Body without an increase locally and a spreading universally, we are wrong. Do not think that we are more spiritual than others. If we do, we are too proud. We must be so living and burning all the time for a certain amount of increase locally and for a measure of spreading universally.

We are living today in the richest country on the earth. Everything is so available, and we are in the very center of the populated world. It is exceedingly easy and convenient for us to go north, south, east, or west. We must spread the Lord's testimony to many cities in this country and Canada, as well as to Mexico, Central and South America and Europe. We must look to the Lord that we will have such an increase locally and such a spreading universally.]

CONCLUSION

The increase and spread builds up the church in each locality as well as the Body of Christ throughout the earth. The Lord will come for His bride when there are built-up local churches spread throughout the inhabited earth. We must give ourselves to pray, to read the word, and to be trained to preach the gospel that we may be part of the great work for the increase and spread of the church life throughout the earth to bring the Lord back. If we are diligent in this matter, we will have a great reward.

Questions

1. Why is the picture of fruit-bearing such a good illustration of the increase of the church?

2. It is wrong for us to preach the gospel using our human effort, however we must preach the gospel; how then do we do it?

3. What is the God-ordained way to increase the church?

Quoted Portions

1. The Practical Expression of the Church (Lee/LSM), pp. 176-179.

2. The God-ordained Way to Practice the New Testament Economy (Lee/LSM), pp. 96-98.

3. The Practical Expression of the Church (Lee/LSM), pp. 181-182.

Further References

1. Church Services One (Lee/LSM), pp. 9-10, 20-21.

2. The Economy of God and the Building Up of the Body of Christ (Lee/LSM), pp. 77-79.

3. Further Light Concerning the Building Up of the Body of Christ (Lee/LSM), pp. 22-35.

4. Further Talks on the Church Life (Nee/LSM), pp. 164-165.

5. The God-ordained Way to Practice the New Testament Economy (Lee/LSM), pp. 37, 63, 93-98, 164-165.

6. On Home Meetings (Lee/LSM), pp. 34-35.

7. Life Study of Ephesians (Lee/LSM), p. 342.

8. Life Study of John (Lee/LSM), p. 420.

9. Normal Christian Church Life (Nee/LSM), p. 35.

10. The New Way to Carry Out the Increase and Spread of the Church (Lee/LSM), pp. 39-43.

11. The Organic Building Up of the Church as the Body of Christ (Lee/LSM), pp. 32-34.

12. Practical and Organic Building Up of the Church (Lee/LSM), pp. 29-30.

13. The Practical Expression of the Church (Lee/LSM), pp. 176, 181-182.

14. Scriptural Way to Meet and Serve for the Building Up of the Body of Christ (Lee/LSM), pp. 183-184.

15. Vision of God's Building (Lee/LSM), pp. 162-165.

Lesson Seventeen

THE MEETINGS OF THE CHURCH
FOR THE BUILDING UP OF THE CHURCH

Scripture Reading

Heb. 10:25; Col. 1:2; Acts 20:7; 1 Cor. 11:20, 23-25;
14:23, 26; Matt. 18:19-20; Acts 2:46; Col. 3:16;
1 Cor. 6:17; 2 Cor. 3:17; Eph. 5:18-19.

Outline

I. The church meetings are ordained by God for the believers

II. The believers are a meeting people

III. The purpose of the church meetings—to exhibit Christ in all the saints

IV. The goal of the church meetings

V. The types of church meetings
   A. Meeting to break bread
   B. Meeting to pray
   C. Meeting to exercise the spiritual gifts
   D. Meeting to read the Word
   E. Meeting to listen to messages

VI. The size of the church meetings
   A. In the believers' homes
   B. In a larger meeting place

VII. Examples of the meetings in the New Testament
   A. The first meeting of the church before Pentecost
   B. The first meetings of the church after Pentecost

VIII. How to meet
   A. Being gathered into the Lord's name
   B. Meeting with the basic factors and elements—the Word, the Spirit, praying, and singing

Text

[Since the church is the assembly called out by God from the world, it should meet continually. Meetings enable God's called out congregation to be supplied, established, and perfected, that the goal of God's calling this assembly may be accomplished.] Meetings are actually the practical expression of a local church. A local church without meetings is not a church. Meetings supply the saints with the Spirit, teach the saints with the Word, and keep the saints in the fellowship of the Triune God. Meetings express the fullness of the Triune God. Meetings defeat the enemy. Meetings save sinners. Meetings build up the church. Meetings are crucial and necessary. Without the meetings, a church cannot go on and will not arrive at the goal of being built up.

I. THE CHURCH MEETINGS ARE ORDAINED BY GOD FOR THE BELIEVERS

Hebrew 10:25 says, "Not forsaking the assembling of ourselves together." [Here the assembling of ourselves together refers to our Christian meetings. God has ordained the way in which every living thing in the universe should exist. God's ordination is the very law by which a particular living thing lives. If the living thing obeys that law, it will survive and be blessed. God is the same towards us who have believed in Christ. God's ordination for us, which becomes our law of existence and blessing, is the meetings. As water is to the fish, and air to the birds, so are the meetings to the Christians. As the fish must live in the water and the birds must exist in the air, so the Christians must maintain their spiritual existence and living by the meetings.]

II. THE BELIEVERS ARE A MEETING PEOPLE

[Every kind of life has its own characteristic, and usually, many characteristics. The spiritual life we believers have received, being the life of God in us, also possesses many characteristics. For example, the hatred for sin and the separation from sin are characteristics of this life. The desire to draw near to God and the willingness to serve Him are also its characteristics. One of the many characteristics of our spiritual life is to flock together, to meet together. John 10:3 and 16 show us that since we are saved, we are the Lord's sheep. The characteristic of the sheep's life is to flock together and to dislike isolation from the other sheep. Hence, the Bible says that we are not only the Lord's sheep, but even more, His flock (Acts 20:28; 1 Pet. 5:2). In order to be a sheep which shares in the blessing of the flock, we must meet together with the flock. The characteristic of the spiritual "sheep life" within us requires this of us.]

III. THE PURPOSE OF THE CHURCH MEETINGS

The purpose of the church meetings is multifaceted. First, the meetings are to remember the Lord and to worship the Father. When the Lord established His supper (Luke 22:7-23), He said that we should do this in remembrance of Him. After the supper they sang a hymn (Matt. 26:30). According to Hebrew 2:12, the Lord may have sung a hymn of praise to the Father with His disciples. Second, the church meetings are for prayer. The Lord said that the church has the authority to bind and to loose what has been bound and loosed in heaven (Matt. 16:19; 18:18-19). This indicates that the church should get together to pray. The church began with prayer (Acts 1:14) and continued in prayer (Acts 2:42). Third, the church meetings are for preaching the gospel to save sinners. The disciples preached the gospel in the temple and from house to house (Acts 5:42). Fourth, the church meetings afford the believers an opportunity to care for one another in love (1 Thes. 4:9) and to grow in life (John 21:15-17). Fifth, the meetings are for teaching the truth to perfect one another (Acts 20:20). Finally, the meetings are for building up the church (1 Cor. 14:26). After seeing the purpose of the church meetings, we should meet as much as possible. Even meeting everyday is not too much.

IV. THE GOAL OF THE CHURCH MEETINGS—
TO EXHIBIT CHRIST IN ALL THE SAINTS

[We have all received the all-inclusive Christ as the good land (Col. 1:12). It is a land flowing with milk and honey. In our daily life we should experience this rich Christ all the time. When we come together we should present this Christ whom we have experienced and offer Him to God to be His food. Then we can all enjoy this Christ together as our enjoyment. If you were to enter into Jerusalem during one of the feasts of the children of Israel, you would have seen the temple surrounded by all kinds of produce of the good land. This is truly an exhibition. It is an exhibition before God of all the produce that the children of Israel harvested.

The way of meeting as revealed in the Bible is not like today's Christian worship services. The way of worship services in Christianity is completely natural and religious. It is a product of habits and traditions. As it takes doctors to handle sickness, and lawyers to handle legal disputes, so some assume that it takes pastors to handle Christian worship. They consider preaching to be the job of the pastors; the rest have nothing to do but listen. The Lord's way for us is not like this. He wants us to gather together to exhibit Christ.]

V. THE TYPES OF CHURCH MEETINGS

A. Meeting to Break Bread

Acts 20:7 says, "And on the first day of the week, when we gathered together to break bread." [To break bread is to eat the Lord's supper, remembering the Lord who died for us (1 Cor. 11:20, 23-25). This should be the first kind of regular meeting for us who have been redeemed by the Lord's death.]

B. Meeting to Pray

In Matthew 18:19-20 the Lord says, "If two of you agree on earth concerning anything, whatever they may ask, it shall come to them from My Father who is in the heavens. For where two or three are gathered together." [Here the Lord is speaking concerning the prayer of a meeting. This kind of prayer is more powerful than the prayer of an individual, being able to bind on earth what has been bound in heaven, and to loose on earth what has been loosed in heaven (Matt. 18:18).] Acts 1:14 says, "These all were persevering with one accord in prayer, together with the women." [Here again, the prayer of a meeting is mentioned. It was this prayer that brought in the blessing of the outpouring of the Holy Spirit on the day of Pentecost.] Then in Acts 4:24-31 it is recorded, "And when they heard this, they lifted up their voice with one accord to God and said. And as they were beseeching, the place in which they were gathered was shaken, and they were all filled with the Holy Spirit, and spoke the word of God with boldness." [It says here that in those days when the disciples were under persecution, they met together to pray with one accord. That kind of prayer caused them to be filled outwardly with the Holy Spirit and to speak the word of God with boldness.] The Bible also says, "Prayer was being made fervently by the church to God concerning him" (Acts 12:5); "where [the house of Mary] a considerable number were assembled together praying" (12:12). [On the day when Peter was imprisoned, the church prayed fervently for him, and a considerable number were assembled together in a sister's house, praying for him specifically. That prayer caused God to perform a great miracle, delivering Peter out of prison.]

C. Meeting to Exercise the Spiritual Gifts

1 Corinthians 14:26 says, "Whenever you come together, each one has a psalm, has a teaching, has a revelation, has a tongue, has an interpretation. Let all things be done for building up." [The meeting mentioned here is for the exercise of spiritual gifts and for mutual building up. In this kind of meeting, there should not be a special person doing a specific thing, but everyone should exercise the spiritual gifts: one has a psalm, one has a teaching, one has a revelation, one does this, and another does that. Each one may participate with the goal of building up and edifying others.]

D. Meeting to Read the Word

Acts 15:30-31 says, "And having gathered the multitude together, they handed them the letter [written by the apostles and the elders in Jerusalem]. And when they read it, they rejoiced at the consolation." [Here it says that when Paul and his companions arrived in Antioch, they gathered the saints together to read to them the letter written by the apostles and the elders in Jerusalem under the leading of the Holy Spirit. Hence, we may also need to meet together occasionally to read the word of God in the Bible.]

E. Meeting to Listen to Messages

Acts 20:7 says, "When we gathered together...Paul discoursed with them, about to go forth on the next day." [On that day, the believers in Troas met together to listen to Paul discoursing with them concerning the spiritual things of God, that they might be edified and established. Therefore, sometimes we should also meet to listen to spiritual messages spoken for God by the Lord's minister of the word that we may be edified and established.]

VI. THE SIZE OF CHURCH MEETINGS

[God's ordained way for Christian meetings is to have two different sizes of meetings: small and large. The smaller size is to be held or practiced in the believers' homes. Do not despise the small meetings.] You may meet with your family or with a few other brothers or sisters. [Apparently, such a small meeting seems insignificant. But you have to realize that human society is composed of small homes with small families. A community or society of millions of people comes from small families. No human society can be built up without the small families in their small homes. In human society big gatherings are not held that regularly. Instead the husband, wife, and children come together in their own home every day. If every family is strong, the community and society will be strong.]

A. In the Believers' Homes

[The believers first met in the homes beginning on the day of Pentecost (Acts 2:46). Three thousand met from house to house. The Greek indicates that they met according to houses, which means that every house had a meeting. There was a meeting in every new believer's house. This could only happen by the Spirit. Furthermore, there were many calling on the name of the Lord (Acts 2:21).

In the home meetings, according to Acts 2:46 and 5:42, they were preaching the gospel, teaching the truth, breaking bread to remember the Lord, and prayers. The saints around the time of Pentecost broke bread every day, that is, they had the remembrance of the Lord by practicing the Lord's table. The saints also prayed in their homes. Acts 12:12 tells us that when Peter was released from prison, he went to the house of Mary where a group of saints were praying.

Meeting in the believers' homes is for all the members of Christ to function. In any big meeting it is hard for the saints to function. But in a small meeting with four or five, or two or three, even a small boy or girl could function. He or she could say, "The Lord Jesus loves me, and it is so good that I love Him." This is a small function, but do not despise it.]

[In Matthew 18:20, in speaking about Christian gatherings, the Lord Jesus used the number of two or three: "For where two or three are gathered together into My name, there I am in their midst." Two or three is a precious number in the Bible, and should be the starting number of the church life. When the church becomes big through the home meetings, the big meetings will be meaningful. But when the church does not have anything and expects to have a big meeting, that big meeting may be empty. To start the church life from a small meeting of two or three is best.]

B. In a Larger Meeting Place

[The church should also have large meetings in a larger place for the whole church to come together (1 Cor. 14:23). There are two kinds of meetings: small meetings in the homes of the believers and large meetings in a larger meeting place.

These large meetings should not be held often. To have these larger meetings should not be a constant practice. If you practice the large meetings constantly, you will deaden the situation. You must learn to have the two kinds of meetings.

We must be balanced. God's design of our body is symmetrical. We have two ears, two eyes, two nostrils, two lips, two shoulders, two arms, two hands, two thighs, two legs, and two feet. On the one hand, we need to begin the meetings in small homes; on the other hand, when the need arises we should hold large meetings in a larger meeting place. In the larger meeting place, we should not have any definite speaker with all the congregation listening to this speaker. We must kill this practice. In such a meeting all the attendants should participate in the building up of the church through their functions (1 Cor. 14:26). When we come together one may have a revelation, another may have a hymn, another one may have a teaching, and others may have another portion. Everyone can and should have something of Christ for the meeting. We all need to have something so that we can function in the meetings for the building up of the church.]

VII. EXAMPLES OF THE MEETINGS
IN THE NEW TESTAMENT

A. The First Meeting of the Church Before Pentecost

[After His resurrection, the Lord came to meet with His disciples, starting from the evening of the first day. Thus, in the Lord's resurrection, the matter of meeting with the saints is crucial. Mary the Magdalene met the Lord personally in the morning and obtained the blessing (Jn. 20:16-18), but she still needed to be in the meeting with the saints in the evening to meet the Lord in a corporate way to obtain more and greater blessings (20:19-23). In this first meeting of the Lord with His disciples after His resurrection, we have the Lord's presence, the peace, the Lord's sending, the breathing, and the authority to bind and loose. These are the blessings which the Lord brought to His disciples in that church meeting.

However good Mary's fellowship was with the Lord during the morning watch, she still needed to come to the evening meeting to obtain all these blessings. These blessings are greater and more important. We may receive something from the Lord and even of the Lord during the morning watch, but this is something we need personally and individually. We must also come to the meetings to receive something more important. The morning watch and the church meetings are two aspects. We need the personal blessing of the first aspect as well as the corporate blessing of the second.

Thomas missed the first meeting the Lord held with His disciples after His resurrection. However, he was compensated for what he missed in that meeting by attending the second meeting (Jn. 20:25-28). Oh, we must not miss any of the church meetings! We should not say that it does not matter and that we shall rest at home. If the Lord comes, we, like Thomas, may miss Him. Thomas missed the Lord's appearing. Due to his absence from that church meeting, he really lacked something. This chapter is full of revelation, but Thomas missed it all. He missed the revelation, the discovery, and the experience of the Lord's resurrection because he missed the morning watch and the church meeting. He missed the revelation that the disciples are the brothers of the Lord and the sons of God. He missed the peace, the breathing of the Holy Spirit, the divine commission, and the authority. He was saved and he was a brother, but because he did not attend that meeting, he missed a great deal.]

After seeing the Lord openly ascend to the heavens on a cloud, the disciples stayed in Jerusalem to wait for the power from on high (Luke 24:49). They did not idly wait but met together for ten days to pray in one accord (Acts 1:14). There was no division, only oneness in the Spirit. Their meeting brought about a major step in God's economy for the building up of the church. On the day of Pentecost, the Spirit was poured out upon them for the formation of the Body of Christ. If they had not met, the Spirit would have had no place to be poured out. If they had been praying at home, the Spirit could not have been poured out upon the assembled believers in order to form the Body. Because they were meeting together, the Spirit was poured out upon them. This again shows us the importance of meeting. After His resurrection, the Lord showed Himself to over five hundred brothers at one time (1 Cor. 15:6); however, many of the brothers were not present. They may have had "more important" things to do. Unfortunately, they missed one of the greatest events of church history.

B. The First Meetings of the Church After Pentecost

On the day of Pentecost, after the outpouring of the Spirit, the disciples preached the gospel and 3,000 people were baptized. The church life in Jerusalem had begun.

[According to Acts 2:46, day by day the believers broke bread from house to house. The early believers remembered the Lord by breaking bread daily in their houses. This shows their love and enthusiasm toward the Lord.

The Greek words rendered "from house to house" also mean "at home," in contrast with "in the temple." The Christian way of meeting together is fitting to God's New Testament economy, differing from the Judaic way of meeting in the synagogues (Acts 6:9). The Christian way of meeting in homes became a continual and general practice in the churches (cf. Rom. 16:5; 1 Cor. 16:19; Col. 4:15; Philem. 2).

In Acts 2:46 we see that the believers "took their food with exultation and simplicity of heart." The Greek word for "simplicity" also means singleness. Here it describes the heart being simple, single, and plain, having one love and desire and one goal in seeking the Lord. These early believers were simple, single, sincere, and pure in heart.

According to Acts 2:47a, the believers in the early church life praised God and had favor with all the people. They lived a life that expressed God's attributes in human virtues, as Jesus the Man-Savior did (Luke 2:52).]

VIII. HOW TO MEET

A. Being Gathered Into the Lord's Name

Matthew 18:20 says, "For where...are gathered together into My name, there I am in their midst." [The most crucial thing in the believers' meeting is to be gathered into the Lord's name. This means that we have to meet in the name of the Lord. Since we are the Lord's and were saved by His name, we should gather only into that name and meet in that name. We must not gather into and meet in any other name, whether it is the name of an individual, of a corporate body, of a mission, or of a denomination.] When we meet in His name, we are meeting in His person, because the name denotes the person. Now the Lord is the Spirit. So, to meet in His name means to call on His name and to be in spirit where His Spirit dwells.

B. Meeting with the Basic Factors and Elements— The Word, the Spirit, Praying, and Singing

[In all of our meetings there should be four basic factors and elements: the word, the spirit, praying, and singing. If we handle these four elements in a proper and living way, there will be a rich display and expression of Christ in all of our meetings.

The word is the holy word revealed in the Scriptures, either the constant Word or the instant word. If we are going to be the speaking ones in our meetings, we must let the word of Christ dwell in us richly (Col. 3:16). The riches of Christ are in His word. The word of the Lord must have adequate room within us that it may operate and minister these riches into our being. Then our speaking of the word in the meetings will be an exhibition of the riches of Christ.

When we refer to the spirit, we are following the Apostle Paul to denote our spirit indwelt by and mingled with the Holy Spirit. According to the New Testament, the divine Spirit and our human spirit are mingled together as one spirit. He that is joined to the Lord, who is the Spirit, is one spirit (1 Cor. 6:17; 2 Cor. 3:17). In a regenerated person, the divine Spirit and the human spirit are no longer two separate spirits. The Spirit of the Lord and the spirit as our inward being are one spirit.]

[Our Christian heritage today is in two things—the Word and the Spirit. We have the Word without and the Spirit within, and these two are one. The Word is the Spirit and the Spirit is the Word. When I have the Word in my hands it is the Word outside of me, but when I pray-read the Word, it gets into me and becomes the Spirit. When I speak the Spirit out to you, the Spirit becomes the word, and when you receive this word into you, it becomes the Spirit. As I am speaking the word, you are receiving the Spirit. But the strangest thing is this—we are supposed to be the speaking people of the speaking God, yet we do not speak. We need to learn how to handle the Word and the Spirit. My intention and my burden is that the saints would learn how to speak forth Christ properly, to speak in the Spirit and with the Spirit.

Another basic factor and element in our meetings is prayer. We have to learn to pray. The word and the Spirit must issue in our praying. In our meetings there should be many prayers.] [Actually, our church meetings need to be full of spontaneous and living prayers. We offer too many religious, duty-fulfilling prayers. Our prayers are not that spontaneous, real, genuine, or true. They are not that much in our spirit. We should not plan what to pray ahead of time. Our prayers should come out of us spontaneously in the way that we breathe. Our meetings are dead because we are short of these living, spontaneous prayers.

Another basic factor and element in our meetings is singing. Both speaking and singing are the issue of the infilling of our spirit. If we are filled in our spirit something will flow out of us in speaking and singing. In Ephesians 5:18-19, Paul tells us to "be filled in spirit, speaking to one another in psalms and hymns and spiritual songs, singing and psalming with your heart to the Lord."]

CONCLUSION

The meetings of the church are crucial to God, the church, ourselves, and others. Without the meetings, there can be no practical expression of the church, and the Lord's speaking is restricted. Without the meetings, the economy of God is not carried out and the church is not built up. Therefore, we must give ourselves to the Lord to be in every meeting of the church. We should never excuse ourselves from the meetings, regardless of the reason; otherwise, we may excuse ourselves from the church life and the kingdom reward.

Questions

1. Why should Christians meet together?
2. List the different types of meetings and their purpose.
3. Explain how "the word, the spirit, praying, and singing are the basic factors and elements in the meetings.

Quoted Portions

1. Scriptural Way to Meet and Serve for the Building Up of the Body of Christ (Lee/LSM), pp. 15-16.
2. The Living Needed for Building Up the Small Group Meetings (Lee/LSM), p. 74.
3. Life Lessons Vol. 2 (Lee/LSM), pp. 20-22.
4. The God-ordained Way to Practice the New Testament Economy (Lee/LSM), pp. 52-55.
5. Life Study of John (Lee/LSM), pp. 565-566.
6. Life Study of Acts (Lee/LSM), pp. 97-98.
7. Life Lessons Vol. 2 (Lee/LSM), p. 22.
8. Speaking Christ for the Building Up of the Body of Christ (Lee/LSM), pp. 7-8, 12.

Further References

1. Life Study of John (Lee/LSM), pp. 298-310, 565-570.

2. Life Study of Acts (Lee/LSM), pp. 41, 91, 97-98, 120-121, 162-163, 293-294.

Lesson Eighteen

THE PRAYER MINISTRY OF THE CHURCH

Scripture Reading

Matt. 16:18-19; 18:18-19; Eph. 6:17-20; Ezek. 36:37; Isa. 62:6-7; 1 John 1:9; Acts 1:14; 4:31; 12:5; 13:2-4; 20:36.

Outline

I. The principles of God's work

II. The prayer ministry of the church—binding and loosing what has been bound and loosed in heaven

III. Examples of prayer in Acts

IV. Two types of prayer
   A. Prayer to have fellowship with God
   B. Prayer for God's work

V. Individual and corporate prayer

VI. Pray specifically and persistently

VII. Pray at set times and all the time

VIII. Pray with the Word and a note book

Text

In this lesson we will fellowship concerning one of the most crucial ministries of the church—the prayer ministry. We agree that Christians should pray. Do you pray? How often do you pray? How consistent is your prayer? Are your prayers answered? If you ask any Christian the same questions, you will find that most Christians rarely pray. Why? Most of us do not realize that prayer is important. We may not know how to pray, or we may not understand the principles of prayer. Our prayer may be non-effective and meaningless. We hope that this lesson will change all that. After you study this lesson and practice accordingly, you will be a proper serving one in the prayer ministry of the church.

I. THE PRINCIPLE OF GOD'S WORK

[When God works, He does so with specific law and definite principle. Even though He could do whatever pleases Him, yet He never acts carelessly. He always performs according to His determinate law and principle. Unquestionably, He can transcend all these laws and principles, for He is God and is quite capable of acting according to His own pleasure. Nonetheless, we discover a most marvelous fact in the Bible, which is, that in spite of His exceeding greatness and His ability to operate according to His will, God ever acts along the line of the law or principle which He has laid down. It seems as though He deliberately puts Himself under the law to be controlled by His own law.]

Do you know the principle of God's work? As in mathematics and science, once people understand a given principle they can achieve predictable and consistent results every time. The law of gravity, Newton's law, and E=MC2 are examples of such principles. If you know the principle of God's work, you will pray much to cause God to work. We know that God's ultimate work is to build the church. There are many steps required to achieve this goal, such as our friends' salvation, reading the Word and prayer, coming to meetings, etc. What principle does God use to accomplish His work? There are seven steps to His principle.

The first step is that God has a will to do something. The second step is that God reveals His will to man through His Word by His Spirit. The third step is that God's church responds to His will by agreeing with it in prayer. The fourth step is that God accomplishes the thing that He wills. The fifth step is that we go and reap the accomplished work. The sixth step is to give God thanks. The seventh step is to enjoy the accomplished work together with God and the church.

II. THE PRAYER MINISTRY OF THE CHURCH— BINDING AND LOOSING WHAT HAS BEEN BOUND AND LOOSED IN HEAVEN

[We have already mentioned how God has His will concerning all things, but that He will do nothing by Himself alone and independently. He will take action only after the free will on earth responds to His will. Were there only the will in heaven, God would make no move; the heavenly move will be accomplished on earth only when He is assured of the same will on earth. This is what we today call the ministry of the church. Believers need to realize that the ministry of the church does not consist merely of the preaching of the gospel—it most certainly does include this, let there be no mistake of that—but also the church's ministry includes the bringing down to the earth the will that is in heaven. But exactly how does the church bring this about? It is by praying on earth. Prayer is not a small, insignificant, non-essential thing as some would tend to think. Prayer is a work. The church says to Him, "God, we want Your will." This is called prayer. After the church knows the will of God, she opens her mouth to ask for it. This is prayer. If the church does not have this ministry, she is not of much use on earth.

Many devotional prayers, prayers of fellowship, and prayers of request cannot be a substitute for prayer as ministry or work. If all our prayers are simply devotional or merely consist of fellowshipping and asking, our prayer is too small. Prayer as work or ministry means that we stand on God's side, desiring what He desires. To pray according to God's will is a most powerful thing. For the church to pray signifies that she has discovered God's will and is now voicing it. Prayer is not only asking God, it is also the making of a declaration. As the church prays, she stands on God's side and declares that what man wants is what He wants. If the church should so declare, the declaration will be at once effectual.]

Matthew 18:18 says, "Truly I say to you, Whatever you bind on the earth shall be what has been bound in heaven, and whatever you loose on the earth shall be what has been loosed in heaven." Who are the "you" here? [They are the church, because in the preceding verse the Lord mentions the church. So that this is a continuation of verse 17. Therefore, the meaning of this verse 18 now before us is: that whatever things you the church shall bind on earth shall be (what has been) bound in heaven, and whatever things you the church shall loose on earth shall be (what has been) loosed in heaven.

Here lies a most important principle: God works through the church today; He cannot do whatever He desires to do unless He does it through the church. This is a most sobering principle. Today, God cannot do things by His own Self alone, because there is in existence another free will; without the cooperation of that will God is not able to do anything. The measure of the power of the church today determines the measure of the manifestation of the power of God.]

[This whole matter can be likened to the flow of water in one's house. Though the water tank of the Water Supply Company is huge, its flow is limited to the diameter of the water pipe in one's house. If a person wishes to have more flow of water, he will need to enlarge his water pipe. Today the degree of the manifestation of God's power is governed by the capacity of the church. Just as at one time earlier when God manifested Himself in Christ, His manifestation was as large as the capacity of Christ; so now, God's manifestation in the church is likewise circumscribed—this time by the capacity of the church. The greater the capacity of the church, the greater the manifestation of God, and the fuller the knowledge of God.]

[How many are the things which God wants to bind and to loose in heaven! Many are the people and things that are contradictory to Him; and all these God expects to be bound. Many also are those people and things that are spiritual, valuable, profitable, sanctified, and being of God; and these He anticipates to be loosed. But just here a problem arises: Will there be men on earth who will first bind what God wants to bind and loose what He intends to loose? God wills to have the earth govern heaven; He desires His church on earth to govern heaven.

This does not imply that God is not all-mighty, for He is indeed the Almighty God. Yet the all-mightiness of God can only be manifested on earth through a channel. We cannot increase God's power, but we can hinder it. Man is not able to give increase to God's power, nonetheless he can obstruct it.

We cannot ask God to do what He does not want to do, yet we can restrict Him from doing that which He does want to do. Do we really see this? The church has a power by which to manage the power of God. She can either permit God to do what He wants or else prohibit Him from doing it.

Our eyes need to foreglimpse the future. One day God will extend His church to be the New Jerusalem, and at that time His glory will be fully manifested through the church without encountering any difficulty.] Today, God wants the church to loose on earth before He will accomplish on earth what has been loosed in heaven; He wants the church to bind on earth before He will accomplish on earth what has been bound in heaven. Heaven will not initiate things on earth. [Heaven will only follow earth in its working. God will not start first; He in His operation only follows the church. Oh, if this be the case, what a tremendous responsibility the church has!]

III. EXAMPLES OF PRAYER IN ACTS

In Acts chapters 1 and 2 we see that 120 disciples were praying. Before receiving the Holy Spirit, the disciples were fighting one another for a position in the kingdom while on the way to Jerusalem before the Lord's crucifixion. After they received the Holy Spirit essentially in John 20 and the instruction from the Lord to stay in Jerusalem to wait for the power from on high—the clothing of the Spirit economically for God's work—they prayed for ten days. On the day of Pentecost, the Spirit came down upon them. The church was formed and the gospel went out; 3,000 people were baptized. By prayer, they loosed the Spirit from heaven and loosed 3,000 souls on earth into God's kingdom. Praise the Lord for prayer. These saints continued in prayer daily.

In Acts chapters 3 and 4 we see that Peter and John were going to pray. On the way, they preached the gospel, and 5,000 were saved. They prayed again with the church after they were threatened by the Jews, and were told not to preach by the name of Jesus. Their prayer caused an earthquake; and they were all filled with the Holy Spirit and spoke the word of God with boldness.

In Acts chapter 12 Peter was arrested for the sake of the gospel. The church prayed fervently concerning him. The Lord answered the prayer of the church and released him.

In Acts chapter 13, while the leading ones of the church in Antioch were praying, the Spirit set apart Barnabas and Saul to be apostles to raise up churches. The rest of the leading ones prayed for them and sent them out. You can see that prayer activates the Spirit to send us out to do His work.

In Acts chapter 20 there was a meeting by the sea at Miletus. After Paul had fellowship with the elders from the church in Ephesus, they prayed by the ship Paul was to take. You can see that the church in the early days always prayed to bind and to loose. They did not care for the approval of other people; they only cared for the Lord's desire.

IV. TWO TYPES OF PRAYER

There are mainly two types of prayer—prayer to have fellowship with God and prayer for God's work. Prayer to have fellowship with God is for us to contact God and to be filled with God. In this type of prayer we confess and repent of the things He enlightens. Prayer for God's work is to pray according to His heart's desire so that He may accomplish His work.

A. Prayer to have Fellowship with God

[The significance of the first aspect of prayer is that we use our spirit to contact God, and to absorb God, and to have our entire being brought back to our spirit to have fellowship with Him. When we contact God, absorb God, and have fellowship with God in this way, God has the opportunity to reveal Himself in us and to infuse Himself into us. As God flows Himself into us in this way, our mind, emotion, and will are gradually mingled with God. As a result, God can open His heart's desire to us, causing us to apprehend His purpose. At the same time, as He is operating and moving within us, He will oftentimes point out our weaknesses, our mistakes, our hindrances, and our difficulties, and then remove them. Therefore, the significance of the first aspect of prayer is to contact God, to touch God, and to let God have the opportunity to mingle with us and to eliminate all our difficulties. Therefore, whenever we come before God to pray, we must look upon this as the first priority. That is to say, whenever we come before the Lord to pray, we should not first petition Him for any other matters. We should rather first turn our entire being back to our spirit and lay our whole being in the light of the Lord's face, waiting for His operating and moving, enlightening, revealing, anointing, infusing, mingling, filling, and saturating. We should also let Him expose our weaknesses, mistakes, hindrances, and difficulties. If we are willing to confess thoroughly and to allow the Lord to remove all these difficulties, our conscience will be at peace, without any accusation. Our spirit would thus be full of the presence of God. At this point, we can then mention to the Lord the things we want to pray for.]

B. Prayer for God's Work

After having the proper fellowship with God in prayer, a foundation is laid for us to go on to petition God for His work. Because of our proper fellowship, the Lord is able to impart into us His burden for a particular person or matter. At this time we can petition God for them. The Lord, upon hearing our petition, will act from His throne in the heavens to accomplish the work. Sometimes He does not act immediately because we may still have some hidden problems not yet confessed; or His timing requires that we wait. At other times Satan and his fallen angels are resisting God's work. If we do not see an immediate answer it does not mean that prayer does not work. It means that we need to persist in prayer.

This type of prayer also energizes us by filling us with the Spirit and with boldness to go to open peoples' eyes with the Word, turn them from darkness to light, and deliver them from the authority of Satan to God, that they may receive forgiveness of sins and the common portion among the saints.

Finally, this type of prayer shows us how to approach our friends, what to say to them, what verses to use, etc. Many times we claim that we do not know what to say, or that we are afraid, or that we cannot get anyone saved. If we pray, God will work within us and within our friends.

V. INDIVIDUAL AND CORPORATE PRAYER

We need to pray individually and corporately. In Matthew 6:6 the Lord says that we should pray in our private room. Certain sins should be confessed privately without anyone knowing but the Lord. It is also more convenient to pray by yourself. But even when we pray by ourselves, our standing should always be in the Body. We are praying individually yet not as an individual.

In Matthew chapter 18 the Lord mentioned praying with two or three. In Acts chapters 1 and 2 the 120 disciples were praying together. We also need to pray together. Corporate prayer is stronger and more effective. In fact, the keys of the kingdom were not given to an individual, but to the church corporately. Therefore, the most powerful prayer for God's work is still the corporate prayer of the church. Some may say, "It is good enough for me to pray by myself. I enjoy the Lord better by myself." It may be true that you can enjoy the Lord by yourself. However, we must ask ourselves, "Is God's work accomplished through your individual enjoyment"? You may be enjoying the Lord for yourself and not for the Lord. Our individual enjoyment is for the corporate work of God. Therefore, we must get together to pray for God's work and to carry out God's work.

VI. PRAY SPECIFICALLY AND PERSISTENTLY

Many times our prayers are ineffective because we are too general; we must pray in a specific way. We may pray, "Lord get many people saved." The Lord does not know which one you desire to get saved. Sometimes we may pray, "Lord get my friend, John, saved." That is better. We can pray more specifically, by saying, "Lord, let me see my friend, John, today at lunch so that I may tell him about the mystery of human life. Lord, prepare him to receive the gospel." This is very specific. You included the person, the time, the message, and what you want the Lord to accomplish. The Lord hears your specific request and accomplishes the work according to your petition.

We also need to persist in our prayer. What do you do, if after your specific prayer you did not meet your friend, John? It seems that the Lord did not answer your prayer. Eph. 6:18 says that we should persevere in prayer. We need to continue to pray. The Lord may reveal to you that you took a pencil from John last year and never repaid him. After you have repented to the Lord and repaid John, the Lord will answer your prayer. If you do not repent, you will waste your time preaching to John, because he will not listen to your message. After your confession and restitution, he will be very open to receive your gospel. So we must persist in prayer until all the barriers are removed in order for the Lord to work.

VII. PRAY AT SET TIMES AND ALL THE TIME

We all know the verse, 1 Thes. 5:17, "Unceasingly pray." How many of us pray unceasingly? We need set times of prayer everyday so that we will be strong in spirit to pray unceasingly. Daniel told us that he prayed three times a day, kneeling down before God (Dan. 6:10). David prayed in the evening, morning, and at noon (Psa. 55:17). Peter and John went to pray at the hour of prayer (Acts 3:1). These brothers had set times to pray; we also need to set aside time to pray individually and corporately if we are to mean business with the Lord. It is not too much to pray three times by yourself and one time with others on a daily basis. We love Him, and we want Him to accomplish His hearts desire; therefore, we must pray at set times and all the time.

VIII. PRAY WITH THE WORD AND A NOTE BOOK

The best way to pray is with the Word (Eph. 6:17-19). We should also have a notebook with us when we pray. Many times we do not know how to pray. Praise the Lord for His Word. We can always read His Word and pray with His Word in order to fellowship with Him. We can also pray according to the burden He gives us through His Word. For example, 1 Tim. 2:4 says, "(God) desires all men to be saved." After reading the verse you may pray, "Lord, you desire all men to be saved; this means all the students in my school are included; this means all my friends are included. O Lord, forgive me for not preaching to them this year. Lord, strengthen my spirit right now and let me preach to my best friend, Mary. Lord, both You and I desire that Mary should be saved." After your prayer, you should write the date and who and what you prayed for in your notebook. If the Lord has not answered your prayer, pray more. After the answer comes, you may give the Lord thanks and write down the date, and how your prayer was answered. You will strengthen your faith by keeping a record. If you become weak in the faith concerning prayer, you can review your record of answered prayer, then you can testify to others that prayer works, and that prayer is the way God works.

Questions

1. List the seven steps of the principle of God's work.

2. What are the two types of prayer? Explain why both are important.

3. Use Matthew 18:18 to explain the church's responsibility in its prayer ministry to God.

Quoted Portions

1. Let Us Pray (Nee/CFP), pp. 23-24.

2. The Prayer Ministry of the Church (Nee/CFP), pp. 16-20.

3. Come Forward to the Throne of Grace (Lee/LSM), pp. 1-3.

Further References

1. Come Forward to the Throne of Grace (Lee/LSM), pp. 1-27.

2. Let Us Pray (Nee/CFP), pp. 23-36.
3. The Prayer Ministry of the Church (Nee/CFP), pp. 7-35.

Lesson Nineteen

THE HOLY, ROYAL, AND GOSPEL PRIESTHOOD FOR THE BUILDING UP OF THE CHURCH

Scripture Reading

1 Pet. 2:5, 9; Rom. 15:16; Heb. 9:14; 1 Jn. 1:9;
Jn. 1:29; Eph. 2:14; Eph. 5:26; Col. 2:9; Heb. 4:16;
Rom. 10:17; Psa. 119:147-148.

Outline

I. The definition of a priest

II. The holy priesthood

III. The royal priesthood

IV. The gospel priesthood

V. How to practice the priesthood
   A. Be revived every morning to be saturated with the Lord
   B. Bear the people on your heart to the Lord in prayer
   C. Beget through gospel visitation
   D. Nourish through shepherding
   E. Teach in small groups
   F. Build through prophesying

Text

The priesthood is crucial to the building up of the church. There are three aspects of the priesthood—holy, royal, and gospel. But although there are three aspects, it is the same priesthood. We need to be priests in the priesthood with all three aspects. The "hood" refers to the building up of the priests. When you have a "priesthood," you have the building up.

I. THE DEFINITION OF A PRIEST

[The dictionary tells us that a priest is a person who serves God professionally. Most Christians would tell us that a priest is one who serves God. This is right, but what does it mean to serve God? Today's Christians would answer that to serve God is to work for God. This answer is wrong! To say that a priest is a person who serves God is right, but to say that to serve God is merely to do something for God, is wrong.

To realize what a priest is, we must first see God's eternal plan. God is a God of purpose. He has a purpose which He wants to accomplish. According to the revelation of the Scriptures, God has a plan to work Himself into a group of people, that He might be their life, and that they might become His expression. Based upon this plan, God created man.

Man was destined to receive God, to be filled, saturated and permeated with God, and to have God flow out of him that he might be the living expression of God. This is a brief definition of a priest. He must contact God, be filled with God, and be possessed by God completely that he may be built up with others in the flow of the life of God. Then the priesthood will be His living corporate expression.

Christianity's concept is that if we love the Lord, we must work for Him. This is a natural, religious concept, not the revelation of the Bible. God never intended to call us merely to work for Him. God's intention is that we must first open ourselves to Him that He may come into us to fill and flood us until He has taken possession of every part of our being. Our whole being must be saturated and permeated with Him. Then we will be one with Him. We will not only be clothed outwardly with Him as power, but permeated inwardly with Him as everything. Then spontaneously, God will flow out cf us, and we will be built up with others in this flow of life.

I must repeat that a priest is not one who merely works for God. God has no intention of calling us to do something for Him. His intention is that we answer His call by opening ourselves to Him and saying, "Lord, here I am, not ready to work for You, but ready to be filled and possessed by You, and to be one with You." Not until we are one with the Lord can we ever work for Him and be a real priest. The main function of a priest is not to work, but to spend time in the presence of the Lord until he is one with Him in the spirit. The priesthood that God plans to have is a corporate man who is saturated and permeated with Himself.]

II. THE HOLY PRIESTHOOD

1 Peter 2:5 says, "You yourselves also, as living stones, are being built up a spiritual house, into a holy priesthood, to offer up spiritual sacrifices acceptable to God through Jesus Christ." The holy priesthood is typified by the priesthood according to the order of Aaron. To be holy is to be separated from the common things, the worldly things, unto the holy God. Positionally or objectively, we need to be separated so that we may be filled with the holy God dispositionally or subjectively. If we are not separated positionally, we cannot come to the holy God. After we come to God, we will be filled with God and His holy nature, dispositionally. Then we will be as holy as He.

How do we come to God as a holy priest? The tabernacle and its furniture is a picture of our actual experience. The first piece of furniture in the outer court of the tabernacle is the altar. The altar signifies the cross where Christ died as our sacrifice (Heb. 9:14). When we come to God, we first need to offer Christ as our spiritual sacrifice, as typified by the five basic offerings—trespass, sin, peace, meal, and burnt offerings (Heb. 9:14). As you come to the Lord, He may expose you on something you said to your mother that was rebellious. You may pray, "Lord, forgive me for speaking in a rebellious way to my mother." By praying this way, you take the Lord as your trespass offering. The Lord will forgive you of your trespass (1 Cor. 15:3; 1 John 1:9). You may continue to pray, "Oh Lord, I spoke in a rebellious way because I have a sinful rebellious nature. Thank You Lord that You have crucified my sinful nature, and were made sin on my behalf." Here, you have offer the Lord as a sin offering (John 1:29; 2 Cor. 5:21).

At this point you may feel peaceful because you sense that the Lord has forgiven you and has cleansed you. Then you may pray further, "Oh Lord, thank You; because You are my trespass and sin offerings, now I have peace with God and with my mother." You have just offered Christ as the peace offering (John 14:27; 20:21; Eph. 2:14). You may then pray, "Lord, I am not a proper and balanced person; that is why I always argue with my mother. But I praise You, You are so fine, balanced, and pure. I thank You that You live in me, and that I can take You as my person." You have just offered Christ as your meal offering (John. 11:15,35; Matt. 21:12-13; 23:33). Finally, you may pray, "Lord, in fact, I argue so much because I am for myself. If I were fully for God and His interest, I would never argue with my mother in a rebellious way. Lord, You are fully for God; You are absolutely for His heart's desire. Lord, I am one with You, and You are one with me for God and His economy." In this prayer you have offered Christ as your burnt offering (John 7:16-18).

The second piece of furniture in the outer court is the laver. The laver signifies the washing of the water in the Word (Eph. 5:26). This water is the Spirit of life. We are cleansed by His Word from the defilement of the world (John 15:3). The first piece of furniture we come to in the holy place is the show bread table. The bread signifies the Word as our food (Matt. 4:4). The second piece of furniture in the holy place is the lampstand. The lampstand signifies the light received from reading the Word (John 8:12; Psa. 119:130). These three experiences are from the Word. When we use our spirit to read the Word, the Spirit will wash us, feed us, and enlighten us.

The third piece of furniture in the holy place is the incense altar. The incense altar signifies our prayer (Rev. 5:8). As we use the Word to pray, we enter into the holy of holies.

The main piece of furniture in the holy of holies is the ark. The ark typifies Christ as the embodiment of God (Col. 2:9). When we arrive at the ark we come "to the throne of grace that we may receive mercy and may find grace for timely help" (Heb. 4:16). This is where we fellowship with God, and where God fills us with Himself to transform us. This is the place where we want to abide. By abiding in the holy of holies, we will know what the Lord desires and what He is burdened for, that we may pray accordingly.

Although we have described the process in a step-by-step way, our experience may not follow this sequence. Do not be too concerned; simply come to the Lord by prayer and with His Word. The Lord will guide us in our experience of Him, until we are saturated with Him.

III. THE ROYAL PRIESTHOOD

1 Peter 2:9 says, "But you are a chosen race, a royal priesthood, a holy nation, a people for a possession, so that you may tell out the virtues of Him who has called you out of darkness into His marvelous light." The royal priesthood is typified by the priesthood according to the order of Melchisedec. According to Genesis 14:18-20, Melchisedec came from God to bless Abraham with bread and wine. He came from God to bless man with the Lord's table. After we go to God as a holy priest, separated unto God, we become saturated with Him. Then we need to go to God's people to bless them with God as the bread and wine. The Lord's table signifies Christ's death and resurrection for man's salvation and enjoyment. This is the gospel, the good news, for fallen, sinful man. In addition, this is what we share in the church meetings to build up the church.

IV. THE GOSPEL PRIESTHOOD

Romans 15:16 says, "That I should be a minister of Christ Jesus to the nations, a laboring priest of the gospel of God, that the offering of the nations might be acceptable, having been sanctified in the Holy Spirit." The gospel priesthood mentioned here is not different from the holy and royal priesthoods. These three terms apply to three different aspects of the same priesthood in the New Testament. We are priests, and we are being built up as a priesthood, having Christ as the high priest.

The main function of the gospel priesthood is to preach the gospel to save sinners, so that they may be offered to God as acceptable sacrifices. Romans 15:16 talks about a minister of Christ Jesus laboring to offer the nations. 1 Peter 2:9 talks about telling out the virtues of Him who has called us out of darkness into His marvelous light. And 1 Peter 2:5 talks about offering up spiritual sacrifices acceptable to God through Jesus Christ. The functions of these three priesthoods are absolutely one. Actually, the gospel priesthood includes the holy and royal priesthoods. As a gospel priest we need to come forward to God to be saturated with Him first. Then the Lord burdens us to pray for a certain friend. We bring God to that friend as a royal priest. How do we bring God to him? We do it by telling him the virtues of Him who called us out of darkness into His marvellous light. "Virtues of Him" means His excellence, His power, His energy, the strength of life received through the gospel that delivered us out of darkness. As you tell your friend about His virtues, the word you speak brings faith into him (Rom. 10:17). This word has the power to deliver him from darkness. Then he will pray with you to receive the Spirit (Gal. 3:5); eventually, he will be baptized into the Triune God. This gospel experience explains how we, as a holy priest, offer someone as a spiritual sacrifice to God.

We need to be the holy priesthood, the royal priesthood, and the gospel priesthood. We should always come to God to be filled with Him, bring God to people by telling out His virtues, and offer the repented sinners as spiritual sacrifices to God. We do this not in an individual way but with others. We are built up as we perform our priestly duties. As we are being built up, more priests become saved and are added to the priesthood to be built up together with us. This is God's way to build up the church.

V. HOW TO PRACTICE THE PRIESTHOOD

A. Be Revived Every Morning
to be Saturated with the Lord

In the Old Testament, the priests start to offer sacrifices to God in the morning. Therefore, [we also must enjoy the Lord in the Word every day early in the morning to have a new start each day (Psa. 119:147-148). According to God's principle in His creation, He ordained to have a new year, a new month or a new moon, and a new day. Within every year we can have three hundred sixty-five new starts. If we failed for three hundred sixty-four days, we still have one more opportunity to have a successful day. We may have failed today, but then the Lord tomorrow is still here waiting for us. Tomorrow morning we will have another chance to have a new start. Within every twenty-four hours, there is a new chance for us to have a new start and be renewed.

To have a new start is not hard. It is so easy. Just rise up a little earlier and say, "O Lord Jesus. O Lord Jesus." You do not need to shout loudly to bother others. Just say, "O Lord Jesus." To say this makes a big difference. Sometimes I forgot to call on the Lord immediately after I woke up. That became a big loss to me. As soon as I realized this I said, "Lord Jesus, forgive me for forgetting You."]

After calling on the Lord, you need to pray-read a few verses. The Holy Word for Morning Revival can be very helpful. Read and pray-read one or two pages a day. Use your spirit with the Word to touch the Lord. Memorize the verse that you enjoyed the most. Then write down what you enjoyed to share with other saints, later. It helps to have your morning revival material by your bed before you go to sleep, so you do not have to look for it in the morning.

By having a morning revival every morning, you will be filled up with God to perform your priestly duty.

B. Bear the People on Your Heart to the Lord in Prayer

You need to pray unceasingly to fellowship with the Lord, by calling on His name and by using the verse you memorized in the morning. You also need to pray specifically for your friends' salvation at set times, by yourself and with others. Praying refreshes us, strengthens us, and directs us in our priestly function. John 15:16 says, "You did not choose Me, but I chose you, and I appointed you that you should go forth and bear fruit, and that your fruit should remain; that whatever you ask the Father in My name, He may give you." The asking is not for anything we want, but is specifically for fruit-bearing. James 4:2b says, "You do not have because you do not ask." Based on these verses, if we ask we will have. The more we ask, the more we will have.

C. Beget Through Gospel Visitation

Sometimes people say that prayer does not work. After they pray, they stay home to wait for the Lord to work. Others may say that they are not effective in the gospel, yet they do not pray. Praying and going are two aspects of our co-laboring with God. On one hand, we need to pray much. On the other hand, we need to go much. We should not pray without going, nor should we go without praying. Eventually, if we do not pray and go, we will be disappointed and stop our praying and going altogether. According to John 15:16, we are chosen by the Lord to bear fruit. The way to bear fruit is to be pruned by the Father, to be cleansed by the Lord's word, to abide in the Lord, to let Him and His word abide in us, to ask the Father for remaining fruit, to love one another, and finally, to go forth. If we do all of the above without going, it is still not adequate. We must go to where the people are, and also invite them to come. We sometimes give up if they do not come. The proper way is to go. Go to visit people as God visited us. Go and speak the word to convert them to the Lord. The little booklet Mystery of Human Life is very helpful in gospel preaching because it summarizes the Bible regarding God's economy, man's condition, and God's salvation. Baptize your friends after they pray to receive the Lord. This is the God ordained way to function as a gospel priest. This is a wonderful exprience that you should have.

D. Nourish Through Shepherding

After your friends receive the Lord, you must continue to pray for them and shepherd them into life, so that they may be established in the faith. This is usually more effective one-on-one. You need to teach them how to pray and to pray-read the Word by doing it with them. You also need to help them to read the Word everyday. Fellowship with them about what they read daily, so that they will continue to read the Word. Another crucial matter is to help them live by the sense of the spirit within them. Whenever we think, speak, or do things that are not of the Lord, we get the sense of death. Sadness, emptiness, and uneasiness, are examples of this sense. Conversely, when we have the sense of life we experience joy, peace, rest, etc. (Rom. 8:6, 13). When we live by this sense, we are living by the spirit. Praying, reading the Word, and living by the spirit are the three foundation stones of our Christian life. You must help your new believing friends to pray, to read the Word, and to live by the spirit.

E. Teach in Small Groups

In Matthew 28:20 the Lord said that after we baptized people, we should teach them "to observe all things, whatever I commanded you." In Acts 20:27 the Apostle Paul said that he "did not shrink from declaring to the saints all the counsel of God." Therefore, you must teach the new ones everything you know about the Lord, His economy, His recovery, His church, etc. The best way to teach the truth is in small groups. When you have a small group of saints meeting together, there are more riches of Christ. If a new one asks a question that you cannot adequately answer, others may be better prepared to answer accurately. This is an example of the priesthood.

F. Build Through Prophesying

The last point concerning our practice of the priesthood concerns prophesying in the church meetings to build up the church. Prophesying, in 1 Corinthian 14, mainly refers to speaking for and speaking forth God. After having been revived for six days by praying and reading the Lord's Word, and having gone forth to bear fruit, we should have much to speak on the Lord's day to build up the church. On Saturday, you can compose a prophesy with the week's enlightenment and enjoyment. In the meetings, we practice as royal priests to speak for God and to speak God into all the saints. You may say that you are young and do not know much. Whatever you currently know and have enjoyed is your portion to build up the church. If you do not prophesy, the saints will miss the portion that you have received from the Lord that week, and the building up of the church will suffer. Not only should you prophesy, you should also train your new ones to prophesy. The church will be built step-by-step as you and your new ones prophesy in the meetings.

CONCLUSION

We should endeavor to be the holy, royal, and gospel priests in the one priesthood. If we are faithful, the life and number in the church will increase and the Lord will build His church through us. Do not say that you are young, and then wait until you are older to get serious. Now is the time for you to start to function as priests. You will learn, and become experienced, mature, and perfected functioning priests as you are growing up. When He comes, you will have a great reward.

Questions

1. With the teacher and the other students in your class, draw a picture of the tabernacle including all the furniture. Discuss the significance of the tabernacle and its furniture.

2. Discuss the function, similarities and differences of each aspect of the priesthood (holy, royal, and gospel).

3. In detail, describe the type of living needed to be a proper priest.

Quoted Portions

1. Speaking Christ for the Building Up of the Body of Christ (Lee/LSM), pp. 36-37.

Further References

1. The New Testament Priest of the Gospel (Lee/LSM), pp. 75-79; 95-110.

Lesson Twenty

OUR ENTRANCE INTO THE CHURCH

Scripture Reading

Eph. 1:3-5, 7; Rom. 4:25; 1 Pet. 1:3; Eph. 2:5-6;
Acts 2:4; 10:44-45;1 Cor. 12:13; Mark 16:16; Acts 2:38;
26:19; 2 Cor. 4:1; Phil. 3:13.

Outline

I. Chosen and predestinated by the Father

II. The redemption of Christ through His blood

III. The resurrection and ascension of Christ

IV. The outpouring of the Spirit on the Body

V. Entering the church by believing and being baptized

VI. Having no exit from the church

VII. Being absolute for the building up of the church
   A. Not disobedient to the heavenly vision
   B. Not discouraged
   C. Always pursuing the goal

Text

In the last seven lessons, we covered the matter of how to build up the church in a general way. In the next five lessons, we will clarify our role in the church life so that we may participate in the building up of the church. People come to the church life from various backgrounds. Most of you were born of parents who are in the church. In this lesson, our burden is to reveal how we came into the church. We were not born into the church physically, nor were we invited by a friend, etc.

We were chosen before the foundation of the world to be in the church. We were redeemed by Christ on the cross to be in the church. We were raised with Christ and seated in the heavenlies together with Christ for the church. We were regenerated by the Spirit to be in the church. We were born of God to be in the church. We are now sons of God in the household of God. We are members of the Body of Christ to be in the church. We are in the church by life and because of life. We are in the church because of the work of the Triune God. We can never leave the church, nor can we ever be dismissed from the church. We were destined to be in the church. We are in the church. The church is our home for eternity. Hallelujah!

I. CHOSEN AND PREDESTINATED BY THE FATHER

In lesson one, we pointed out that the church was in God's eternal plan. Here, we state that not only is the church in God's eternal plan, we also are in that plan. Our being here is not a matter of happenstance. Ephesians 1:3-5 says, "Blessed be the God and Father of our Lord Jesus Christ, who has blessed us with every spiritual blessing in the heavenlies in Christ, according as He chose us in Him before the foundation of the world that we should be holy and without blemish before Him, in love, having predestinated us unto sonship through Jesus Christ to Himself, according to the good pleasure of His will." It is clear that the first blessing we receive from the Father is His choosing and predestinating of us to be His sons. We know that Ephesians is a book on the church. Chapter one ends with the revelation of the Head with the Body, the church, to be the fullness of the Head. We can therefore say that the Father's choosing and predestinating of us to be sons is for the church. Because the church is made up of the many sons of the Father, we who were chosen and predestinated are the constituents of the church.

II. THE REDEMPTION OF CHRIST
THROUGH HIS BLOOD

Ephesians 1:7 says, "In whom we have redemption through His blood, the forgiveness of offenses, according to the riches of His grace." When man was created, God said that he was very good. He had no sin, yet he still needed God to come into him. But before God could come into him, man fell into sin and came under the curse of the law. Therefore, God must redeem us, forgive us, and cleanse us from our sins to prepare us to be building material for the church. He accomplished redemption, as a man, on the cross for all mankind, once and for all. When we believe into Him, we receive the forgiveness of sins.

III. THE RESURRECTION AND ASCENSION OF CHRIST

After Christ was delivered because of our offenses, He was raised because of our justification (Rom. 4:25). We were regenerated unto a living hope through His resurrection (1 Pet. 1:3), and we were made alive together with Christ (Eph. 2:5). As a result, the eternal life of God came into us to make us divinely human. This qualifies us to be the constituents of the church. Furthermore, we were raised up together and seated together in the heavenlies in Christ Jesus (Eph. 2:6). All things are under our feet. We have the authority in heaven and earth to carry out God's desire—to build up the church. Having obtained all these blessings from the Father, we can never be discouraged or down-trodden. Nobody can stop us, not even the devil himself, from accomplishing God's purpose—the building up of the church.

IV. THE OUTPOURING OF THE SPIRIT ON THE BODY

The Triune God's final accomplishment was the outpouring of the Spirit to form the one Body. This was done in two steps for two peoples. The Spirit was first poured out on the day of Pentecost for the Jewish believers (Acts 2). The Spirit was then poured out in the house of Cornelius for the gentile believers (Acts 10). Therefore, Paul said in 1 Corinthian 12:13, "For also in one Spirit we were all baptized into one body, whether Jews or Greeks (representing the gentiles), whether slaves or free, and were all given to drink one Spirit." The baptism is our initiation into the Body and is once for all. To drink the Spirit is continuous, and is to be practiced by us constantly for eternity.

V. ENTERING THE CHURCH
BY BELIEVING AND BEING BAPTIZED

Our participation in the Father's choosing and predestinating, the Son's redemption, resurrection, and ascension, and the Spirit's infilling and outpouring is for our entrance into the church. We had no choice in these matters, because we were not yet born. Nevertheless, we have been fully prepared to be members of the Body of Christ for the building up of His Body. The way we experienced all these things is by believing and being baptized after hearing the word of the truth, the gospel of our salvation. By believing, we receive the Spirit of reality, who brings us all the divine realities. By being baptized, we are put into the Spirit once and for all to remain in the Body. All these spiritual realities accomplished by the Triune God long ago have become real to us today. Our entrance into the church is due entirely to the Triune God. We entered the church by the Father's choosing, the Son's redemption, the Spirit's regeneration, our believing, and our baptism. Our being in the church is eternal, of the Father, of the Son, of the Spirit, and of the eternal life. It is not of us or of anyone else. What can we say except, "Hallelujah!" We must thank Him for His mercy and grace.

VI. HAVING NO EXIT FROM THE CHURCH

After seeing how we entered the church, we can conclude that there is no exit from the church. Our entrance began from eternity past, before anything was, before we had done anything good or bad. It continued through Christ's incarnation, crucifixion, resurrection, ascension, and the Spirit's outpouring. We experienced a rich entrance by believing and being baptized after hearing the gospel. Our entrance is eternal; it is according to the divine and uncreated life of God. It was not accidental, nor was it based on anyone's decision. No one hired us or signed us up. Can we drop out from such a church? No, never! One day, heaven and earth will pass away, but we will still be in the church. There is no back door, no way to escape. No one can dismiss us from the church because we were born into the church, spiritually. If God is for us, who can be against us? There is no going out, whether by our choice, by somebody else's choice, or by God's choice.

VII. BEING ABSOLUTE FOR THE BUILDING UP OF THE CHURCH

Have you seen the vision of the church and the building up of the church? Do you know why you are in the church and how you entered in? If you see this vision, your spontaneous reaction will be to give yourselves absolutely to Christ for the building up of the church. You realize that there is nothing else to do in the universe but to build up the church.

A. Not Disobedient to the Heavenly Vision

Many people have seen this heavenly vision and have consecrated themselves for Christ and the church. Unfortunately, many of them have left this way. Do you wonder why? Apostle Paul said in Acts 26:19 that he was not disobedient to the heavenly vision. This means it is possible to be disobedient. We need to pray for the Lord's mercy to keep us obedient to the heavenly vision so that we will continue to be absolutely consecrated until the end. We believe the Lord will be faithful to answer our prayer.

B. Not Discouraged

Sometimes you may be discouraged by the condition of the church, or because the condition of the church does not match the heavenly vision. Some may say that after having been in the church life for ten years they still have not seen the fulfillment of God's purpose, as revealed in the Bible. We should tell them that heaven and earth will pass away, but His Word will not pass away until everything is fulfilled (Matt. 24:35). God is building the masterpiece of the universe. It is less difficult to create the physical heaven and earth than it is to build the church. It requires more love, wisdom, time, and energy to build the church. The material He uses to build the church comes from the heap of collapse. All were evil sinners, full of filth and corruption. God needs to redeem man then transform him into the right material for His building. It takes time. This age, and most importantly, our life-time is for this work. Therefore, we should not lose heart because we have the New Testament ministry to encourage and supply us for the building up of the church (2 Cor. 4:1).

C. Always Pursuing the Goal

We must focus our attention on the goal—Christ and the church. Paul said in Philippians 3:13 that he forgot the things which are behind and stretched forward to the things which are before, that is, he pursued toward the goal—Christ and the church. We must have the same attitude as Paul. Do not say, "I am not like my brother Paul." Paul said that he is a pattern for the believers to imitate (2 Thes. 3:9). We all should imitate him because he is an imitator of Christ (1 Cor. 11:1). Therefore, young brothers and sisters, set your whole heart, whole mind, and whole soul to love the Lord Jesus for the building up of His church. Pray like this, "Lord, You gave Yourself to me and to the church. You chose me, redeemed me, regenerated me, and baptized me into Your Body. Lord, I want to give my whole being, all that I am, have, and can do to You. I consecrate my whole life, my whole future to build up Your church. All that You have is mine, and all that I have is Yours. Your will becomes my will, and My will is Your will. Lord, build up the church through the saints and through me."

Questions

1. Use the Bible to write a prophecy regarding our entrance into the church.

2. We have seen in this lesson that it is possible to be disobedient to the heavenly vision—but is it possible to leave the church? Explain.

3. What role did the Triune God—the Father, the Son, and the Spirit—have in our entrance into the Church?

Further References

1. Body of Christ (Lee/LSM), pp. 19-24.

2. The One New Man (Lee/LSM), pp. 47-61.

3. Organism of the Triune God in the Organic Union of the Divine Trinity (Lee/LSM), pp. 39-45.

Lesson Twenty-One

OUR ATTITUDE IN THE CHURCH LIFE

Scripture Reading

Rom. 12:3-5; 1 Cor. 12:12-27; 1 John 3:14; Heb. 13:17.

Outline

I. Being conscious of the Body

II. Loving the brethren

III. Having no division

IV. Being delivered from independence

V. Staying in fellowship

VI. Learning to be a member

VII. Submitting to authority

VIII. Having no ambition

Text

In this lesson, we need to consider our attitude in the church life. Having the proper attitude helps to build up the church. Having the wrong attitude helps the devil to destroy the church life. Some may say that they see the Body, yet their attitude is wrong; having a wrong attitude creates problems in the church. Therefore, the young people must learn to have the proper attitude for the building up of the church.

I. BEING CONSCIOUS OF THE BODY

We were saved as members of the Body of Christ; therefore, we must be conscious of the Body. Many who do not see this vision, consider themselves as individual Christians, saved by the Lord from going to hell so they can go to heaven. They do not realize that God's purpose is the church, nor do they realize that they are members of the Body; therefore, they are not conscious of the Body. They live as individuals separate from the Body. They care only for themselves and their own spirituality. They live independently from other believers, acting as though they are not needed. It is pitiful for a believer to have such an attitude. We must pray and study the Word until we fully see the vision of the Body, and are conscious of the Body of Christ.

II. LOVING THE BRETHREN

[Let us first approach it from the standpoint of love. One thing is quite marvelous when we contemplate this verse: "We know that we have passed out of death into life, because we love the brethren" (1 John 3.14). All who have passed out of death into life love one another. All who have become members of the same spiritual Body love one another. Such love comes from life and it flows spontaneously. Could a person be considered a child of God if, after answering affirmatively in a church meeting that he is a Christian and after being reminded that as a Christian he ought to love other Christians, he then says, "I will start to love other Christians tomorrow if you say so"? Oh, let us see that everyone who is truly born from above and has the life of God spontaneously loves all who are members together with him in the Body of Christ. Whether he is reminded or not, he has a consciousness of loving the brethren. He unquestionably needs many times to be reminded to love the brethren. Yet this reminder does not add anything to him which is not already within him, it instead merely stirs up into more fervency what is already present in him. If the love of God is present in a person, the love of the brethren is there. And if God's love is absent, brotherly love is not there. It is that simple. Nothing can be created or manufactured. When a believer meets another person who belongs to God he strangely but quite naturally loves him because he has that inner consciousness within him which must express itself in love towards that other person.]

All of us who were born of God and have been baptized into the Body of Christ cannot help but love one another. When we live in the flesh, we have the tendencies to insult others by our offensive remarks. We need to repent from such behavior. We must take care of one another's feelings by living in the spirit.

III. HAVING NO DIVISION

[One who has seen the Body of Christ and who thus possesses the consciousness of the Body feels unbearable inside when he does anything which may cause division or separate God's children. For he loves all who belong to God and cannot divide His children. Love is natural to the Body of Christ, whereas division is most unnatural. It is just as in the case with our two hands: no matter for how many reasons one hand may be raised against the other hand, there is no way to sever their relationship: division is simply impossible.]

[The Body of Christ will deliver us from sect and sectarianism; it will also save us from self and individualism. How sad that the life principle of many is not the Body but the individual self. We may discover this principle of individualism in many areas.] For example, [sometimes three or five, even ten or twenty brethren at a meeting will all speak only whatever concerns themselves, without showing any interest in the affairs of the others or listening to the others' thoughts. Or, as the case might be, as you or others sit with such a person as has been described, he may talk with animation for an hour or two about his own business; but when you or the others talk, he does not pay the slightest attention—for if you ask him afterwards, he evidences the fact that he hardly seems to have heard anything. In small things such as these, you can tell if a person has truly discerned the Body of Christ.

The plague of individualism can grow from simply expressing one person's individualism to that of several persons. You may notice in the church that three or five, perhaps even eight or nine persons will sometimes form a small circle. Only these few are of one mind and love one another. They do not fit in with the other brothers and sisters. This indicates that they too have not perceived the Body of Christ. The church is one, it cannot be severed. If a person has really known the Body, he cannot endorse any kind of individualism. He cannot form a party or any small circle.

If you have genuinely experienced the Body of Christ you will be conscious of something wrong whenever you begin to show your individualism, and obviously you dare not take any action. Or else, when you or several others should make a wrong move, this Body consciousness will cause you to be aware of being disconnected from the other children of God, thus preventing you from proceeding further. There is something in you which restrains, speaks, reproves, warns, or hinders. This consciousness of life can deliver all of us from any taint of division.]

IV. BEING DELIVERED FROM INDEPENDENCE

[If we have Body consciousness we will comprehend immediately that the Body is one. Thus, in spiritual work, it cannot be individualistic in its scope. In order to participate rightly in the Lord's work, it is imperative that we deal with this matter of independent labor. In the thinking of some people, a person must lay his own hand on things or else that person will consider those things to be good for nothing. Whatever is done by him is deemed as having spiritual value; what is not done by him has no value at all. When he preaches and nobody is saved, he feels depressed. When he preaches and people are saved, he shows pleasant surprise. This is because he looks at the work as his own personal labor. But the moment God's children perceive the oneness of the Body, they immediately comprehend the oneness of the work. The instant they see that the Body is one, they are delivered from their individual endeavor since they now see the work of the Body. This does not imply that a person can no longer labor as an individual. It simply means that he can no longer consider work as belonging solely to himself. Whether the work is done by him or not is no problem anymore, so long as it is done by someone.

As Christians, we should admire and seek for spiritual things, but we ought not have any emulative pretensions nor any trace of jealousy. Our attitude individually towards spiritual work should be: What I can do I hope others can also do; and what I cannot do I wish someone else can do; I would like to do more as well as I would expect other people to do more. How I need to realize that I can only be a single vessel in the work; I cannot monopolize it. I dare not consider the work and its result as altogether mine. If I insist that everything must be done by me, I have not apprehended the Body. The moment I apprehend the Body, immediately I realize that both my labor and that of others mean gain to the Head as well as to the Body. And let all glory be to the Lord and all blessings be to the church.

The Lord distributes His work to all, and everyone has his share. We must not think of ourselves more highly than we ought to think. We should be faithful to the portion which the Lord has given each of us; but we should also respect the portion He gives to others. Many young people possess a kind of competitive attitude in which they are always comparing what they have with that which others do not have and what they do not have with that which others have. Actually, such comparison is absurd. How can we add a chair to a table? Are they one or two? A table plus a chair equals a table and a chair. If we are asked which is better, the hand or the eye, we can only answer that the hand and the eye are both good. He who has seen the Body recognizes the functions of all the members. He looks at himself as only one among many members. He will not project himself to a distinctive position in order to compare himself favorably with others or even to occupy another's place.]

V. STAYING IN FELLOWSHIP

[He who sees the Body of Christ most spontaneously sees not only the stupidity of independent action but the need for fellowship as well. Fellowship is not an external exercise in social intercourse; it is the spontaneous demand of body life. What is erroneously but commonly assumed to be fellowship by God's children is a visiting of homes of some brothers and sisters at times of leisure and chit-chatting with them a while. In actuality, fellowship means realizing the total inadequacy of my own self. I am desirous of doing all things with the other members of the Body. Although for doing many things I am not able to gather all the brothers and sisters in the church, I still can do them with two or three brothers and/or sisters according to the principle of the Body.

Oftentimes we need to learn fellowship in prayer, to learn fellowship in difficulties, to learn fellowship in seeking God's will, to learn fellowship concerning our future, and to learn fellowship regarding God's word. What fellowship means is that, knowing that I am inadequate in the matter of prayer, I seek out two or three others to pray with me. I by myself am incompetent in solving difficulties, hence I ask two or three brethren to deal with the situations together with me. Alone I am unable to know God's will, therefore I solicit the help of two or three others. I in myself am rather confused as to my future, consequently I request two or three brothers and sisters to fellowship and decide with me what my future should be. I cannot understand God's word alone, so now I study the word of God with two or three brothers and sisters. In fellowship, I acknowledge my insufficiency and incompetency, and I also acknowledge my need of the Body. I confess that I am limited and liable to make mistakes; for this I plead with those brothers and sisters who have spiritual discernment to help me (and not just ask those to help me who are affectionate towards me). I am inadequate, and hence I need the help of other brethren.

The Body of Christ is a life, and there is therefore also a consciousness involved. You yourself will become conscious or aware of the fact that without fellowship you cannot live.]

VI. LEARNING TO BE A MEMBER

[If a person has Body consciousness he at once recognizes his place in the Body; that is to say, he sees himself as being one of its members. Each member has his distinctive usefulness. A member of a physical body is different from a body cell. Lacking a cell does not matter much, but the lack of a member in a body is unthinkable.]

[Because we are members of the Body of Christ and members each in its part, we must seek how to help the Body in gaining life and strength. In any gathering, even if we do not open our mouths, we may pray silently. Even though we may not speak, we can still look to God. This is Body consciousness. If we have seen the Body, we cannot say we are a person of no consequence. We will rather say: I am a member of the Body, and hence I have a duty to perform. I have a word which I should speak, I have a prayer which I should utter. When I come to the meeting I must do whatever God wants me to do. I cannot afford to be a spectator. Such things as these are what we will say or do if we truly apprehend the Body. And as we all function, the life of the entire gathering will swallow up all death. Many meetings fail to exhibit such power to overcome death for there are too many spectators.]

VII. SUBMITTING TO AUTHORITY

[Whoever knows the life of the Body of Christ and is conscious of being a Body member will invariably sense the authority of the Head, who is Christ Jesus the Lord.

We must not only submit to the direct authority of the Head, we need also to submit to the indirect authority of the Head. My physical hand is under the direct authority of the head of my body, but when my arm moves, my hand moves together with my arm—for my hand submits to the head through the arm. Consequently, whoever sees the Body of Christ sees also the authority which God has set in the Body of Christ for him to submit to.]

[If you truly perceive the authority of the Head, you will also perceive that one or more members of the Body are ahead of you, and that to them you must learn to submit. Hence you recognize not only the Head but also those whom God has set in the Body to represent the Head. If you are at odds with them, you will also be at odds with God.]

[If a person does not know what authority is, how can he say he knows the Body of Christ? Let us see that the one who knows the Body can discern—even when only three or five people are assembled together—who among those assembled is his authority; because there is manifested in their midst the authority of the Head to which he needs to submit. How natural and how beautiful it is in the human body for the fingers to submit to the wrist, the wrist to the arm, the arm to the shoulder, and so on. And this same beauty can be displayed in the Body of Christ.

Certain Christians are so careless in action as well as in speech that they will not listen to anyone. They seem to regard themselves as being the greatest to such an extent that they fail to recognize anyone to whom they could submit. This proves that such believers have never known the restraint of the Body nor have ever submitted to the authority of the Head. May God have mercy on such members. If we have genuinely been dealt with by the Lord and if our flesh has received such dealings as to have had the backbone of the natural life broken, we will immediately acknowledge how neither our hands nor our mouth have unlimited freedom—since all are under the control of the body—and how we cannot fail to submit ourselves to the authority which God has set in the Body of Christ.]

VIII. HAVING NO AMBITION

According to our experiences over the past years, ambition has been the source of all the problems in the church life. Ambition leads to power struggle. The source of ambition is Satan. His ambition is to rise above God and His authority. Satan was cast down and judged because of ambition. Today, you can see power struggles everywhere. You see it among your friends. Once you try to rise above others to have authority over others, you will create problems in the church life. We do not mean that there should not be authority in the church life. The foregoing lessons have already described the matter of authority in the church. The more life of God one has, the more authority he has. Authority does not come by struggling, back-biting, or arguing. It comes from God and it comes with the life of God. God is the source. Satan was created by God. How then can

Satan rise above God? This is Satanic ambition without the capacity to exercise the proper authority. We must learn to submit.

The Lord humbled and emptied Himself to be a slave unto death. How about us? Paul said that we should let the mind of Christ be in us (Phil. 2:5). If we would do this, there will never be any Satanic ambition in us. Rather, we will always serve as a slave in the church life to build up the church.

Questions

1. How does the "consciousness of life" deliver us from division?

2. When you visit with the brothers and sisters can you discern the difference between fellowship and chit—chat? What is the difference? Can you quote from memory a verse from the Bible referring to fellowship? If so, quote it to the other students in the class.

3. What is the difference between" power struggle" and authority? What is the source of each?

Quoted Portions

1. Body of Christ (Lee/LSM), pp. 9-22.

Further References

1. Life Study of Romans (Lee/LSM), pp. 295, 303-305, 320-325.

YOUNG PEOPLE FOR THE BUILDING UP OF THE CHURCH

Scripture Reading

1 Sam. 2:18; 16:11-13; Dan. 1:4, 8, 17;
2 Tim. 2:22; 3:1-4; Eccl. 4:12.

Outline

I. God calling the young people for His move

II. Being caught and occupied by God

III. Purposing in our heart not to be defiled

IV. The need for companions

V. Praying and seeking the truth with companions

Text

It is good that while you are young you see the vision concerning the church and are developing a burden to build up the church. After seeing the vision of the church, we all have the feeling that we want to give ourselves to the Lord to build up the most wonderful thing in the universe—His church. Some may see this vision when they are older. The older one is, the less time he has to build. You have time because you are young. Be careful, your time may run out like everyone else if you do not set your heart on the Lord's building today. You should do everything possible, including studying hard, reading the Word, praying, learning to preach, being in the meetings, and offering to the Lord, to prepare yourselves for the work of the ministry and for the building up of the church.

I. GOD CALLING THE YOUNG PEOPLE FOR HIS MOVE

[It is so good to be young persons in the Lord's recovery. In every age and generation God has come to the young people for the carrying out of His move. Both the Bible and church history show us that God wants to use the young people. We may say that Adam was very young when God was with him because he had just been created. Abel, the second generation of man in the line of life, was probably also young when he offered sacrifices to the Lord (Gen. 4:2, 4). Enoch was young when he began to walk in God's presence. He was sixty-five years old when he began to walk with God, but at his time a man who was sixty-five years old was still young. He walked with God for three hundred years, and God took him at the age of three hundred sixty-five (Gen. 5:21-22).]

The first time God called Abraham, he was in Mesopotamia. At that time he was very young. [Moses was called by God and began to serve Him when he was eighty years old, but his preparation for service began when he was a small boy being nursed by his mother.] [Samuel was a very young boy when he was caught by God (1 Sam. 2:18). David also was a young man when he was anointed to be king (1 Sam. 16:11-13). Likewise, Daniel was young when he was an overcomer in the palace of the king of Babylon (Dan. 1:4, 17).

In the New Testament, none of the apostles whom Jesus called was an old man. They all were young people. When the Lord walked along the shore of the sea of Galilee, He called the young people. Zebedee was with his two sons, John and James, but the Lord called only the sons and not Zebedee (Matt. 4:21-22). It was God's divine way and economy to call the sons and not the father. The elders in the first church on the earth, the church in Jerusalem, were young people.

The Bible also tells us that Timothy became an apostle (1 Thes. 1:1; cf. 2:6) as a young man to carry on the Lord's testimony. In 2 Timothy 2:22 Paul wrote, "Flee youthful lusts." This indicates that the receiver of that Epistle was still a young man. I am happy that I was called by God when I was a teenager. All those who were in the initial stage of the Lord's recovery of the proper church life over fifty years ago were young people in their twenties. Very few were over twenty-five. Most were either in high school or in college.]

Therefore, you should not consider yourself too young to be serious with the Lord. You are at the right age to be called for the Lord's move in His recovery of the building up of His church.

II. BEING CAUGHT AND OCCUPIED BY GOD

· [The goal of Satan, God's enemy, is to spoil and occupy mankind. In 2 Timothy 3:1-4 Paul says, "But know this, that in the last days difficult times shall come; for men shall be lovers of self, lovers of money... nonlovers of good... lovers of pleasure rather than lovers of God." Today throughout the whole earth, young people are lovers of pleasure. Sports, amusements, and entertainment are simply pleasures.]

[Paul told Timothy to be aware that difficult times would come when men would be lovers of self. History tells us that at the time of the fall of the Roman Empire, the Romans were self-lovers. They did not care for anyone but themselves. Of course, they were also lovers of money. Self, money, and pleasure always go together. Where self is, money is loved and pleasures are sought. Men in this condition are fully spoiled and occupied with something other than God. They are lovers of themselves, of money, and of pleasures, but not lovers of God or of anything good.]

[Praise the Lord that in the midst of such a situation of ruin, He has visited many of us. Many of the young people among us have not only been caught by God but also occupied by Him. They have been "wrecked" by Him. Satan spoils people, but God "wrecks" people. Satan spoils people to make them useless for God's purpose, but God wrecks people to make them useless for Satan's purpose, the purpose of loving money and pleasure. Why would so many young people attend the meetings of the church? Why would they not seek sports or entertainment? It is because they are wrecked. Over sixty years ago, I was wrecked by God. I was a very active, ambitious, and somewhat smart young man. However, one day I was wrecked by God. Several times I tried to go back to my old way, but because I was wrecked, I could not make it. We have been caught and occupied by Him.]

Why did God "wreck" us and why does He want to "wreck" some of our friends? He needs to build His church. He needs material and co-laborers for the building up of the church.

III. PURPOSING IN OUR HEART
NOT TO BE DEFILED

[Daniel was taken into captivity as a young man. He and his three friends, who were of the children of Judah, were selected to come into the king's palace to be taught. There they had to decide whether or not they would eat the food sacrificed to idols. That meat was no longer merely food; it had become related to the demons. To eat it was not a small thing. Daniel and his three friends purposed in their heart not to be defiled, not to have any share in that defiling element (Dan. 1:8).

For Daniel and his three friends not to eat the king's food was to protest, to be God's testimony, against the tide of idolatry. This was a great matter in the eyes of God and also in the eyes of the Devil. This was the fighting of a spiritual warfare. In such a situation, Daniel was one who was caught by God. From his very youth, he was called, captured, and fully occupied by God. Eventually, it was he who brought in the return from captivity.]

[Young people today are also in a situation of captivity. God's testimony has been spoiled, and the riches, the vessels, of God's testimony have been taken captive. Everything in this age is defiling, including religion and society with its pleasures. Today all religions are in a form of idolatry. Religion takes God's name, but worships something other than God. This is idolatry. God needs some young people to keep themselves from being defiled by the idolatrous worship. Once some young people see the situation of today's religion, they will purpose in their heart. They will say, "Lord, from today I would never become polluted with this religion. I would stay away from this defilement." To flee youthful lusts is to keep from being defiled.]

[Do not go along with the present situation. At the time of Daniel, some young people might have said, "What is wrong for us to eat the king's meat? Everything created by God is clean. We do not care whether or not this food has been offered to idols. We will just take advantage of it." This is a word of failure and defeat. They should rather have said, "I will never go along with this current. I will keep away from it. I protest against the present situation. Let others eat, but I will not." If the young people today would make a purpose such as this deep in their heart, God will use them.]

[The young people need to flee youthful lusts, and they should also pursue, that is, seek after, righteousness, faith, love, and peace (2 Tim. 2:22b). Righteousness, faith, love, and peace are all Christ. To pursue these things is to pursue Christ in different aspects. Flee youthful lusts, and pursue Christ as your righteousness in your relationship with others, as your faith in your relationship with God, as your love in your relationship with one another, and as your very peace. Such fleeing and pursuing is a living for God's testimony. It is a daily gospel life. A daily walk which expresses righteousness, faith, love, and peace is the best gospel preaching. It is the life that opens the way for the gospel to reach people.]

IV. THE NEED FOR COMPANIONS

[You must have such a life of fleeing and pursuing. However, when you endeavor to flee and pursue, you will find that you are not able to do so by yourself. The way to flee youthful lusts and pursue Christ is in the last part of 2 Timothy 2:22. This verse says, "But flee youthful lusts, and pursue righteousness, faith, love, peace with those who call on the Lord out of a pure heart." You need "those who call on the Lord out of a pure heart." By yourself you are inadequate. The key is to be "with those."]

[The young people must make the decision to pick up some others as companions. Daniel had his three friends. Under the Lord Jesus in the New Testament none of the disciples were individuals. They were sent two by two; they all had companions. Peter and Andrew and James and John are referred to in the Gospels in pairs (Matt. 4:18, 21).]

[If we have four companions to support us from each direction, we will not fall, regardless of what storm may come. If one stands by himself, he will possibly be captured by the enemy. It is best for four or five young ones from junior high school to come together as companions. Let the young brothers be companions to one another, and let the young sisters be companions to one another.

We need companions not only because we are weak to stand by ourselves, but also because we are all so natural. According to our natural disposition, it is very hard for us to have companions. Our individualism is a pleasure to us. We enjoy our individualism so much. We may not care for a brother or a sister because they are not like us. We demand that others be like us. Wanting people to be like us is devilish. If we love the Lord, we should be able to go to any young brother or sister, not caring for what they are like. They may be slow or quick, dull or smart, like you or one hundred percent different from you. We should forget all the differences. We must have companions. If the young people would be grouped in this way, Satan will be put to shame. This is a great matter.

If five junior high school students would be grouped together as one, their school will be "overthrown." If they start with five, after not long a time, perhaps two months, there will be fifteen. The preaching of the gospel in their school will be like wildfire. Even the college age and working age saints need companions. They need to work together, live together, and have their daily walk together. Ecclesiastes 4:12 says, "A threefold cord is not quickly broken." If one person has four companions, the five of them will even be a fivefold cord. Nothing can break this cord. The gospel preaching of these five will be prevailing. They will subdue people. Their grouping together will convince people, and Satan will be put to shame.

Do not have companions in a loose way. Do not take a brother as a companion because you like him and tomorrow reject him because you do not like him. If he is a brother, you must take him. This will subdue and break you. You need to be broken. Who will break you? Wives are good "breakers," but I do not trust the wives to completely break the husbands. The good "breakers" are the brothers and sisters with whom you group yourself.

The young people must look to the Lord to get four or five companions. Even the people in the world say that union is power. By myself I would not dare to do many things, but when I have four companions, I would dare to do anything.]

V. PRAYING AND SEEKING THE TRUTH WITH COMPANIONS

What do companions do when they get together? If they talk about worldly things, they will be distracted from the Lord. If they insult one another with offensive words, they destroy one another. [The five companions should always call on the name of the Lord together (2 Tim. 2:22). They should always come together to fellowship, pray-read, pray, and take care of new ones. One brother's new ones should be another brother's new ones also. In this way one group of five saints will have fifteen new ones under their care. All these new ones will be saved. The principle for the saints in both the Old and New Testaments is that they should be grouped together. The young people need to flee youthful lusts and pursue the Lord with some companions.]

They need to pray. Prayer strengthens their spirit. Prayer will move the Lord to work. Prayer will give them the guidance on how to go on with the Lord. Paul said in 1 Tim. 2:1, "I exhort therefore, first of all, that petitions, prayers, intercessions, thanksgivings be made on behalf of all men." Prayer is the first thing we must do. We like to talk; we do not like to pray. We need to develop a habit of praying. Daniel prayed three times a day kneeling before God. That was his habit. Therefore, young people should pray together to develop such a holy habit. Paul also charged the saints to pray unceasingly. The young people need to develop a spiritual habit to pray unceasingly. The best way to develop such a habit is to pray every time we think about someone and every time we have to do something or say something. If the young people will pray together, they will afford the Lord a chance to perfect them for the work of the ministry and for the building up of the church.

They should research [the things concerning Christ and the church. When a group comes together, one brother may ask the others if they can speak something concerning the assurance of salvation. The young people in the church may know how to call on the name of the Lord, and they have been saved. However, some may not know assuredly that they are saved. Eventually, their assurance of salvation will be tested. The young people should thoroughly fellowship matters such as the assurance of salvation and regeneration in their groups.

There has not been enough time for the church as a whole to cover these matters. As a result, the knowledge and experience of the young people is too general. The young people should take care of their own needs in their groups of five. If they do not, we may eventually have a good number of saints among us, but they will not be thoroughly rooted in spiritual matters. If five young people cannot speak clearly to each other about the assurance of salvation, how can they help others? They may only be able to help them to call on the name of the Lord in a general way. In their groups the young ones should help each other to be clear about the life experiences.]

[We need to lay a foundation for the young people's work. The young ones should be helped to know what the assurance of salvation is, what regeneration is, and what eternal life is. If each group covers one or two points a week, after half a year they will have covered thirty or forty basic points. This will lay a good foundation. It is not enough to come together and pray in a general way. The young people must do something specific, just as we eat something specific and definite at every meal.

To practice meeting in small groups is not a difficult thing to do. Every week after a church meeting, five young people could go to a brother's home for fellowship. To spend even only fifteen minutes will be a help to them. They should not fellowship there in a general way. This is the time to cover two or three specific points.]

CONCLUSION

We hope that all the young people will have a burden for the building up of the church. In order to do the building-up work, they need to be caught and occupied by God, to purpose in their heart not to be defiled, and to flee youthful lusts with their companions. The companions need to fellowship with one another, pray, seek the Lord in the Word, and preach the gospel together. The Lord will prepare these young ones for His move, His recovery, and for the building up of His church.

Questions

1. Name three people from the Old Testament who were called by God in their youth. Discuss their circumstances and calling.

2. List four things that a group of companions should do when they are together.

3. Can you quote from memory 2 Timothy 2:22? Discuss.

4. Why does God "wreck" people? Are you "wrecked" for God's purpose? Discuss.

Quoted Portions

1. Fellowship with the Young People (Lee/LSM), pp. 7-15, 29-30.

Further References

1. Completing Ministry of Paul (Lee/LSM), pp. 366-370.

2. Life Study of Ephesians (Lee/LSM), pp. 161, 324.

3. Fellowship with the Young People (Lee/LSM), pp. 32-36.

4. A Living Sacrifice (Nee/CFP), pp. 67-82.

Lesson Twenty-Three

OUR NEED TO SERVE
FOR THE BUILDING UP OF THE CHURCH

Scripture Reading

Matt. 24:14; Acts 20:24; Rev. 1:9; 1 Tim. 2:4; Eph. 5:27;
Mark 16:16; Matt. 28:20; 5:11-12; 2 Cor. 1:4.

Outline

I. The gospel needs to be preached

II. The saved ones need to come to the full
knowledge of the truth

III. The local churches need to be established in
every city

IV. We must pray for His move

V. We must go to disciple all the nations

VI. We must teach them what we have been taught

VII. We must go and establish local churches
throughout all the earth

VIII. We will bring the Lord and the kingdom to
earth and will receive a reward

Text

I. THE GOSPEL NEEDS TO BE PREACHED

In Matthew 24:14 the Lord said, "And this gospel of the
kingdom shall be preached in the whole inhabited earth for a
testimony to all the nations, and then the end shall come."
[The "gospel of the kingdom," including the gospel of grace
(Acts 20:24), not only brings people into God's salvation, but
also into the kingdom of the heavens (Rev. 1:9). The emphasis
of the gospel of grace is on forgiveness of sin, God's
redemption, and eternal life; whereas the stress of the gospel
of the kingdom is on the heavenly ruling of God and the
authority of the Lord. This gospel of the kingdom shall be

preached in the whole earth for a testimony to all the nations before the end of this age comes. Hence, this preaching will be a sign of the consummation of this age.] We who love the Lord and want to serve Him should go and preach the gospel of the kingdom until there is no place left to go.

In 1 Timothy 2:4a the Apostle Paul said, "Who (God) desires all men to be saved." Having all men saved is God's desire. Many Christians pray to know God's will for their life, but they are ignorant of God's will for humanity. All have sinned. All have been condemned. All will be in the lake of fire unless they are saved. If they are not saved, they are not useful to God who created them. They will not be members of the glorious church the Lord is building. Therefore, God desires all men to be saved for His purpose.

II. THE SAVED ONES NEED TO COME TO THE FULL KNOWLEDGE OF THE TRUTH

Paul continued in 1 Timothy 2:4b, "and come to the full knowledge of the truth." It is crucial to see the word "and." We may only see that God desires all men to be saved, and neglect to see that God also desires that they come to the full knowledge of the truth. Getting saved is the initial step for men to be in God's purpose. Men are not useful for the building up of the church unless they have come to the full knowledge of the truth. We also need to come to the full knowledge of the truth in order to help others come to the full knowledge of the truth.

The term "full knowledge" does not merely mean understanding; it includes understanding and experience. To really know that sugar is sweet, you must taste it. After tasting its sweetness, you will know sugar is sweet, experientially, and no one will be able to convince you otherwise. All men need to come to the full knowledge of the truth the same way. Too many people know only "hear-say" truth. They do not really know nor have they experienced the truth to the extent that no one could convince them otherwise. All should know the truth item by item, point by point, and also know it experientially, until they have come to the full knowledge of the truth.

III. THE LOCAL CHURCHES NEED TO BE ESTABLISHED IN EVERY CITY

The Lord said, in Matthew chapter 16, that He will build the church - the ruling and overcoming church. The church is glorious (Eph. 5:27). The universal church is comprised of many local churches; therefore, local churches need to be established throughout all the earth. The local churches need to be built up with the Spirit and the Word. The churches should be full of God, essentially. They should be full of Christ as the testimony of Jesus. They should be full of the Spirit to express the Triune God as lampstands in the dark, evil, and perverse world. The Lord's as well as our work is not complete until all of the preceding points have been accomplished.

IV. WE MUST PRAY FOR HIS MOVE

The gospel of the kingdom must be preached to the whole inhabited earth in order for all men to be saved and come to the full knowledge of the truth, and for the local churches to be established throughout all the earth. This is God's desire, Christ's commission, and the Spirit's work. We are co-laborers with God, partners of Christ, and the reprint of the Spirit to carry out this great purpose of God.

Hymn 1248
verse one

Recall how David swore,
"I'll not come into my house,
Nor go up to my bed,
Give slumber to my eyelids,
Until I find a place for thee,
A place, O Lord, for thee."
Our mighty God desires a home
Where all His own may come.

This verse was written according to Psalm 132. It describes how David felt about God's house, the church. We should have the same feeling towards His church.

If we mean business with the Lord, we will consecrate ourselves for this glorious commission. Firstly, we must pray. Prayer fills us up with the Triune God. Prayer causes the Father to give us those we ask for, and enables the Lord to bring to earth what has been done in heaven. Prayer also energizes us to accomplish this great work. We must pray. Pray at set times and pray all the time. Pray individually and corporately with our companions. Pray in spirit and with the Word. Pray until the Lord increases the church with flocks of men for the building up of His habitation (Ezek. 36:37). Pray until the Lord makes Jerusalem, the builded church in spirit, a praise in the earth (Isa. 62:6-7).

V. WE MUST GO TO DISCIPLE ALL THE NATIONS

After praying, we must go to disciple all the nations. In Matthew chapter 28, the Lord commissions us to disciple all the nations. In Mark 16, He charged us to preach to all the creation. In Luke chapter 24, He told us to be His witnesses to all the nations. In John chapter 15, He appointed us to go forth and bear remaining fruit. Therefore, in conjunction with our prayer, we must go. The unbelieving people will not come to us. We must go to them. The Lord went forth from His throne in the heavens to come to us. The unbelievers do not know the address of our meeting halls. Even if they knew, they may not want to come. The best way to disciple all the nations is to preach to all the creation, to witness to all the nations, and to bear much fruit. This requires us to pray and go.

When the nations believe and are baptized they will be saved (Mark 16:16). They become sons of God and members of the Body of Christ. As a result the church will increase in number. There will be more called-out ones in the assembly, more material to build up the house of God, and more members to function in the Body of Christ. This is a crucial part of the church-building process. The building work will cease if we are not faithful to disciple all the nations.

VI. WE MUST TEACH THEM
WHAT WE HAVE BEEN TAUGHT

After baptizing new believers into the Triune God, we must continue by "teaching them to observe all things, whatever I (the Lord) commanded you; and behold, I (the Lord) am with you all the days until the consummation of the age" (Matt. 28:20). This is very important. It fulfills the second half of 1 Tim. 2:4 - that they may come to the full knowledge of the truth. You may say that you have not yet come to the full knowledge of the truth. This is the fifth summer school of the truth you have attended. What you have learned is not insignificant. You have learned the major points of the truth of the Bible. Most seminary students have not learned what you have already learned. They may know many things from the Bible, but they do not know the crucial truths concerning God's full salvation. Most of them do not know the three stages of salvation, nor do they know the truth concerning sanctification and transformation. They may not even know the difference between justification and reconciliation. However, you already have much truth to teach the new ones. Teach them everything you know. Learn more and teach more. If you continue to learn, you will always be equipped to teach. Hallelujah!

You can pray, go, baptize, and teach. As you do these things, the processed Triune God will be with you. You will be able to bind Satan and loose people for God's church.

VII. WE MUST GO AND ESTABLISH LOCAL
CHURCHES THROUGHOUT ALL THE EARTH.

The last thing we must do is to establish local churches. If you are faithful to do all the things listed above, you will have begun to build up a local church. Some people desire to preach the gospel in the uttermost parts of the earth, yet they do not preach where they presently live. If we are able to preach the gospel where we presently live, we will be able to preach the gospel anywhere. If you do not know how to preach, then learn by praying, fellowshiping, and practicing with your companions. If you know how to preach, continue and teach others to preach. In the meantime, study diligently, exercise properly, and develop a good character. After you graduate from college, attend a full-time training to be fully prepared for the Master's use. You and your companions will be trained, formed into a team, and sent out by the Lord to establish churches.

VIII. WE WILL BRING THE LORD AND THE KINGDOM TO EARTH AND WILL RECEIVE A REWARD

As you are faithful to carry out His burden to build up the church, He will be there to supply you. It is not that you will be without problems, but you will have the bountiful supply of the Spirit of Jesus Christ to carry you through every crisis. You may be attacked from without and from within, yet you will stand. You may be persecuted for the Lord's sake, yet you will not give up because you know that great is your reward in the heavens (Matt. 5:11-12). You may be very discouraged at times, yet simply touching the God of all encouragement will revive your spirit (2 Cor. 1:4). After you have labored faithfully all your life, many churches will be established. All the other faithful brothers and sisters will do the same. Together, we will bring the Lord back. When He comes, He will bring His reward with Him to award all the faithful ones (Rev. 22:12).

Are you willing to be faithful? Are you ready to go on? Are you on the Lord's side? Hymn 473 tells us that when we give up all things for Christ, we own everything in this universe. We give up a fragment and in exchange the Lord will give us the whole. Pursuing Christ in such a way will lead us to the throne of Christ and enable us to rule with Him as co-kings. Amen! Hallelujah!

Questions

1. What is God's will for all of humanity?

2. Memorize 1 Timothy 2:4.

3. How do you help young Christians come to the full knowledge of the truth?

4. Based on this lesson what steps are taken from the time we are saved until we reach the New Jerusalem?

Quoted Portions

1. Recovery Version (Lee/LSM), Matt. 24:14, note 1.

Further References

1. Living Uniquely for the Gospel (Lee/LSM), pp. 31-37.

2. Talks Concerning the Church Services (Lee/LSM), pp. 15-22, 41-44.

3. Truth Lessons Level 1, Vol. 2 (Lee/LSM), pp. 154-160.

4. Words of Training for the New Way (Lee/LSM), pp. 36-39.

Lesson Twenty-Four

OUR PATTERNS FOR THE BUILDING UP OF THE CHURCH

Scripture Reading

Phil. 2:5-10; Acts 4:18-20; 26:16-19; 1 Tim. 1:16.

Outline

I. Jesus Christ our Lord being a pattern for us

II. Peter being a pattern for us

III. Paul being a pattern for us

IV. John being a pattern for us

V. Being faithful to the end for the building up of the church

Text

In this final lesson we will reveal the lives of four men whose human living became our pattern for the building up of the church. These men began to seek the Lord when they were young. Some came at a young age, some came at an older age; nevertheless, they all were considered young men when they first started to pursue the Lord. Therefore, do not look down upon yourselves, but look to these patterns.

I. JESUS CHRIST OUR LORD BEING A PATTERN FOR US

Jesus Christ our Lord is our first pattern for the building up of the church. He is not only the Head of the Body, He is also a pattern. He humbled and emptied Himself for the church (Phil. 2:5-10). He gave up His position, status, glory, comfort, and throne to become a man. He was inside Mary's womb for nine months. He was under the authority of Joseph and Mary for thirty years. He submitted Himself to His own creatures. He allowed Himself to be apprehended, mocked, tried unfairly, and crucified by His own people. He passed through these human sufferings to redeem His chosen people. Then He resurrected that they may be regenerated to be the sons of God and members of His Body. He ascended in order to pour out the Spirit upon the members to form His Body. He went through the process of incarnation, human living, crucifixion, resurrection, and ascension for the building up of the church. He did not sit on the throne in the heavens and command us to build the church. He took the lead in self-humbling and self-emptying to do the Father's will. There is no other way to build the church. We are not capable of building the church as sinners. Therefore, He took the first steps to lead us through the process necessary for the building up of His church. He was faithful and He is our pattern.

II. PETER BEING A PATTERN FOR US

Peter is also our pattern for the building up of the church. Peter is the first one to whom the Father revealed Christ. He is also the first one to whom Christ revealed the church. Throughout the Old Testament, no one was clear about Christ and the church. In Matthew chapter 16, Peter saw the revelation of Christ and the church at the same time. He was very blessed. It is a blessing to see Christ and the church. Have you seen Christ and the church? If you have seen this vision, you are also very blessed.

He was faithful to the Lord's vision, though not in himself. He failed in himself, yet he succeeded in Christ. After Christ breathed the Holy Spirit into him in John 20:22, and poured the Spirit upon the Body in Acts 2:4, Peter took the lead to preach the gospel to save the Jewish sinners and establish the church in Acts 2. This was the use of the first key of the kingdom of heavens to unlock the kingdom for the Jewish believers. He continued to preach Christ to save sinners for their regeneration in Acts 3 and 4 even though he was threatened by the Jewish rulers and charged not to teach in the name of Jesus (Acts 4:18). Peter and John were bold and said to them, "Whether it is right in the sight of God to hear you rather than God, you judge; for we cannot but speak the things which we saw and heard" (Acts 4:19-20). He also used the second key of the kingdom to open the kingdom to the gentile believers in Cornelius' house (Acts 10). He continued to preach Christ to build up the church despite the fact that he was threatened, beaten, and put in jail.

When he was older, he wrote in 1 Peter 2:5 that we are living stones being built up into a spiritual house. He did not forget the vision he saw in Matthew chapter 16. Praise the Lord for our brother, Peter, who was faithful to the end, preaching and laboring for Christ and the building up of the church. He certainly is our pattern for the building up of the church.

III. PAUL BEING A PATTERN FOR US

Paul is a very good pattern for the building up of the church. In Acts 26:19 Paul told King Agrippa that he "was not disobedient to the heavenly vision." If he said that he was not disobedient, that means that one can be disobedient. He was faithful. He did not disobey what he saw. Will you obey or disobey what you see?

What did he see in the heavenly vision? He saw Christ and the church. At that time his name was Saul, and he was persecuting the church (Acts 9:1). On the day of his conversion, he was on his way to Damascus to bind all who call upon the name of the Lord (Acts 9:14). "And as he went, it came about that he drew near to Damascus; and suddenly a light from heaven shone around him; and he fell on the ground and heard a voice saying to him, Saul, Saul, why are you persecuting Me? And he said, Who are You, Lord: And He said, I am Jesus, whom you are persecuting" (Acts 9:3-5).

[Saul did not have this revelation, thinking that he was persecuting Stephen and other Jesus-followers in the way he considered heresy (24:14), not knowing that when he persecuted these he persecuted Jesus, for they were one with Him by being united to Him through their faith in Him. He considered that he was persecuting people on earth, never thinking that he touched anyone in heaven. To his great surprise a voice from heaven told him that He was the One whom he was persecuting, and His name was Jesus. To him this was a unique revelation in the entire universe! By this he began to see that the Lord Jesus and His believers are one great person—the wonderful "Me." This must have impressed and affected him for his future ministry concerning Christ and the church as the great mystery of God (Eph. 5:32), and laid a solid foundation for his unique ministry.] The wonderful "Me" that he saw was the universal new man, the Body of Christ, with the Head in the heavens and the Body on the earth.

The vision of Christ and His church delivered him from everything, and transferred him into Christ. He had been deeply involved with the Jewish religion. He was zealous for it. He tried his best to excel in the Jewish religion even to the extent of persecuting the church with threatening and murder. But he became blinded to all that at the sight of Christ and the church. He dropped everything and came to Christ for His church.

From the vision came a commission from the Lord. [Acts 26:17-18 says, "Taking you out from the people and from the Gentiles, to whom I send you, to open their eyes, to turn them from darkness to light and from the authority of Satan to God, that they may receive forgiveness of sins and an inheritance among those who have been sanctified by faith in Me." These verses show us the five items of Saul's commission: (1) to open their eyes; (2) to turn them from darkness to light; (3) to turn them from the authority of Satan to God; (4) that they may receive forgiveness of sins; (5) and that they may receive an inheritance among those who have been sanctified by faith in the Lord Jesus.]

He was faithful to the vision and the commission. Immediately after his baptism, he proclaimed Jesus in Damascus, and gathered disciples (Acts 9:18, 20, 26). When he was persecuted, he went to Jerusalem and "spoke boldly in the name of the Lord" (Acts 9:28).

He had a strong beginning and continued even more strongly. He went throughout Asia minor and Europe to preach Christ (Acts 13-28), shepherd new believers (Acts

20:18-38), teaching them what he knew about the Lord (Acts 20:18-28), and establishing churches (Acts 13-28; 14:23; Titus 1:5). He was faithful to the end. He said in 2 Tim. 4:7-8, "I have fought a good fight, I have finished the course, I have kept the faith; henceforth, there is laid up for me the crown of righteousness, which the Lord, the righteous Judge, will award to me in that day; and not only to me, but also to all those who have loved His appearing." Because he was faithful, a crown was reserved for him.

You may say that Paul was special and that you could never be like him. We may never get a direct heavenly vision of Christ and the church as Paul did, but we can receive an indirect heavenly vision through the word of Paul's ministry. There is actually no difference. The Lord said to Thomas in John 20:29, "Because you have seen Me, you have believed. Blessed are those who have not seen and have believed." We are those who have not seen and have believed. We are those who did not have a direct heavenly vision like Paul, yet we see from his ministry in his epistles. We are more blessed. But we must be faithful to what we have seen. Paul said in Philippians 3:17, "Be imitators together of me, brothers and observe attentively those who thus walk as you have us for an example." He is our pattern. He went before us. He first saw the heavenly vision. All that he has seen is for us to receive and imitate as a pattern.

[This young man, Saul of Tarsus, is a real example to us. It may be that in the entire Scriptures only the Lord Jesus as a man could exceed this man Saul, who was later called Paul. Paul even told us in 1 Timothy that he was a pattern to the believers (1:16). Saul was religious and natural, yet one day he received the heavenly vision and was converted from all things other than Christ to Christ Himself. From that day he became very useful in the hand of God and had a prevailing impact. The Lord was able to accomplish many wonderful things through him. This is the kind of person whom God can use today. May we all go to the Lord and pray, "Lord, here I am. I am open to You, to Your vision, to Your commission, and I am ready to pay any cost, any price. I want to count all things loss and count only Christ as gain. I am ready to be occupied, possessed, and filled by Christ." If we go to the Lord and spend some time with Him to receive the heavenly vision, we will have a living contact with Christ and be a living, functioning member of His living Body. Then we will be persons in God's plan.]

IV. JOHN BEING A PATTERN FOR US

John is another pattern for us. You may say that John did not seem to have accomplished much in the gospels and in Acts. That is true. But he was always there, and he was there faithfully. He was there with the Lord during His earthly ministry for three-and-half years. When the Lord was arrested and judged, Peter denied the Lord three times and left (Matt. 26:75), yet John stayed there (John 18:15-16). When the Lord was crucified, the other disciples were not seen around the cross, yet John was still there (John 19:16). After hearing the news of the Lord's resurrection, John arrived at the Lord's grave first (John 20:4). John was present at the first meetings to receive the breathing and the outpouring of the Holy Spirit. He was also with Peter at the conversion of the 3,000 and 5,000 souls. He was there faithfully in everything that the Lord was doing to build up the Body of Christ. He was not taking the lead, yet he was one with and in full support of Peter, who at that time was taking the lead. He had a clear vision of Christ and the church. He saw the need of oneness (John 17) and kept the oneness of the Spirit.

The Lord preserved him until all the original disciples passed away. He was faithful until the end, even during his exile on the island of Patmos. Then the Lord showed only him the last revelation—the New Jerusalem, the ultimate consummation of the mingling of Christ and the built-up church. John is definitely a pattern for us to follow for the building up of the church.

V. BEING FAITHFUL TO THE END FOR THE BUILDING UP OF THE CHURCH

Have you seen the vision of Christ and the church? Peter, Paul and John saw the vision in their spirit. All you have to do is pray with the Word in spirit and fellowship with your companions. Eventually, you will see the same vision they saw. Based upon the vision of Christ and the church you will receive a commission from the Lord to preach the Word, to bring new members into the Body of Christ, to nourish them in life, to teach them the truth, and to build them up into the church. Together, you will raise up many local churches on the earth to bring the Lord back.

Seeing the vision and receiving a commission is still not enough. You need to be obedient to the heavenly vision, and you need to be faithful to carry out the commission. Peter, Paul and John will receive a reward, and so will you. Do not put them on a pedestal and down-grade yourself. They are our elder brothers. They had the same problems that we have. They also had the same spirit we have. Whatever they had we have. We must be faithful as they were. Hallelujah! One day, we will all line up together to receive a reward having been faithful in enjoying Christ for the building up of the church.

Questions

1. What patterns do you find to follow in the following:

   a. The Lord Jesus?, b. Peter?, c. Paul?, d. John?

2. Have you seen the vision of Christ and the Church?

3. Having finished this lesson book and seeing the vision of the building up of the church, will you be obedient to the heavenly vision?

Quoted Portions

1. Life Study of Acts (Lee/LSM), p. 206.
2. A Young Man in God's Plan (Lee/LSM), pp. 33, 37.

Further References

1. The World Situation and God's Move (Lee/LSM), pp. 9-18.
2. A Young Man in God's Plan (Lee/LSM), pp. 7-37.